INTERNATIONALISATION OF SINGAPORE

F&B COMPANIES:

Critical Success Factors and Challenges

chefatwork
REDEFINING F&B EXPERIENCES

DR JAMES MOK

To order additional copies of this book, contact
Toll Free +65 3165 7531 (Singapore)
Toll Free +60 3 3099 4412 (Malaysia)
www.partridgepublishing.com/singapore
orders.singapore@partridgepublishing.com

ISBN
978-1-5437-7319-4 (sc)
978-1-5437-7321-7 (hc)
978-1-5437-7320-0 (e)

Print information available on the last page.

03/28/2023

PARTRIDGE

INTERNATIONALISATION OF SINGAPORE F&B COMPANIES:

CRITICAL SUCCESS FACTORS AND CHALLENGES

DR JAMES MOK

CONTENTS

LIST OF FIGURES

LIST OF TABLES

In loving memory of my late parents, Francis Mok Boon Yeo and Lisa Ng Kiok Hua.

Thank you for having this book, and may you find useful information in strategising your voyages beyond Singapore.

Best wishes.
Dr James Mok

EXECUTIVE SUMMARY

The voyages of Singapore food and beverage (F&B) companies out of Singapore over the last few decades have encountered both successes and failures. There is a lack of research in this area. The book is based on an exploratory case study of the internationalisation of thirty Singapore food service companies.

The multiple-case study was conducted from 2017 to 2018 to examine the critical success factors for internationalisation. These Singapore F&B companies were categorised in the stages of internationalisation into *aspirants*, *actives*, and *achievers*. To strengthen external validity and data triangulation for this study, eleven industry experts, termed as *advisers*, and seven other foreign individuals who have acquired a Singaporean brand were included.

This study has made several significant contributions to the field of internationalisation as well as the critical success factor literature. The book has the following takeaways for anyone interested in internationalisation and for industry leaders keen on venturing overseas.

First, the study refines the conceptual process model of the internationalisation model including Uppsala's stage theory, transaction cost analysis, internalisation theory, the theory of organisational evolution, and literature on international franchising as well as the critical success factors for internationalisation.

Second, the book promotes the view that internationalisation is not homogenous and that aspiring companies have faced different challenges from those who are in the field for some time. The critical success factors for these companies, challenges, competencies, and consequently their strategies for venturing overseas are different.

Third, this study also lends support to Choo's (2005) study on multiple-unit franchising and expands to include a new hybrid of joint-venture (JV) franchises in Asia. The modes of entry employed by various companies have shown that these are like different tools in a toolbox to be selected subject to a host of internal and external factors in this study.

Fourth, this study also looks at those overseas-based entrepreneurs who acquired the Singapore brand and what motivated them to accept the brand. It gives a comprehensive view from the 'other side', the buyers' perspective, providing insights to Singaporean companies interested in venturing overseas.

Fifth, this study has also sought the views of another set of critical stakeholders, the industry experts or advisers who are often consulted by Singapore F&B companies in seeking expansion overseas. These advisers are part of the network of experts assisting Singaporean companies in their internationalisation drive. Therefore, advisers exerted considerable influence on the development of their internationalisation capabilities and strategies.

Sixth, there has been a lack of theoretical and empirical research on the developmental process and critical success factors for internationalisation in Asia so far. This study reveals the diversity and dynamism of companies in their various stages of internationalisation in Asia. It is, therefore, critical for companies to continually benchmark themselves against the various critical success factors inherent in the various stages of internationalisation.

Finally, the research provides a diagnostic tool to ascertain readiness as well as for auditing the internationalisation of Singaporean companies in the food service sector. This tool will be a reality check for international firms in considering shifts in capability building or strategies as they continue their efforts towards achieving success in internationalisation.

Dr James Mok

Dr James's first degree was a Bachelor of Social Science (Honours) from the National University of Singapore, and he obtained an MBA degree from the University of Strathclyde in 1998. In 2021, he graduated with a Doctor of Business Administration from the University of Western Australia. Dr James also obtained a Certificate of Education from the Institute of Education and was a teacher.

Dr James worked with many established Singapore companies such as Singapore Airlines, United Overseas Bank, and Shangri-La. He managed a Singapore F&B company with a turnover of about $20 million before becoming a business consultant with FT Consulting in 2004. Since 2006, Dr James focused on assisting Singapore companies venturing overseas. He is currently the director of Chef at Work Pte Ltd and managing director of Successus Consulting. He is also a Singapore Certified Management Consultant since 2020.

FOREWORD

A useful and important reading for all who are interested in internationalisation, the book provides information on how to work smarter by setting up systems as well as focusing on driving revenue from international ventures.

Edwin Phua
CEO
CAW Holding
Malaysia | Vietnam | Cambodia
Executive Director

CHAPTER 1

INTRODUCTION

The Push for Internationalisation – the Singapore Experience

To the young and the not-so-old,

I say look at that horizon,

follow that rainbow, go ride it.

—Lee Kuan Yew, 7 June 1996

This famous quote by Singapore's founding prime minister, Lee Kuan Yew, is highlighted on the official website of the Singapore Malay Chamber of Commerce to highlight its efforts to assist companies to internationalise (see appendix 2 for the website link). The push for Singaporean companies to venture beyond Singapore started in 1993, which was termed the *year of the second wing* (Mahizhnan, 1994). Mr Lee Kuan Yew, then senior minister, urged Singaporean companies to venture overseas and to create an external economy for Singapore as had happened in other advanced economies. The Economic Committee advocated the initiative to internationalise against a backdrop of a stagnating Singapore economy in 1986.

With the feedback from the public and private sectors, the committee's report (*The Singapore Economy: New Directions*) identified regionalisation and globalisation as crucial drivers for the Singaporean economy. Mr Lee, in a keynote address to business leaders in 1993, promised that the government would expedite and enable this internationalisation effort, which has been a driving force ever since.

Despite the Singapore government's push for companies to expand beyond its island, a recent survey of some 400 companies showed that only 14 per cent were interested in venturing overseas (QBE Research, 29 January 2019). A significant 56 per cent of the companies stated they would focus on the local market instead.

The road to success in internationalisation is a long and winding one. The United States (e.g. Apple, GE, Citibank, and Microsoft), China (e.g. Alibaba, Tencent, and Huawei), Japan (e.g. Toyota, Honda, and Sony), and South Korea (e.g. Hyundai, Samsung, and LG) all have global successes. Despite being a small nation, Singapore also has some international successes such as Singapore Airlines, Tiger Balm, Tiger Beer, Creative Technologies, Gardena, and CIAS.

On a brighter note, the *Sunday Times*, in an article dated 2 September 2018, noted:

Dozens of Singaporean restaurants and food brands are available around the world. The island's reputation as a culinary hot spot with an inherent passion for food has helped brands like Song Fa, Bak Kut Teh and Ya Kun Kaya Toast enter competitive foreign markets.

Besides listed companies, such as Singapore Airlines and Jumbo, many Singaporean companies that ventured overseas are small and medium enterprises (SMEs), such as Sushi Tei, Fish & Co., Paradise, Putien, Founder Bak Kut Teh, Wee Nam Kee Chicken Rice, and Old Chang Kee. Bowen's (2017) many parameters are used to define an *SME*, such as the number of employees, capital, profits, or market position. *Small and medium enterprises* in Singapore are defined as organisations with annual sales turnover of less than $100 million or less than 200 workers (Skills Connect, 2013). As expected, almost 99 per cent of Singapore's enterprises are SMEs. They employ about 70 per cent of the workforce and contribute more than 50 per cent of the nation's gross domestic product (Wang, 2019).

However, there is little research into the factors that lead to Singaporean companies venturing abroad successfully, particularly SMEs, despite the government's long-standing efforts and funding to build an external economy.

This book addresses the following hot topics.

1. The critical success factors for Singaporean F&B companies venturing overseas
2. The implications on these companies' capabilities
3. Impact on go-to-market strategies when companies venture overseas

There is also a need to understand better the interactions between micro-, internal, and organisational factors on the one hand and macro-, external, and host country factors on the other. The research used a multiple-case research approach to examine these issues. Data were gathered from Singaporean companies in various stages of internationalisation, overseas franchisees or companies that had acquired Singaporean brands, and business advisers in relevant overseas countries, whose primary role was to assist Singaporean companies in expanding into those countries.

Chapter 1 provides an overview of the research and outlines its rationale and objectives as well as background information on Singapore's food service industry.

Chapter 2 then reviews prior research that examined the critical success factors in internationalisation.

Chapter 3 describes the research methodology adopted in the research and the profiling of the forty-eight participants.

Subsequent chapters 4 to 10 present the findings for the different case companies in various stages of internationalisation.

Chapters 11 and 12 discuss the findings of the acquirers and why they take on the Singapore brand.

Chapters 13 and 14 cover the findings of the advisers' group and their expert views on the keys to success.

Chapter 15 revisits the new 'tsunamis' of the pandemic, the war in Ukraine, and the shocks on the supply chain and how external shocks can be the key overriding factor for internationalisation.

Chapter 16 concludes the book with strategic issues and propositions which Singapore F&B companies must consider in venturing out.

When the research was completed, Covid-19 occurred in early 2020 and created tsunamis that disrupted the world's economies and affected the economic, social, and psychological states of life. Chapter 16 discusses the ensuing effects of the pandemic, resulting in severe supply chain disruptions. The subsequent invasion of Ukraine led to further supply disruptions, inflation, and food insecurity. These are external shocks and change the dynamics of the critical success factors of internationalisation for Singapore's F&B companies overseas.

Chapter 17 summarises the key issues in internationalisation and relates how the various stakeholders from the case studies viewed them. Business leaders, entrepreneurs, academics, and general practitioners would be interested in the implications of these pertinent issues in internationalisation. How they might vary across national boundaries would be of interest.

Finally, in the concluding chapter, the contributions of the research, implications, and suggestions for future research will be discussed.

1. The Rationale for the Research – Why Singapore?

Singapore is a prosperous city state, a multiracial and religious nation in the heart of the Association of Southeast Asian Nations (ASEAN) that, together, have a population of more than 600 million people. By 2030, ASEAN will be the fourth largest economic bloc in the world with annual consumer spending of around US$2.3 trillion. Singapore has the highest per capita income (US$90,500) within the ASEAN group, which also includes countries such as Indonesia, Malaysia, and the Philippines (Figure 1.1).

FIGURE 1.1:
KEY SOCIOECONOMIC STATISTICS

KEY ECONOMIC DATA FROM THE COUNTRIES INCLUDED IN THE BENCHMARKING SURVEY

Countries / Questions	USA	Australia	Singapore	Philippines	Malaysia	Indonesia
1. Total Population	325.5M	23.3M	5.9M	104.3M	31.4M	260.6M
2. Urbanization	83.7%	90%	100%	44.2%	76%	55.2%
3. Median Age	37.8	38.7	34.6	23.5	28.5	30.2
4. GDP Per Capita	$US53.3K	$US49.9K	$US90.5K	$US8.2K	$28.9K	$US12.4K

(1)Data obtained from United Nations Statistics & CIA World Fact Book

Figure 1.1: Key socio-economic statistics

As Singapore had a small population of 5.69 million in June 2020, according to the Department of Statistics, and a limited domestic market, Singaporean companies must look towards the more extensive ASEAN hinterland if they wish to expand. Despite its size, this small island state is an open market, and English is the primary spoken language. It is known for its ease of doing business and the ease of repatriation of income (Choo, 2005), making it an attractive 'home and base' for many foreign companies. Indeed, Singapore is one of the few ASEAN countries that does not have regulations governing franchising, and the repatriation of income earned is permitted in most spheres of business (Wong, 2017). It is, therefore, not surprising that Singapore has one of the highest franchise units per capita in the ASEAN region (Figure 1.2).

While Singapore is one of the world's most densely populated cities, its limited population and competitive landscape affect business survival; and thus, many local businesses are driven (a push factor) to consider international expansion.

Figure 1.2: Total number of franchise brands

Service sector franchises account for a much higher percentage in developed markets due to the maturity of the markets and other socio-economic factors.

Definitions of industry segment may vary by country and respondent but for the most part the franchises identified as falling into the Other Sectors segment could be classified as Services Franchises.

The USA has 1 franchise brand for every 85.8K residents while Australia has a franchise brand for every 22K residents. At 1 brand for every 8K residents Singapore has the highest ratio, at 207.5K residents for every franchise brand Indonesia has the lowest ratio. Malaysia and the Philippines fall between the USA & Australia.

Source: CIA World Fact Book

We see a proliferation of Singapore brands overseas and probably on a per capita basis; it is more than in most countries. Also, Singapore brands tend to go overseas much earlier than those from other countries. (Troy Franklin, COO, World Franchise Associates)

Some of the companies that embarked on internationalisation will form part of the multiple-case studies in this research. Besides its expansion overseas, the Singapore food brand is world trusted and highly regarded in terms of food safety and quality; thus, Singapore food companies are good case studies in understanding the critical success factors in their internationalisation efforts.

Table 1.1 illustrates that amongst the top five ASEAN nations, Singapore is top of the list, and thus, contextualising Singapore as case research will seemingly make sense in furthering the understanding of internationalisation for the other ASEAN countries. Thus, there are many examples of Singapore companies that have embarked on their internationalisation journey, and they will form part of the multiple-case studies in this research.

Table 1.1: The number of brands in each country that ventured overseas

Country	Singapore	Malaysia	Philippines	Indonesia	Thailand
No. of the concepts ventured overseas	81	11	12	3	20
Prominent concepts	• BreadTalk Group • Sushi Tei • Ya Kun • Crystal Jade • Jumbo • Paradise Group • SaladStop! • Old Chang Kee • Wee Nam Kee • Fish & Co.	• Marrybrown • Secret Recipe • PappaRich • OldTown • Ipoh Chicken Rice • Manhattan Fish Market • The Chicken Rice shop • Lavender • Morganfield's • Malaysia Boleh	• Jollibee • Potato Corner • Binalot • Yellow Cab Pizza • Figaro Coffee • Julie's Bakeshop • Fiorgelato • Sweet Corner • Maxi Mango • Max's • Goldilocks • Bibingkinitan	• J.CO • Bebek • Ayam Pak Ndut • Excelsior • OJJU • Kebab Turki • Es Teler 77	• Kamu Tea • Greyhound Cafe • After You • Doi Chaang • Patara • Took Lae Dee • Hokkaido Milk • Chokdee Dim Sum • Cafe Amazon • S&P • Inthanin Coffee • Black Canyon • MK • Bar B Q Plaza • Coca • Daddy Dough • Mango Tree • Basil • The Pizza Company • ChaTraMue • Coffee World

Source: Author's compilation based on extensive internet searches as of 6 August 2019.

2. *Justifications for a Single-Industry Research*

Earlier internationalisation and performance studies have been 'undertaken at too high a level of aggregation' (Aggarwal et al., 2011, p. 571). These studies are focused on the relationship between internationalisation and performance. Hennart (2007, p. 446) suggested that future research should focus on 'a detailed industry level'. This research looks at the food service industry and attempts to understand the critical success factors of internationalisation for this industry.

Another justification for such single-industry research is that there are notable prior examples of such studies. Many scholars have concentrated on the fast-food sector in the United States given its prominence as it accounts for 40 per cent of retail sales in that country (Sen, 1998). In recent years, there have been many single-sector studies on internationalisation; some examples include the following:

- Shih, 2017 – F&B svector in Taiwan
- Zhang, 2018 – internationalisation of higher education
- Ooi and Richardson, 2019 – the service sector
- Ridha and Hidayat, 2020 – halal certification and the F&B sector in Malaysia and the Philippines
- Rienda et al., 2020 – Spanish hotel industry
- Sasha et al., 2020 – Thai F&B sector

While Verberien (2008) recommended looking beyond restaurant franchising, the fact remains that little is known about franchising or, for that matter, the internationalisation of this industry in Singapore, heightening the need for the present research.

3. *The Food Service Industry*

The term *food service* can be spelt differently (the UK version is food service, and the US version is foodservice), and it can have different meanings across the Atlantic (Edwards, 2013). This research accepted the UK convention, defining *food service* as

The serviced provision of food and beverages (meals) which may be consumed both in and out of the home. (Edwards, 2013, p. 223)

Industrialisation and urbanisation have brought about a higher incidence of eating out of homes. Eating out has become more common for a variety of reasons (e.g. entertainment, business, or celebration) (Edwards, 2013). So significant is eating out that it is a US$2.1 trillion global industry that employs about 10 per cent of the workforce and contributes 10 per cent of the gross domestic product (Euromonitor International, 2009). It is an industry worthy of research.

4. *The Stage: Singapore Food Service Industry*

Singapore is at the geographical crossroads of Southeast Asia. According to the Euromonitor International report (2017), Southeast Asia is one of the four critical regions for international expansion within the consumer food service industry. ASEAN has a well-developed food culture, as well as consumer preference for dining out and a rapidly growing young middle-class segment that is curious and experimental in its capital cities, which explains this desired expansion.

ASEAN's regional restaurant sales, a vital component of the food service industry, amounted to more than US$100 billion in 2015, a market size equivalent to that of India or Brazil. The compound annual growth rate (CAGR) of sales value in the six leading ASEAN economies from 2010 to 2015 was 2.65 per cent, with Vietnam having the highest (6.5 per cent) and Singapore having the lowest (0.3 per cent) growth rates.

You cannot imagine Singapore without its food. (Tharman Shanmugaratnam, deputy prime minister, 4 January 2019)

Singapore's international recognition as a 'food paradise' comes from the wide variety of food found in the republic with its unique blend of ethnic Asian cuisines with a cosmopolitan touch. It is also due to many food outlets. In 2017, there were more than 35,000 such outlets in Singapore. On a per thousand population basis, Singapore has more restaurants than Moscow, Helsinki, Istanbul, and Edinburgh (Word Cities Culture Forum, 2020).

Further, the country's 'Made in Singapore' brand gives confidence due to Singapore's world-class food security standards, which are increasingly crucial against a backdrop of 'food scares' and a higher demand for 'healthier' and 'quality' food choices (Global New Product Database, 2015).

Enterprise Singapore, a merged government entity made up of the previous SPRING Singapore and International Enterprise Singapore, noted that Singapore's food service industry contributed 0.8 per cent to the nation's gross domestic product. The industry employed 180,000 workers or 4.5 per cent of Singapore's total workforce in 2016, again highlighting the sector's importance.

5. *The Actors: Singaporean Companies in the Food Service Industry*

Although growing in number, the total of Singaporean food service companies venturing overseas is still not significant. In a directory compiled by Asiawide Franchise Consultants in 2006, only twenty-eight Singaporean food service companies had intentions to venture or had ventured overseas (Table 1.2). From 2006, only ten out of the twenty-eight companies in the Asiawide listing had made progress in venturing overseas.

Table 1.2: Food and beverage companies that had an interest or ventured overseas

S/N	Concept	Overseas units 2006	2019	Year of incorp.
1	BreadTalk Group	115	717	2000
2	Seoul Garden/BREEKS!	3	67	1985
3	Ya Kun	17	52	1940
4	Fish & Co.	6	29	1998
5	Sakae Sushi	12	28	1997
6	Pastamania	16	27	1998
7	Old Chang Kee	1	12	1956
8	Cavana	0	4	1982
9	Thai Village Restaurant	0	4	1991
10	O'Coffee Club	8	3	1991
11	Palm Beach Seafood	0	0	1956
12	Do & Me Fried Chicken	0	0	2009
13	Ritz Apple Strudel	0	0	2000
14	Spizza	0	0	2002
15	PrimaDeli	0	0	1992
16	Jollibean	0	0	1995
17	Jack's Place	0	0	1968
18	Komala's Fast Food	0	0	1995
19	Bakerzin	10	0	1998
20	Kinara Restaurant	0	0	2005
21	Long Beach Seafood	0	0	1946
22	Kim's Fried Hokkien Prawn Mee	0	0	1960
23	Pasta Fresca Da Salvatore	0	0	1988
24	Sins Choc Shoppe	0	0	1996
25	China Jump	0	0	1999
26	House of Sundanese Food	0	0	2005
27	Phin's Steakhouse	0	0	2005
28	Sanur Indonesian Restaurant	0	0	1983

Source: Asiawide Directory 2006 and compilation by the author

BreadTalk Group is a leader as it now has more than 700 overseas outlets, while Zingrill Holdings Pte Ltd – which owns Seoul Garden, BREEKS!, and others – increased sales by more than 21 times over this period. Notably, Bakerzin and O'Coffee Club have retreated from internationalisation. Bakerzin currently has no overseas outlets, while O'Coffee Club's overseas outlets fell by more than 60 per cent. Concisely, internationalisation has been a mixed bag for Singapore food service industry companies.

The Franchise and Licensing Association is the trade group that facilitates and coordinates internationalisation for Singaporean companies. Its membership base in 2019 is 130 companies that own or represent some 170 brands. However, only twenty-four Singaporean food service companies were members of the association.

Positively, the food and beverage industry in Asia had the highest rate of growth in the world (Euromonitor International, 2016). Consequently, Singaporean companies that venture into other ASEAN countries should benefit from the expected growth rate of more than 5 per cent (Singapore Business Federation, 2016). However, the challenges in the food service sector are severe. The Singapore F&B industry 2015 statistics report suggested that the average Singapore local F&B business was running at an annual loss of 8 per cent and that it took an average of two and a half years to recoup an initial investment. With a steep hurdle to climb, Mr Tan Chor Sen, executive vice-president of OCBC Bank, Global Enterprise Banking, speaking at the Enterprise Awards tenth anniversary ceremony on 11 April 2017, suggested:

If a food and beverage company can succeed in Singapore with its high cost of rent and labour, they can survive anywhere else. (Siow, 2017 'SMEs Going Places', *Business Times*)

With the local Singapore market reaching saturation and dwindling profitability, venturing overseas has become even more critical. The first few Singaporean companies in the food service sector that ventured overseas and have sustained and maintained their overseas presence are the BreadTalk Group, Ya Kun International, and Sushi Tei. However, overall, the performance of Singaporean companies in the international arena has been mixed. BreadTalk Group, with more than 1,000 outlets in and away from Singapore, is the most successful food service company in Singapore with the highest number of outlets overseas. Many others have ventured overseas but have quietly retreated, particularly because Singapore society amplifies successes and shuns failures. Failures are shunned due to what is known amongst locals as *pai sei* (Hokkien slang, a local Chinese dialect, for a 'loss of face' or being embarrassed).

In a directory compiled by the author in 2019, based on personal interviews, checks on companies' websites, internet news, and media reports, about eighty food service companies have ventured out of Singapore, a sevenfold increase over the number reported by Asiawide Franchise Consultants in 2006. Table 1.3 shows the top ten such companies for the number of overseas outlets. The leader is the BreadTalk Group, which has more than 700 overseas outlets and is still growing.

Table 1.3: Top ten Singaporean companies that have ventured overseas

S/N	Concept	Company
1	BreadTalk	BreadTalk Group Ltd
2	Bee Cheng Hiang	Bee Cheng Hiang Hup Chong Foodstuff P/L
3	Roti Mum	Roti Mum Pte Ltd
4	Shihlin Taiwan Street Snacks	SSTS Pte Ltd
5	Pezzo	Pezzo Singapore Pte Ltd
6	Killiney	Killiney International
7	Sushi Tei	Sushi-Tei Pte Ltd
8	Seoul Garden/BREEKS!	Zingrill Holdings Pte Ltd
9	Ya Kun	Ya Kun International Pte Ltd
10	TWG Tea	TWG Tea Company Pte Ltd

Figure 1.3 shows the countries these Singaporean companies chose for their inaugural overseas launch. The top destinations were Malaysia (twenty-five companies) and Indonesia (twenty-two companies), followed by Hong Kong, China, and the Philippines.

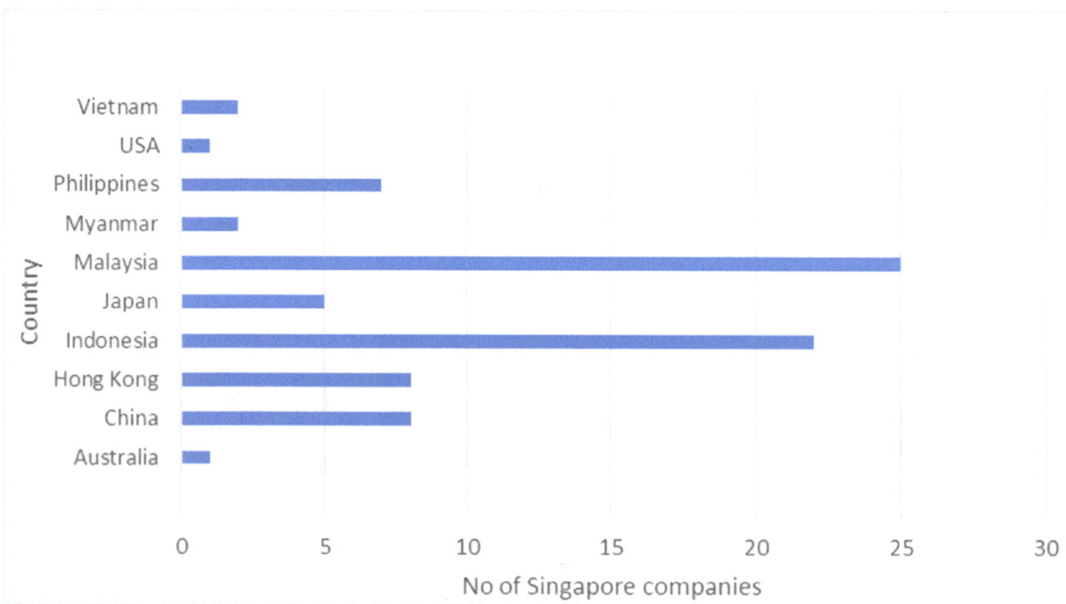

Figure 1.3: Choice of the country for the first overseas outlet (compiled by the author)

The TungLok Group was the first company to internationalise, opening an outlet in Jakarta in 1993. During the 1990s, only four companies ventured overseas. While it was a slow start, expansion gathered speed, with a 250 per cent increase over the next decade and another 350 per cent increase from 2010 to the present. Figure 1.4 shows the increase in the internationalisation of Singaporean companies since the 1990s.

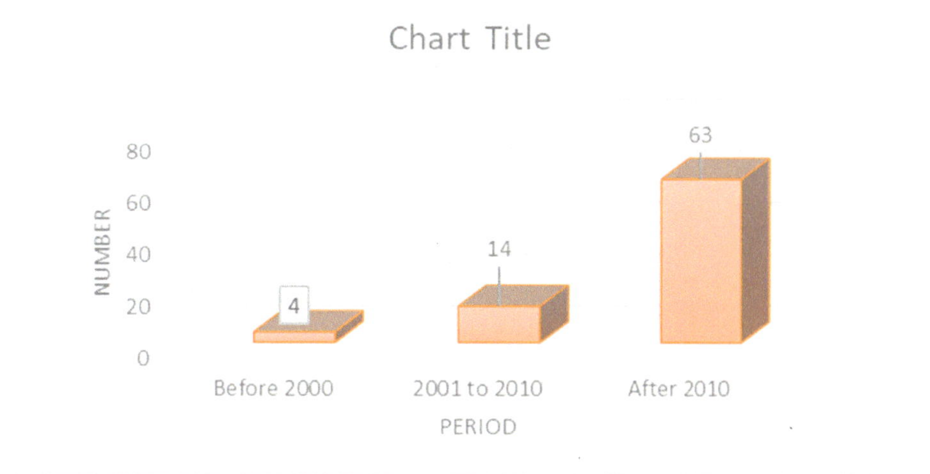

Figure 1.4: Number of companies venturing overseas (compiled by the author)

Of the eighty-one Singaporean companies that had internationalised, 61 per cent had more than 30 per cent of their total outlets outside Singapore (Figure 1.5).

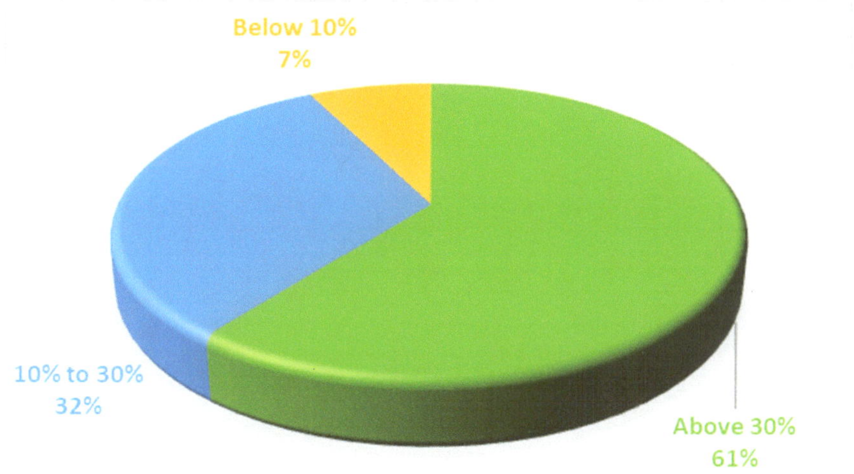

Figure 1.5: Percentage of overseas outlets for Singaporean companies that ventured overseas after 1990 (compiled by the author)

Knowing the critical success factors or, conversely, the lack of success, which is the crux of this research, is essential for Singaporean companies already in the international arena and for those aspiring to step onto the regional or global stage. A Euromonitor (2002) report on the food service industry in Singapore suggested that failures of foreign brands in Singapore are due to a weak brand, food selections that were not suitable to the market, or a weak concept. The other significant factor is the choice of a local partner (Choo, 2005) as working relationships with overseas partners will determine whether there is a harmonious and successful partnership, which affects a venture's success or failure (Fladmoe-Lindquist, 1996).

6. *Singaporean SMEs Going Overseas*

Most of the Singaporean companies that have ventured overseas started as SMEs. Some have grown large enough and are listed on the Singapore stock exchange (i.e. the BreadTalk Group, Jumbo, No Signboard, Old Chang Kee, Paradise, Crystal Jade, and the TungLok Group). However, some are still SMEs, which are defined in Singapore as companies with at least 30 per cent local shareholding, a group annual sales turnover of less than $100 million, or fewer than 200 workers (Skills Connect, 2013). Around 99 per cent of Singapore's enterprises are SMEs. They employ about 70 per cent of the workforce and make up more than 50 per cent of the economy (Wang et al., 2019).

The drive to internationalisation, as is the case in many countries, has been spearheaded by Singapore's SMEs (Figure 1.6). However, only a few SMEs are interested in venturing overseas. A recent QBE research found that only about 14 per cent of Singapore's SMEs intend to internationalise, while about half preferred to keep their business within Singapore. The two top barriers cited in the report were a lack of funding and a lack of knowledge about the standards and processes used in overseas markets (*Business Times*, 18 May 2018). This lack of interest is despite the Singapore government providing funds to promote internationalisation, including the $600 million International Partnership Fund, a co-investment scheme that local firms can use to increase their presence in overseas markets (Seah, 2017).

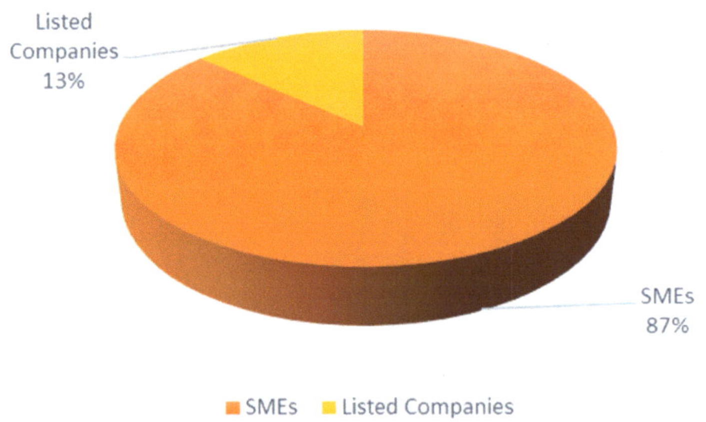

Figure 1.6: Singaporean SMEs going global (compiled by the author)

The Singapore government has consistently maintained that, as domestic growth slows, businesses must expand internationally. However, many Singaporean SMEs are reluctant to expand. SMEs in general and those in Singapore are no exception, facing many challenges when venturing overseas.

A. Financial Barriers

Most SMEs have limited financial capability and need to allocate their funds for their core business as this helps ensure the survival of their existing business. Consequently, they often do not have the financial resources needed to venture overseas as the upfront investments required for overseas expansion can be prohibitive (Rahman, 2014; Bowen, 2019). Internationalisation can be challenging for SMEs as they risk having insufficient working capital to cover short-term liabilities if they divert their cash flow overseas.

B. Human Resources

The Institute of Policy Studies report *Supporting a Dynamic SME Sector: Challenges Faced by SMEs in Singapore* suggested that workforce was also a significant challenge (Yahya et al., 2016). While economic restructuring had hurt companies, especially SMEs, many were struggling with scarce human resources.

In contrast, others moved their operations to Malaysia. Singapore's prime minister Mr Lee Hsien Loong commented that 'if we squeeze them too hard, they may not survive and that will mean many jobs will be at risk' (Chuang, 2014). Nonetheless, there has been no reversal in government policies, especially with the announcement about the tightening of foreign labour quotas (*Straits Times*, 18 February 2019) to ensure that growth in the foreign labour force is sustainable. Indeed, many SMEs are unlikely to have people with the specialised skills and capabilities needed to manage cross-border operations. Of the seventy-one SMEs that have internationalised, only twenty-three (32 per cent) employed a franchise manager or equivalent to oversee international operations, with the others using the founders or business owners in these roles.

C. Capacity to Expand Overseas

Many SMEs have limited capital and little access to financing options. Indeed, 40 per cent of Singapore's SMEs did not have access to bank finance (Deloitte, 2015). Further, Singapore's tight labour market means most SMEs run a lean operation and cannot scale their production to meet additional demands, limiting their capability to explore growth opportunities abroad. SMEs are also often unable to capitalise on the efficiencies and economies of scale that multinational corporations can achieve. Consequently, it might not be profitable for them to ship products overseas (Murphree and Anderson, 2018).

D. Knowledge and Networks

Successful internationalisation requires extensive knowledge of foreign markets, regulations, and business norms. Membership in appropriate networks in target markets is also essential. Enterprise Singapore encourages Singapore's larger enterprises and MNCs to help SMEs in their internationalisation efforts. Their mission is to reduce the lack of knowledge about venturing overseas and expand the SMEs' limited networks.

7. The Research Objectives

This research aims to fill various gaps in the literature on internationalisation firstly by focusing on a 'lower level of aggregation' and examining a single industry in detail as Hennart (2007) has suggested. This research looks at Singapore's food service industry to improve understanding of providers' underlying considerations and to identify success factors. Secondly, most internationalisation studies have examined Western-style franchises with little consideration of Asian options (Dant, 2008). Indeed, Singaporean companies need to control opportunism to avoid brand hijacking (Choo, 2005; Luoma-aho et al., 2018), an issue rarely examined in prior research. Other research has suggested that franchising has become a popular market-entry strategy (Rosado-Serrano et al., 2018; Robson et al., 2018) even in local contexts (Sanghavi, 1991). This research will add to our understanding of franchising's value in a new context (i.e. Singaporean food service providers).

There has not been much research on the critical success factors for internationalisation, and this research attempts to provide insights into the challenges that Singaporean companies have faced. Finally, internationalisation has been examined from a Western developed country perspective. Consequently, it is unclear whether the findings are relevant in Asia. Indeed, Frazer and Merrilees (2012) have suggested that there might be a distinctly Asian franchising model (Trans and Marginson, 2018; Wang et al., 2019). Does the fact that many Singaporean companies are family-run enterprises affect their selection of partners based on shared values and alignment of familial goals, and does this process affect the likelihood of success?

This research has been both a descriptive and exploratory research project and has aimed to find answers to three major research questions:

1. What are the critical success factors for Singaporean companies in the food service industry when they consider or undertake international operations?
2. What capabilities do Singaporean food service companies consider essential when considering or undertaking cross-border expansion?
3. What strategies do Singaporean food service companies consider to ensure success when operating internationally?

8. *The Importance and Contributions of the Research*

One of the research's contributions is that, while many prior studies on internationalisation and franchising focused on developed nations such as the United States and Germany, this research added to the few studies undertaken in Asian nations and Singapore. Another contribution is the research's examination of the importance of brand and its role in internationalisation, which has received insufficient research attention (King et al., 2013). The research will examine the role of the entrepreneur and founder and the presence of a professional management team in internationalisation.

Further, there have been few studies that have examined the spectrum of the internationalisation process. This research examined critical success factors of each phase of the journey (i.e. from being an aspirant to an active and successful operator). The question whether there is an 'Asian model of internationalisation' that might be different from the 'Western' model (Frazer and Merrilees, 2012) was examined.

The research's contribution to managers and owners of Singaporean companies, especially SMEs, will be the information on profiling and benchmarking from case research data obtained from the selected cases. The research's results could also prove useful to Singaporean academics, the franchising industry, government agencies, and the public who are interested in understanding internationalisation, which was an integral part of Singapore's plan as stated in the Report of the committee on future economy 2017. The critical success factors found in this research could help Singaporean companies learn from practising companies, suggesting how they could avoid pitfalls and increase their chances of success. The research also has developed diagnostic tools that can assess a company's readiness for internationalisation (appendix 2). The results can identify gaps and suggest how these could be closed.

The research sought to improve understanding of the critical success factors that help SMEs going overseas remain successful. These results provide strategic recommendations for aspiring entrants and suggest some practical strategies for government agencies responsible for assisting potential entrants.

9. Conclusions

The present chapter began with an overview, rationale, and justification for focusing on a single industry. It then provided a review of Singapore's food service industry and discussed the internationalisation of Singaporean food service companies. The chapter ended by discussing the relevance of the research, outlining the research questions, and suggesting some of its hopes for contributions. The next chapter provides a review of the relevant literature, while subsequent chapters discuss the research, its results, and its implications.

CHAPTER 2

THEORETICAL FOUNDATION

This chapter reviews the literature relevant to internationalisation in emerging markets in Asia and the importance of critical success factors for internationalisation. This review provides a guide to the present research of Singaporean companies seeking success in internationalisation. The review has seven major sections.

Section 1 provides an overview of the literature on the internationalisation of Asian firms.

Section 2 looks at the emerging Asian variant of internationalisation.

Section 3 discusses the concept of success in internationalisation.

Section 4 defines the concept of the critical success factor.

Section 5 reviews the general literature on critical success factors.

1. The Internationalisation of Asian Firms

Bowen (2017) noted that there are many definitions of *internationalisation.* Many early studies examined the international activities of multinational enterprises (e.g. Beamish and Banks, 1987). Johanson and Vahlne (2003) discussed this in terms of the outward movement of individual organisations to a foreign country, while Welch and Luostarinen (1988) suggested that *internationalisation* could be defined in terms of a firm's increased involvement in international operations. A broader definition has suggested that internationalisation is 'a process through which a firm moves from operating solely in its domestic marketplace to international markets' (Javalgi et al., 2003, p. 185). Table 2.1 differentiates four suggested strategies for internationalisation that provided insights used in the present research.

Table 2.1: Four strategies for internationalisation

Category	Definition
Global	More than 20% in all three regions
Bi-regional	More than 20% in the two regions but less than 50% in the home region
Home region oriented	More than 50% within the home region
Host region oriented	More than 50% of sales in one region besides the home region

Source: Teramae et al., 2019

Many 'global' companies have most of their sales within the home leg of the 'triad', namely, North America, the European Union (EU), or Asia. Beyond the triad, a broader definition of the region includes North America, Europe, Asia-Pacific, and others (Rugman and Verbeke, 2004).

Alouiche and Schlentrich (2009) sought to answer two key questions about internationalisation, namely,

1. Where should the firms expand overseas?
2. What is the optimal entry mode into the priority target countries?

They suggested a prescriptive three-phase international franchise expansion model that is shown in Figure 2.1. That was a conceptual and analytic framework that integrates academic research and business experience. The authors were able to use the model to objectively determine the relative attractiveness of many countries as potential franchise expansion markets.

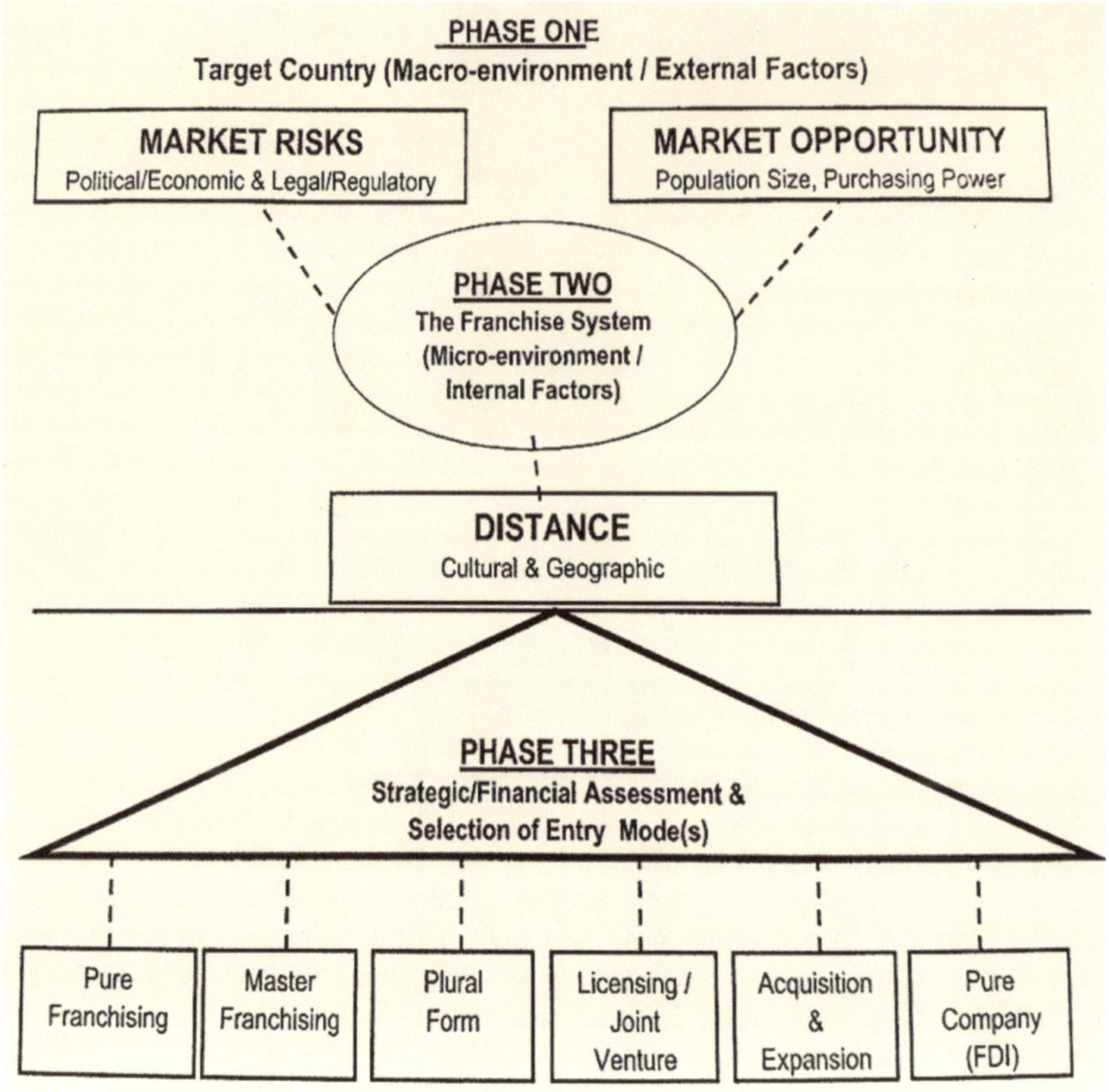

Figure 2.1: An international expansion assessment model

Source: Aliouche and Schlentrich (2011)

The model also highlighted the importance of explicitly assessing the relative influences of the key determinants of internationalisation decisions. Finally, the model enabled the creation of a comprehensive international franchise expansion index that ranked 143 countries according to their attractiveness as an expansion market.

In the literature, there are many studies about the internationalisation of developed nations' companies entering Asia, but the reverse (i.e. Asian companies, including those in the food service sector) is still lacking (Uzhegova and Baik, 2020).

The rise of Asia and the internationalisation of Asian firms (Paul and Dikova, 2016) is the latest wave in globalisation, and that could be Globalisation 4.0 in the coming decades. Asian firms are beginning to challenge companies from developed nations (Luo and Tang, 2007; Demirbag et al., 2009). These Asian firms from China and India (Bhasin and Paul, 2016) as well as those of South Korea, Japan, and Taiwan could make up the leading force in the next century. There is a need to understand Asian firms and their characteristics in their internationalisation journey (Paul and Dikova, 2016; Galloway et al., 2020).

However, internationalisation literature on Asia and other emerging markets (Table 2.3) is still largely underdeveloped, and it says much about the relative infancy of this area (Frazer and Merrilees, 2005). Some of the recent works include Wang et al. (2008), Anderson et al. (2018), and Lo and Pan (2020), who have written about internationalisation in China, Vietnam (Nhan and Le, 2019), and India (Paswan, 2008; Dar, 2019).

Asia attracted many foreign franchisers in the 1980s and 1990s. Within a few decades, Asia has the most considerable number of franchising networks in the world: 13,900 international franchisers with 1.3 million franchise establishments, which surpasses North America (Antonowicz, 2011). Given that Asia has half of the world's population with a rapidly growing middle class, Asia leads the franchising networks of the developed world (Ghantos and Das, 2018).

The next wave of international franchising in Asia is the proliferation of Asian franchise concepts in Asia (Hussain et al., 2020). Some strong players include Jollibee from the Philippines, with more than 302 outlets and expanding its footprint in Asia and acquiring other established brands like Pho 24 from Vietnam (Liddle, 1998, 'Cash-Up Filipinos Feast on Fast Food 2000'). Other notable international franchisers are from Singapore, such as BreadTalk Group with some 1,000 international outlets, and Ya Kun.

However, there is little understanding of Asian franchising brands (Frazer and Merrilees, 2005). Besides, there is a lack of knowledge on the factors affecting internationalisation in Asia and how much Asian franchise brands have used Western approaches to franchise management or in what ways these systems adapt to the Asian context (Laroche et al., 2020). This research strives to contribute to this understanding from the perspective of Singapore's SMEs in the food service sector.

2. *Is There an Asian Variant of Internationalisation?*

Frazer, Merrilees, and Bodey (2007) proposed an Asian variant model of franchising that requires further research. There are different approaches taken by Asian and non-Western countries in internationalisation in the more recent literature (Wang et al., 2019; Galloway et al., 2020).

Distinctively, there are gaps in the literature on the preferred governance modes for Asian franchisers. Choo (2005) highlighted that brand hijacking in East Asia occurred amongst many other forms of franchisee opportunism (Shane, 1996; Hussain et al., 2020). Against this backdrop, there are reasons to believe that non-US franchisers in this part of the world differ in their choice of governance compared with US companies in their internationalising experience.

Given the conditions of internationalisation, would there be consequences on the choice of market entry that will improve success rates for SMEs in their internationalisation effort?

SMEs follow the Uppsala internationalisation process model (Vahlne and Johanson 2017). Still, there have been cases of them leapfrogging from low to high commitment in distant markets like 'instant' or 'born global' companies (Frazer et al., 2007; Liu, 2017). McKinsey & Co. (1993, p. 9) was the first to develop the 'born global' concept, suggesting:

These firms view the world as their marketplace from the outset and see the domestic market as a support for their international business.

It is a mindset and a management view that the world is their marketplace. Born global firms plan to start international activities right from their birth. Frazer et al. (2007) suggested firms can take a reactive as well as a proactive approach to internationalisation. The proactive approach involves purposeful planning and the execution of a deliberate international expansion strategy. The question is whether a company conceptualises such plans from inception or as their systems mature.

This new picture of internationalisation came with changing global market conditions and the development of new transportation and communication technologies and frequent travel (Rasmussen and Madsen, 2002). These new firms have been given different labels, such as international new ventures (Oviatt and McDougall, 2005, Moen, 2002), high-technology start-ups (Jolly et al., 1992), and born globals (McKinsey & Co., 1993; Knight and Cavusgil, 1996; Madsen and Servais, 1997). This new development was so significant that Cavusgil (1994) suggested gradual internationalisation was dead.

While many born global firms are high-tech firms (Madsen, 2013), born global firms of different sizes, ages, and experiences are emerging (Knight and Liesch, 2016). However, there has been little research into born globals in the food manufacturing and food service area, and Madsen (2013) reported that only 4 out of 900 born global companies he examined were in the food or textiles sector. This lack of research begs the question whether food service companies in Asia can be born global.

Therefore, unlike the Uppsala model, the current thinking is that internationalisation is multilateral. It is a network model that examines the relationship between firms and analyses external internationalisation. Firms forge new networks and relationships in new markets by connecting with existing systems in other countries (Gerschewski et al., 2020). Internationalisation, then, is about exploiting the firm's group of network relationships rather than just focusing on the firm's specific advantages.

Therefore, the understanding of the internationalisation of SMEs should focus on the use of different approaches and theories and, as Ruzzier et al. (2006) proposed, 'integration of process models, innovation models, network approach, resource-based view, and international entrepreneurship theory. The final analysis is that there is no single theory of internationalisation that can explain this phenomenon.

3. Definition of Success in Internationalisation

Internationalisation success can be a difficult concept to grasp. It depends on the objectives of internationalisation. The measurement of that success is dependent on the parameters used (Coelen, 2009). The *Oxford Dictionary* (2020 edition) defines *success* as

[t]he accomplishment of the aim or purpose, or a good outcome of an undertaking.

Depending on the reason for internationalisation, success in internationalisation can have quite different meanings (Coelen, 2009).

One of the questions for internationalisation will be why certain firms are more successful than others in their expansion overseas and what the prerequisites for success are. For many participants in the present research, stepping out of Singapore was already a success according to Albert Kong, managing director of Asiawide Consulting Pte Ltd who is an industry expert in assisting Singaporean companies to venture overseas for the last thirty years.

A financial yardstick often measures success, and many will only dare to claim it if they have overseas outlets that are consistently returning a revenue. Another measurement of success is the number of outlets abroad. This is positively related to market share, power, credibility, and economies of scale in purchasing, operations, and marketing promotions. Yet another is the rate of growth (Alon, 2006). Growth is interrelated with internationalisation (Gruenhagan et al., 2018). The rate of growth is a more robust measure where there is a lack of financial data, such as overseas sales as a percentage of overall sales (Shane, 1996a). A more recent study by Demir et al. (2021) suggested that strategic agility and internationalisation speed influenced international success, which was measured in terms of profitability, sales growth, and the realisation of organisational goals.

Critical success factors, therefore, are key areas of this research. However, success can be elusive, and many participants in the research have required that the measurement of success be sustainable. There is no point in declaring success in internationalisation in a year where many overseas outlets were opened, and then subsequently, these outlets 'disappear' for a host of reasons, such as during a pandemic. In general, to achieve an acceptable measure of success, Singaporean companies must identify the critical success factors for internationalisation and develop the necessary capabilities, skills, knowledge, or personnel when venturing overseas.

4. *What Are the Critical Success Factors?*

The critical success factor (CSF) approach to management has existed for a considerable time. Daniel (1961) is regarded as perhaps one of its earliest proponents, and the approach has been applied extensively to the information systems (IS) field and extended to more 'generic' approaches to management over the past two decades (Fayaz et al., 2017; Mazzarol et al., 2001; Moueff et al., 2020). There are several definitions of *CSFs*. Daniel (1961) mooted the concept of success factors, which was refined by Rockart (1979, p. 85):

The limited number of areas in which results, if they are satisfactory, will ensure successful competitive performance in an organisation.

Brotherton and Shaw (1996) identified and classified a set of critical success factors, and their adapted model can be seen in Figure 2.2, which depicts the multidimensional interactions between critical success factors, firm goals, and implemented strategies. Their study provided a typology of critical success factors for the various categories examined in this research (i.e. aspirants, actives, achievers, acquirers, and advisers).

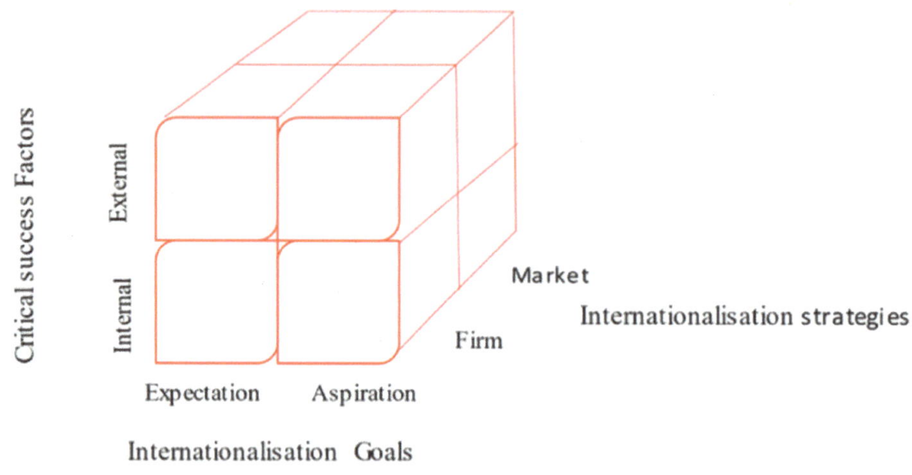

Source: An adaption of Brotherton and Shaw's model (1996)

Figure 2.2: A multidimensional interactive model of CSFs, goals, and strategies affecting internationalisation success

Given the many definitions of *CSFs*, Rockart's description is the most comprehensive because it makes the connection between internal and external factors for a particular company (Pfoser et al., 2016). The classification of CSFs into a 'useful many' or a 'vital few', together with the understanding of the external environment and the competitive marketplace, will aid the formulation of strategic decisions that will affect the success (Aaker, 1984).

Choo (2003) defined *CSFs* as capabilities and critical activities that companies must possess or perform particularly well to outperform their competitors. These factors also must be managerial and continually monitored to lead to high performance (Aich et al., 2018). It is clear that CSFs have a meaningful impact in the real world and that there is a need to identify them and establish their relevance (Bose, 2016).

There is, however, no single factor for success in internationalisation (Paul and Dikova, 2016; Pham et al., 2020). The extant literature in the next section revealed that there could be several significant factors for the success of internationalisation.

5. *The Literature on Critical Success Factors*

Chiang and Chathoth's (2013, p. 204) exploratory study of three Hong Kong food service firms noted, '[T] he issue of international expansion strategy formulation and evolution arguably deserves closer scrutiny.' Thus, this section covers some of the literature on CSFs and how they affect competencies and strategies that influence the outcomes for internationalisation. Table 2.2 illustrates the critical theories on CSFs in the general literature. There is a reasonable consensus on the capabilities that companies or franchisers must have to achieve a higher probability of successful international operations (Nogy, 2017).

Table 2.2: Research Papers on Critical Success Factors in Internationalisation

Key Research Papers	Critical Success Factors	Key Implications
Bose (2016) **Bowen (2019)** **Pham et al. (2020)**	Firm characteristics as determinants of internationalisation. Domestic success as key to international success Domestic capabilities concerning marketing, distribution, and location selection auguring well for internationalisation	• The study tends to be firm-centric and lacks the vigour to accommodate external factors of the host countries which will affect the success of internationalisation. • It could not manage the rise of 'born global', which defines the need for domestic success. • Recent research highlights that current internationalisation successes affect the outcomes of future international endeavours. • While domestic success is key to international success, consequent international success enhances, consolidates, and further fuels success in the domestic market as firms learn from the handling of customers in foreign markets. This will also affect their production technology, improve domestic sales, and enhance long-term competitiveness.

Key Research Papers	Critical Success Factors	Key Implications
Wong and Merrilees (2007) **Hinson, Osabutey, and Kosiba (2020)**	Importance of brand	• A brand is an abstraction of social values, and it embodies social and emotional benefits to the consumers. The consumer associates with the brand, and that results in success for the owner of the brand. • Brand and product congruence are CSFs. • The brand is a CSF for the long-term sustainability of overseas franchises. • SMEs do not place emphasis on branding as an internationalisation strategy. • Brand awareness, equity, and performance are interrelated to the financial performance of a company venturing overseas.
Doherty and Quinn (1999) **Dube et al. (2016)** **Bowen (2017, 2019)**	Suitability of taste	• Not much prominence is accorded to the suitability of taste as a CSF in internationalisation in the literature. • More recent studies shed light on this CSF. If the focus is on the Muslim population in Southeast Asia, halal certification of food is vital in ensuring that the food is suitable for this group for patronage and success. • Stronger cultural affiliation of food with the consumers of the host country will result in acceptance and generate success in internationalisation.

Key Research Papers	Critical Success Factors	Key Implications
Lafontaine and Shaw (1999) **Klein (1995)** **Chaplin (2017)** **Kirschling (2019)** **Lee and Lee (2020)**	Attractive franchise terms	• Friendly and acceptable terms are essential to ensure brand acquisition for overseas expansion. • Unattractive and overprotective terms for the licensee and franchiser can impede development in the host country. • The focus should be on not just monetary terms but also the whole franchise contract and all the terms in that agreement. • Fairness in the contract will subsequently lead to the re-contracting of the franchise agreement. • Unfavourable contract terms can lead to conflict in the franchiser and franchisee relationship and satisfaction. It can stifle entrepreneurship and thwart innovation and continuous development overseas.
Choo (2005) **Saraogi (2009)** **Oliveira (2017)** **Jin (2017)**	Right overseas partner	• It is one of the key determinants for international success. • Giving the right support to the partner during expansion as well as in times of conflict is key to sustainability and long-term performance. • Forging a partnership in internationalisation requires the company to look at not just economic considerations but also the sustainability of the concept in the host country. Companies must focus on the motivations, aspirations, and expectations of overseas partners to forge a long, sustaining relationship.

Key Research Papers	Critical Success Factors	Key Implications
Antoncic and Hisrich (2000) **Bradford et al. (2017)** **Cahen et al. (2017)** **Igwe and Kanyembo (2019)**	Understanding and management of internal and external factors Firm – internal (enterprise) Firm – external (entrepreneurial and business environment) factors	• The exploratory study requires further testing of the propositions. • Financial data furnished on the measurement of success were based on the opinions of the owners and managers. • Institutions such as the government play a significant role in SMEs overcoming internal and external barriers to going international. • Internal and external factors are barriers and impediments to internationalisation, and the impact varies across industries and types of firms.
Choo (2003) **Nogy (2017)**	Developing key capabilities for internationalisation Administrative efficiency Cultural adaptability Host country policy Foreign exchange	• Managerial capabilities have overarching consequences in internationalisation amongst other skills such as networking, technology, fiscal management, or marketing. • The ability to respond to external challenges with a dynamic managerial capability development will augur well for internationalisation. • A global mindset is key in internationalisation that manages much uncertainty in the host country.

Key Research Papers	Critical Success Factors	Key Implications
Campbell et al. (2009) **Kyvik (2011)** **Kamata et al. (2017)** **Ooi and Richardson (2019)**	Role of entrepreneurs and the management team in internationalisation	• Entrepreneurs and the management team are the vital driving force of internationalisation. • Entrepreneurial involvement and decision-making are critical for SMEs in their internationalisation efforts. • The team's attitudes and values towards venturing overseas can be critical. • Having the right mindset is also key. • The international attitude of the entrepreneurs in non-family firms registered a higher level of internationalisation as compared with family-oriented firms.
Choo (2005) **Frazer, Merrilees, and Bodey (2007)** **Kruesi, Kim, and Hemmington (2017)** **Lin and Ho (2019)**	Right 'modus' for expansion	• The firm's resources dictate the choice of market entry. • A more recent study showed that the size of the organisation, the importance of intangible assets, the investments in these assets, and external factors such as legal and political risk and the availability of the right local partner determine the mode of entry into a foreign market. • Franchising is more suited to smaller SMEs for internationalisation. • The emergence of a hybrid governance structure in Asia will suit the target of foreign territory.

Key Research Papers	Critical Success Factors	Key Implications
		• With limited financial and personnel resources, innovation, product characteristics, advertising intensity, export intensity, and industry have a positive effect on deciding the choice of a high-level resource commitment for SMEs in foreign markets. • Is there an Asian variant in the choice of market entry?

Source: Compiled by the author

5.1. Firm Characteristics Determine International Success

Firm characteristics are explanatory variables in internationalisation success, especially for new manufacturing firms that ventured overseas (Brodzicki, 2017). Cicic et al. (1999, p. 90) noted that 'unique firm advantages would range from variables such as superior, patented or competitively priced products, domestic market experience, technological orientation, experience in distribution and management expertise'.

The other outstanding characteristic is the firm size (Idris and Saridakis, 2018). Although success in domestic development may not necessarily mean international success, Huszagh et al. (1992) noted that experience in local development provides the firm with the knowledge for internationalisation. Except for a born global concept where internationalisation occurred from the very first outlet, most others would follow the 'make global' route as postulated by Frazer, Merrilees, and Bodey (2007). In this context, franchisers in Australia will ride on the success of domestic franchising in Australia before embarking on any internationalisation (Macek et al., 2019).

Alon and McKee (1999) went further to suggest that firms ought to consider internationalisation only when they have run a minimum of two outlets over three years or three outlets for two years. This local development will equip the firm with the needed capabilities first in the domestic arena to tackle issues of franchisee opportunism before proceeding to manage the more complex international stage (Huszagh et al., 1992). Franchisers with a vast domestic geographic dispersion of franchisees are more likely to seek international franchisees, and other scholars supported this view (Sun et al., 2019).

A recent study by Bose (2016) highlights that current internationalisation successes affect the outcomes of future international endeavours. In another study by Pham et al. (2020), the authors noted that while domestic success is key to international success, consequent international successes enhance, consolidate, and further fuel success in the domestic market as firms learn from the handling of customers in foreign markets. This will also affect their production technology, improve domestic sales, and enhance long-term competitiveness. It is a circular loop of success begetting further success.

5.2. Brand

A brand is one of the critical firm characteristics as it has recognition and sustaining power that makes it distinctive from the competition. In the literature, the power of the brand does not have much prominence, yet brand power and dominance are some of the CSFs in the continuing success of internationalisation.

The challenge for companies venturing overseas is to create awareness and market the brand using local culture and stereotypes and adapt it to the local context to win the hearts and minds of foreign customers (Kotler and Gertner, 2002). In the same light, Wong and Merrilees (2007) highlighted that branding is accorded emphasis in domestic marketing research and has been neglected in the international context. The author further pointed out that the success of the international marketing strategy contributes to international performance.

Before embarking on internationalisation, the brand and concept must be attractive to the host country and the potential partners or franchisees initially who intend to bring the brand to the overseas market (Gikonyo et al., 2015). The power of the brand, therefore, is a CSF for sustainability and long-term viability (Gikonyo et al., 2015; Hinson et al., 2020). While competitors can replicate the outlet operations, menu, and service delivery, they cannot copy a brand name (if it is trademarked), and that is a competitive advantage (Shane and Spell, 1998). Despite this, many studies still find that branding strategies are lacking in all but the most mature SMEs (Wong and Merrilees, 2008).

5.3. Taste Suitability

This research is on the food service sector, and inevitably, the food concept and product offering must fit the taste palates of the customers in the host country. The choice of the concept for the host country should have relevance in terms of taste preference and be culturally aligned to achieve any success (Doherty and Quinn, 1999). Bowen's (2017) study showed that between the SMEs in Wales and Brittany, the Breton SMEs' strong cultural identity of their food products and branding was more successful in internationalisation compared with the Welsh SMEs. Taste suitability is often assumed to be a given, but if the original taste is not suitable for the customers in the host country, the expansion of the brand is restrictive.

Dube et al.'s (2016) study showed that for local firms to internationalise in Muslim-populated countries such as Malaysia, regions in the Philippines, and Indonesia, having suitable food for Muslims by obtaining halal certification is the single most important and core factor for success.

5.4. Franchise-Friendly Terms

For the brand or concept to gain a foothold in the host country, overseas partners must adopt it. Companies would have to consider friendly terms for their foreign partners to secure their expansion overseas (Gikroyo et al., 2015; Combs and Castrogiovanni, 2004). As highlighted by Doherty and Quinn (1999) for international expansion, companies must adapt and appraise the franchise agreements for global development that would give them the most significant levels of control.

A recent study by Kirschling (2019) argued that unattractive terms and obsession with what he called 'the nickel' could result in investors, licensees, and franchisees not generating the required returns relative to risk. Lee and Lee (2020, p. 509) highlighted that 'distributive fairness and informational fairness increase the relationship quality, which franchisees perceive under the franchise system'. Both distributive and informational fairness matter for domestic and global franchises. The study also shows that the key relationship quality is trust, and that affects significantly when it comes to performance and re-contracting after the initial agreement expires.

5.5. The Right Overseas Partners

Over and above the CSFs described in Fladmoe-Lindquist's (1966) model, authors have highlighted several other essential factors. One of the crucial success factors is the selection of a right and good international partner (Choo, 2005; Oliveira, 2017). The success of a franchise relationship hinges on both the franchiser and franchisee, and the selection of the right partner enhances its long-term survival, while poor choices can spell disaster (Saraogi, 2009; Shockley and Turner, 2016; Jang and Park, 2019).

The implication of this is a proper and systematic screening process and investment in finding the right partners. Mahizhnan (1994) noted that Singaporean companies face the challenges of trust, compatibility, and competence in selecting international partners overseas, and this is particularly true for SMEs. Once the overseas partners are selected, the next crucial task is to provide continuing support to these international partners. Services such as training and product updates are critical for maintaining good relations with partners and are critical to the performance of internationalisation (Michael and Combs, 2008; Combs et al., 2011). Besides support, communication, an essential aspect of proper relationship management, is vital to franchisees' satisfaction (Kirschling, 2019).

The CSF for any international partnership is to create satisfaction for the overseas partners, and this satisfaction can be economic and non-economic, and that contributes to the psychosocial aspect of the relationship (Kirschling, 2019). While conflicts are inevitable in any partnership, the key is to be able to manage these conflicts so that they are not disruptive to the international objective (Saraogi, 2009). Jin (2017) suggested that forging partnerships in internationalisation requires the company to look at not just economic considerations but also the sustainability of the concept in the host country. Companies must focus on the motivations, aspirations, and expectations of overseas partners to forge a long, sustaining relationship.

5.6. Internal and External Success Factors

CSFs typically dwell in a particular company's 'internal' environment. 'Differential firm advantages' such as marketing mix management, operations strategy, organisational size, corporate entrepreneurship, and management structure affect the company's specific core capabilities and competencies critical for its competitive advantage (Felzenstein et al., 2020).

Bradford et al. (2017) uses the CAGE (cultural, administrative, geographic, and economic) framework to suggest that SMEs need to overcome internal and external barriers to internationalise successfully. One feature of these external CSFs is that they 'are less controllable than the internal ones, though they may still be subject to varying degrees of measurement and control' (Brotherton and Shaw, 1996, p. 115).

The debate about whether it is the internal or external factors that deter firms from internationalisation lingers, and the verdict is still pending. For some scholars, the main obstacle is the firm itself rather than externalities (in terms of market opportunities) as the firm struggles with limited resources, capabilities, and capacities (Virglerova et al., 2020). The issue for these firms would be whether they are 'internationalisation ready'. Christiano (2018) studied family businesses venturing overseas and discovered that entrepreneurial, managerial, and financial resources were key as were how these factors affect the decision-making process in internationalisation. The entry of young successors in the family business provided the impetus and drive for this development in achieving success. The author noted that the timing, the choice of target markets, and the methods of internationalisation may vary with the life cycle of the family business and the governance structure.

Internal and external success factors have been studied concerning the motivations or drivers for internationalisation and have been categorised in many ways including push and pull factors (Madanoglu et al., 2017), proactive and reactive motivations (Bowen, 2019), and internal and external drivers (Brochado et al., 2020). Push/reactive drivers relate to negative aspects of the domestic market, while pull/initiative-taking drivers relate to attractive elements of foreign countries.

5.7. Capabilities

Graves and Thomas (2006) noted that successful international expansion requires the managerial capabilities necessary to configure and leverage a firm's resources in the global marketplace. Bose (2016) built her conceptual model on the key competencies and capabilities that determine successful future internationalisation outcomes. Seige and Weers (2020) suggested that amongst networking, technological, and marketing skills, managerial capabilities had overarching consequences for internationalisation.

Huszagh et al. (1992) identified two categories of capabilities that are critical, and the first is closely related to what is known as administrative efficiency, defined as the management of the franchise relationship at the international level. The second group of capabilities relates to managing risk in the company's conduct of business in a foreign territory (Fladmoe-Lindquist, 1996; Choo, 2003).

5.8. The Role of the Entrepreneur

Most internationalisation literature tends to focus on the firm and its characteristics. Newer studies have suggested that the roles of the founder/entrepreneur and manager are the vital driving force for SMEs' internationalisation (Wach, 2017).

The founder of the company has an essential influence on strategic orientation, resource allocation, management structure, reward philosophy, growth, and entrepreneurial culture of the firm (Cortellazzo et al., 2020). Kyvik (2011) noted that the attitudes and motivations of the decision-makers of the firm determined the path and pace of the internationalisation of SMEs. Global mentality and mindset are most crucial in internationalisation (Torkkeli et al., 2018; Goxe and Belhoste, 2019). Wach's (2017) study measured the transnational index (TNI) of both family-oriented and non-family firms in Poland and found that the international attitude of the entrepreneurs of non-family firms registered higher TNI than family-oriented firms. The entrepreneur's involvement in decision-making and initiatives was the driving force of SMEs in their internationalisation (Christmann, 2019).

As the company grows beyond a certain threshold, these attributes of the founder must cascade down to the management team and be part of the organisational culture (Crick et al., 2020). Successful internationalisation firms must have a committed, supportive, strong management team (Buzavaite and Korsakiene, 2019) and competence (Korsakiene and Bekesiene, 2019) for long-term, sustainable performance.

5.9. Choosing the Right 'Modus'

The degree of control a firm has with the intangible and tangible resources that it possesses dictates the mode of entry (Hollender et al., 2017). As noted by Buckley and Casson (2018), while foreign direct investment as an entry mode constitutes a much higher commitment at one end of the spectrum, exporting will be at the other end.

Franchising is suitable for SMEs as it fits the make-up and mindset of SMEs, and it is one of the popular choices and routes of SME expansion globally (Rosado-Serrano, 2019). A more recent study by Kruesi et al. (2017) showed that the size of the organisation, intangible assets, investment in these assets, and external factors such as legal and political risk and the availability of the right local partner determine the mode of entry into a foreign market. Aliouche and Schlentrich's (2011) study reinforced the importance of undertaking a comprehensive and systematic assessment of the various risks involved in international franchising decisions and the need to develop effective risk management methods to deal with rapid changes in the global marketplace.

For SMEs, Lin and Ho's (2019) study highlighted that with limited financial and personnel resources, SMEs are likely to base their choice of foreign market entry mode on the resources available. The authors found that innovation, product characteristics, advertising intensity, export intensity, and industry have positive effects on the choice of a high-level resource commitment for SMEs in foreign markets. Alon et al. (2020, p. 43) concluded that international franchising was the preferred mode of market entry for 'firms to develop new markets with very little risks but also little control'. While only pure franchising and master franchising are listed in Figure 2.1 as Asian approaches, there are typically four modes (i.e. master franchising, area development franchising, multi-unit franchising, and direct franchising with or without a subsidiary), which are discussed in subsequent sections.

A. Master Franchising

This entry mode is a commonly used strategy by organisations in developed nations such as those based in the USA and European countries to develop distant territories (Preble, 1995; Burton and Cross, 1997). Their major advantages are low costs, fewer risks, increased speed of business and market development, the local supervision of outlets, and better local knowledge (Justis and Judd, 1986). The franchiser assumes little political and market risk and has less direct involvement and can develop a territory expeditiously (Burton and Cross, 1997). The strategy's downside will be a loss of control, lower profits as these are shared with the master franchisee, and monitoring issues (Alon, 2000).

B. Area Development Franchising

Unlike. master franchising, area franchisees or area developers are only permitted to open franchises on their own. They are not allowed to sub-franchise independent franchisees (Burton, Cross, and Rhodes 2000). This mode gives the franchiser the advantages of master franchising but removes some disadvantages, such as a loss of control due to the sub-selling of rights to incompetent independent franchisees and increased monitoring issues (Burton, Cross, and Rhodes, 2000). This mode is also used as a complementary strategy to master franchising as some franchisers have found that this mode lets them 'hedge their bets' by setting up a smaller-area franchise territory and evaluating performance before upgrading the area franchisee to a master franchisee (Steinberg and Lescatre, 2004). Indeed, this mode is used by many Singaporean companies as they franchise to neighbouring countries.

C. Multi-Unit Franchising

Multi-unit franchising is a significant alternative to master franchising and has gained increasing popularity in Asia (Altinay and Altinay, 2003; Choo, 2005). Indeed, an International Franchise Association (2002) study found that multi-unit franchisees (MUF) operated 53 per cent of all franchised outlets across different sectors.

Multi-unit franchising is similar to area franchising as multi-unit franchisees have to invest in outlets, and sub-franchising is not permitted. However, commitment in terms of the number of outlets and the size of these outlets is much reduced. The advantage of this is a reduction in the franchisee's upfront commitment while they enjoy territory rights over a designated area. A significant disadvantage involves the creation of franchisee mini-chains that can erode a franchiser's power as there is evidence that franchisees will often seek preferential treatments like 'bulk purchases' (e.g. they may want to pay discounted rates for rebranding stores or demand discounted advertising levies). This can affect the power relationship between a MUF and a franchiser and may lead to brand hijacking (Choo, 2005; Luoma-aho et al., 2018) or affect the renewal of a franchise agreement or the survival of the franchise system (Grunhagen and Mittelstaedt, 2001).

D. Direct Franchising with or without a Subsidiary

In direct franchising, a franchiser signs up a foreign franchisee in the same way as domestic franchising; but in this case, it is a foreign host country. Direct franchising with a subsidiary is similar to direct franchising, with the franchiser establishing a presence in a host country to conduct its franchising activity. The advantages of such a mode are better monitoring of the franchisee as the franchiser has a presence in the host country, a better understanding of the local situation and increased local knowledge, and the ability to benefit from any government or tax incentives that come to a presence in the host country.

The downside is that the subsidiary is subject to the ideologies and regulations of the host country. Indeed, Kentucky Fried Chicken was forced to change its name to Kuwaiti Fried Chicken (KFC) because the local government was against American cultural imperialism.

In summary, the choice of mode may affect the success of the internationalisation of companies in any new and foreign territories.

5.10. Conceptual Models of Internationalisation

The interactions between internal factors such as firm-specific characteristics and externalities or the environment determine success in internationalisation (Rask, 2014) (Figure 2.3).

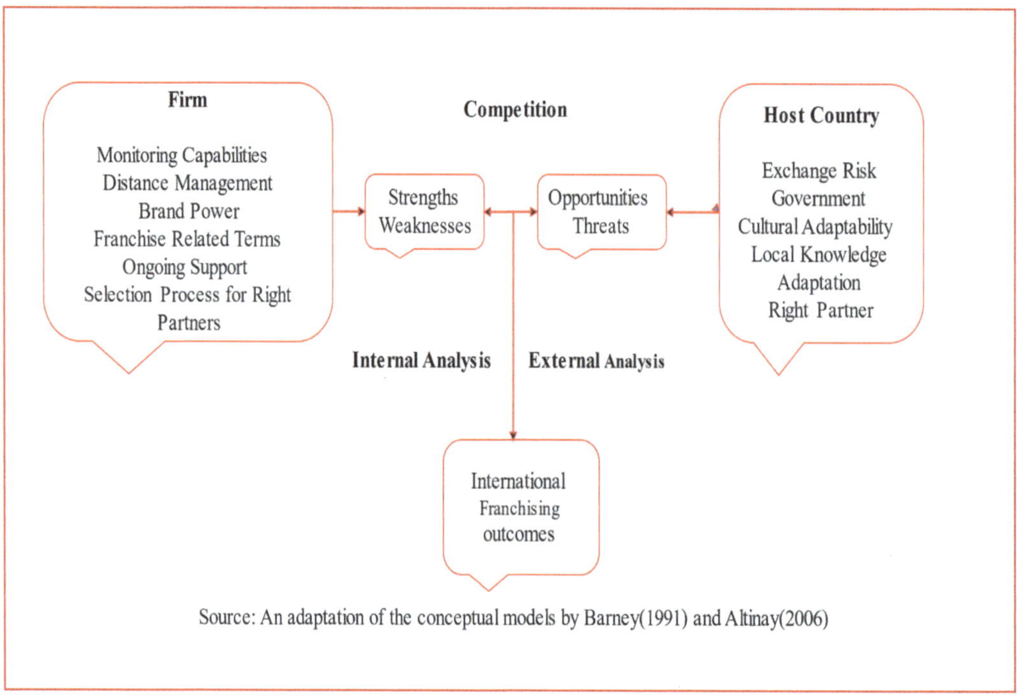

Figure 2.3: The interactions between organisational factors' effectiveness and external factors' impact on outcomes in international franchising

5.10.1. Critical Success Factors for SME Internationalisation – A Conceptual Model by Bose (2016)

Bose (2016) suggested four CSFs in SME internationalisation and built a conceptual model based on the key competencies and capabilities that are required for successful future internationalisation outcomes, which are shown in Figure 2.4. The four CSFs she identified were current internationalisation, future internationalisation prospects, internationalisation competency, and internationalisation strategy. Bose developed a model with those variables and established a relationship for showing the sequence. The model tends to be more focused on the firm and to neglect some of the critical external factors that will affect the success of internationalisation.

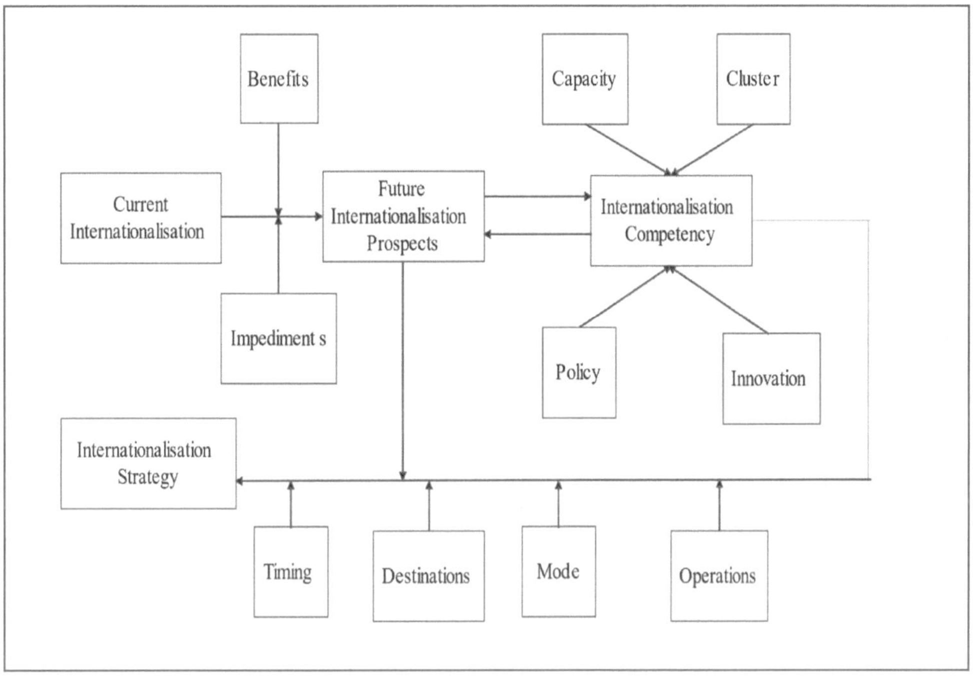

Figure 2.4: Bose's (2016) conceptual model for SME internationalisation

In her study, Bose mentioned management, a vision that could be an impediment and barrier to internationalisation. These barriers are primarily related to management and include lack of vision, fear of losing control, lack of knowledge, lack of resources, lack of consolidation in the domestic market, and the external environment – legislation, currency, cultural differences, and logistics. As she noted, psychic distance plays a vital role in the internationalisation of family SMEs. Bose's (2016) conceptual model is a synthesis of the stage and process-based models found in the general literature. Current internationalisation experience, she suggested, will affect future internationalisation prospects, a view supported earlier by Aaby and Slater (1988). In Asian societies, where failures are shunned, an unsuccessful overseas venture will be a key learning point or, at worst, may even deter subsequent efforts.

There are some inherent limitations in this study because it is confined to export activities, and a cross-industry application will be useful. It presupposes that SMEs have current internationalisation experience, but many of them are pre-internationalisation; it will be necessary to include this vast population. The external effects of the macro-environment of the host country are non-existent in the model, and it tends to be firm-centric and specific. Nonetheless, the model opened possibilities for verifying the constructs and variables for different countries.

6. Conclusion

This chapter has defined and reviewed the literature on internationalisation from an Asian perspective and the CSFs for internationalisation. The empirical research gathered in this study will shed light on the CSFs for Singaporean companies venturing overseas. In addition, it will relate how these CSFs will affect the capabilities and competencies and therefore the success of Singaporean companies in their internationalisation experience. This review has suggested several gaps in the literature, especially in terms of Asia-focused research. These gaps have led to the present study, which is discussed in subsequent chapters.

Table 2.3: Summary of relevant articles from the past twenty years

Year	Title	Authors
2000	'Intrapreneurship Modelling in Transition Economies: A Comparison of Slovenia and the United States'	Antoncic and Hisrich
2001	'Critical Success Factors for International Franchising: Case Studies of Foreign Franchisors in Asia'	Choo
2003	'Determining the Critical Success Factors of International Franchising: Cases of Foreign Franchisors in East Asia'	Choo
2005	'The Selection of International Retail Franchisees in East Asia'	Choo, Mazzarol, and Soutar
2008	'The Development of Franchising in China'	Wang, Zhu, and Terry
2009	'Equity-Based Entry Modes of Emerging Country Multinationals: Lessons from Turkey'	Demirbag et al.
2012	'Pioneering Asian Franchise Brands: Pho 24 in Vietnam'	Frazer and Merrilees
2015	'Critical Success Factors for Franchised Restaurants Entering the Kenyan Market'	Gikonyo et al.
2016	'The Halal Certification System Is a Key Determinant of Firm Internationalisation in the Philippines and Malaysia'	Dube et al.
2017	'Franchising in Southeast Asia: Prerequisites, Progress, and Prospects' 'An Empirical Study of Food and Beverage Chains' Internationalisation: Advancing Intangible Resource Theory and Research'	Terry and Grunhagen Shih
2019	'Internationalisation of SMEs: How Do Global Mindset and Network Relationships Impact India'	Dar
2020	'The "Internationalisation", or "Englishisation", of Higher Education in East Asia'	Galloway et al.

Source: Compiled by the author

CHAPTER 3

RESEARCH METHODOLOGY

1. Overview

As noted in chapter 1, the principal objective of the present study was to identify the critical success factors that affected Singaporean companies' internationalisation outcomes. The study was undertaken because there has been little research into the internationalisation of Singaporean companies. A qualitative methodology was chosen because it should improve our understanding of the what, how, and why when organisations pursue this course of action (Choo, 2005; Nogy, 2017). Indeed, the complexities involved in entrepreneurs' choices provide a good rationale for the use of a qualitative approach such as the one used here (Alonso and Kok, 2020).

A multiple-case study approach, during which the author interviewed thirty Singaporean managers and owners of food service companies, was used. Other people were also interviewed (i.e. industry experts, franchisees, and overseas partners of Singaporean companies operating in Indonesia, Malaysia, Australia, and the Philippines). Yin (2013) has suggested that such an approach (i.e. a multiple-case study) is more dependable and robust than a sole case study. Further, such an approach should generate rich data as it tracks the complexities and dynamism in each case. Miles and Huberman (1994, p. 10) have also suggested that the data collected through such an approach are 'real' as data collection 'focuses on naturally occurring, ordinary events in natural settings'. In other words, the data collected are specific to a case or situation and are realistic and vivid when compared with other types of data. Such qualitative data allows researchers to obtain a 'snapshot' of events that suggests what happened, how it happened, and why things happened.

2. The Case Study Method

Yin (1994, p. 13) defined a *case study* as 'an empirical inquiry that investigates a contemporary phenomenon within its real-life context; especially when the boundaries between phenomenon and context are not evident'. In the social sciences and management, the case study method has been used to examine business and organisational issues, education, child development, youth policy, family studies, international affairs, evaluation, technology development, and social problems (Yin, 1983).

Case studies were once considered appropriate only for exploratory research. However, Yin (2003) has pointed out that some of the best and most famous case studies have been both descriptive (e.g. Whyte's (1955) *Street Corner Society*) and explanatory (e.g. Allison's (1971) examination of the Cuban missile crisis). Indeed, Eisenhardt (1989) suggested that the case study approach can provide a description (Kidder, 1981), test a theory (Anderson, 1983; Pinfield, 1986), or generate a theory (Harris and Sutton, 1986). There are diverse types of case studies that can be classified according to their purposes (e.g. descriptive, explanatory, evaluative, or exploratory) (Robson, 1993).

In a descriptive case study, researchers organise data according to constructs and try to relate constructs. Themes formed during the data analysis identify the salient features of a case. Robson (1993) suggested that descriptive research provides an accurate profile of relevant people, events, or situations and that such patterns require extensive knowledge if researchers are to identify relevant aspects. However, Yin (2003) pointed out that descriptive case studies can also find information that answers research questions and should not be purely descriptive.

Haverland and Blatter (2012) suggested that explanatory case studies focus on identifying systematic patterns. When such patterns are considered relational, they might be termed *causal*. Further, evaluative case studies allow researchers to make judgements (Gall et al., 1966). Exploratory case studies have been described as the purest method, and it has been suggested that they can help form theory (Choo, 2005). Here, researchers ask new questions, assess new phenomena, and look at events in a new light to understand the how and why of current events (Robson, 1996). An exploratory case study is useful when there is little existing knowledge (Yin, 2003). As there is currently little research in this area, the present study can be considered an exploratory case study.

3. *Criticisms of the Case Study Method*

The case study method has faced several criticisms. Some regard the case study method as inferior to other techniques such as experiments and surveys (Yin, 1994). One of the strongest criticisms is that case studies lack the rigour of some other research methods, especially as researchers' biases can influence findings and conclusions (Yin, 1994). Further, some have argued it is inappropriate to generalise from a solitary case (Yin, 2003). To be accepted as a new scientific finding, phenomena need to be examined many times and in different conditions. However, by not relying on one case, a multiple-case study approach should provide better evidence. According to Eisenhardt (1989), there is no optimal number of cases in a multiple-case study, although she suggests that between four and ten cases suffice. When there are fewer than four cases, it is challenging to generalise, while when there are more than ten cases, data can be challenging to process and manage.

While the case study method uses analytical generalisations, other approaches, such as surveys and experiments, rely on statistical generalisations. This distinction is the most critical challenge when undertaking case studies (Yin, 1994). It is a common flaw, when using a case study method, to think in terms of statistical generalisation and to make inferences about a population (Yin, 1994). Rather, in a case study, a previously developed theory is used as a template with which to compare empirical results from the new research; and if two or more cases have the same results, replication can be assumed (Choo, 2005).

3.1. Triangulation

The case study method has some advantages as multiple sources of evidence (e.g. interviews and secondary data sources) can be included (Yin, 1994). Experiments and surveys are limited by what is measured. They do not record behaviour or look at records that can provide valuable insights, especially when the phenomenon of interest is not well understood. The case study method, on the other hand, allows researchers to examine a wide range of historical, attitudinal, and behavioural data (Yin, 1994). The use of multiple sources of evidence allows triangulation of the obtained data, which allows researchers to see whether various aspects converge. The task is to see whether 'independent measures of [a phenomenon] agree or, at least, do not contradict' (Miles and Huberman, 1994, p. 266). Case studies are convincing if such convergence occurs (Yin, 1994). Here, triangulation was examined through comparisons of the interview data obtained from the Singaporean companies and the interviews undertaken with their franchisees and industry experts who assisted these companies to expand internationally and through an examination of secondary sources of data (Patton, 2002).

4. The Case Study Approach

As the present study was explanatory and descriptive, with a focus on the what, why, and how questions, a case study approach was preferred (Yin, 2003). The use of multiple case studies was justified in this instance as it is challenging to find a solitary case that is unique, revelatory, and critical (Yin, 1983). The use of a multiple-case design also enabled various sources of evidence to be obtained that were used to triangulate the obtained data. It also supported theoretical replication (i.e. an ability to predict different results for expected reasons) and literal replication (i.e. an ability to predict comparable results) (Choo, 2005), allowing a comparison of similarities and differences within the cases, as well as allowing cross-case comparisons, which can suggest new categories and concepts and different relationships.

The number of Singaporean food service companies that have internationalised has grown over the past decade. One of the earliest directories of such companies, published by Asiawide Consulting in 2006, had only twenty-eight companies interested in venturing overseas or operating overseas outlets. An internet search (e.g. Singapore food companies + abroad) and relevant government websites (e.g. www.enterprisesg.org) found only twenty such companies that had internationalised. One site (Franchising and Licensing Asia, Singapore, www.flasingapore.org), which provides information about companies that have a common interest in franchising or licensing, included information about twenty-nine such companies. Further searches on various franchise directories, such as the Singapore Franchise Directory, found forty-five popular franchises that operated in Singapore. By integrating the data from these directories, the internet, and companies' websites, the number of Singaporean companies that have internationalised grew from eight in 2006 to eighty-two in 2019.

4.1. The Selection of Cases

There is no ideal number in the selection of cases, although Eisenhardt (1989) has suggested between four and ten cases should be examined. On the other hand, Patton (2002) argued the number of cases should depend on the quality of the information obtained as this will affect the validity and reliability of the findings. Yin (2003) also argued each selected case should be based on its ability to predict comparable results (literal replication) or different results (theoretical replication). Further, Miles and Huberman (1994, p. 28) have argued that cases should be selected to maximise variation during data analysis to see if there are 'outlier cases while the main patterns still hold'. The use of conforming and disconfirming cases increases the confidence researchers can have in a study's findings and conclusions (Miles and Huberman, 1994). All these factors were considered when choosing the cases in this study.

Oxenfeldt and Kelly (1969) classified franchise types based on two dimensions (firm size and firm age) and suggested that four stages should be examined:

1. New franchises
2. Rapidly growing franchises
3. Prosperous franchises
4. Mature and declining franchises

This suggestion was also considered when choosing the cases. Thus, the selection of the cases here was based on theoretical underpinnings and was not done for statistical reasons (Glaser and Strauss, 1967). Consequently, the selection of cases was based on Oxenfeldt and Kelly's (1969) suggestions, with some revisions (Table 3.1).

Table 3.1: Cases based on the typology of internationalising companies

Category suggested by Oxenfeldt and Kelly (1969)	Proposed category (by the researcher)	Classifications (by the researcher)	Proposed cases
New	New	Aspirants	9
Rapidly growing	Rapidly growing	Actives	7
Prosperous	Prosperous	Achievers	14
Maturing	Overseas partners	Acquirers	7
	Industry experts	Advisers	11
Total			**48**

To better triangulate the data, the study added an 'acquirers' category for overseas partners who had 'taken up or purchased' Singaporean brands. It was hoped an understanding of the motivations of those who had bought a Singaporean brand and the critical success factors for continuing their collaboration would enhance the richness of the obtained data. The definitions of the groups shown in Table 3.1 were as follows:

- Achievers are Singaporean companies that have outlets in three or more countries.
- Actives are companies that have internationalised but have outlets in fewer than three overseas countries. They are actively seeking further overseas expansion.

- Aspirants are Singaporean companies with an interest in venturing overseas that are actively pursuing franchise interest through their website and have participated in national or regional franchise expositions, although they do not have international outlets at this point.
- Acquirers are overseas companies that have acquired a Singaporean brand through franchising, licensing, or some other form of joint-venture arrangement.
- Advisers are industry experts or consultants who have helped Singaporean companies expand overseas. These include Singapore-based and internationally based consultants or experts.

The rationale for selection was on an a priori criteria that the internationalisation experiences and journeys of Singaporean companies are not homogeneous. Consequently, it was assumed there are variations worth examining, and the chosen group should improve the study's validity and reliability.

4.2. The Interview Protocol

The interview protocol is a set of broad questions for participants. The interview questions were used as a guide to ensure consistency across the interviews. These questions were not asked in each order but were used to ensure all relevant issues were covered. The interview protocol guided the interview process, and when necessary, probing ensured greater insights were obtained.

Given the study's research objectives, it was crucial that key decision-makers were interviewed, such as members of business development teams or franchising teams or founders/owners of the participating companies, to ensure participants knew about the companies' internationalising experiences and journeys. Participants had all been given false names in the reported results to maintain confidentiality.

As an icebreaker, participants were asked to share their brand's history and the story of their company, outlining critical milestones and suggesting why they felt there was a need to go or should not go overseas. This opening paved the way for more searching questions later in the interview.

5. Data Collection

A pilot study with the owner of a Singapore-based company was undertaken in December 2017. The pilot study was used to check the phrasing of the interview questions and to ensure all the needed information was included. The pilot study also helped in the rewording of some of the issues before the full-scale data collection occurred (Parkhe, 1993). Between December 2017 and December 2018, forty-eight interviews were undertaken. The interviews served two purposes:

1. To achieve triangulation, enhan4cing the validity of the data collected from the franchisees
2. To generate more data, thereby enhancing the robustness of the findings and assisting in suggesting themes for more intensive investigation

The main challenge in the data collection process was to find time with the key decision-makers as many found it difficult to spare the thirty minutes to an hour or more needed for the interview. Before a meeting, the researcher sent an email or a WhatsApp message to the participant. Subsequently, the researcher followed up with a telephone call to secure an appointment, which was usually at a time and date set by the participant. There were some rejections for a variety of reasons, such as confidentiality, a corporate policy not to be interviewed, or merely a polite rejection.

Of the fifty-eight people approached, forty-eight agreed to be interviewed (Table 3.1). One business owner did not want to be interviewed face to face as that would add to the myriad tasks she needed to schedule and fulfil. However, she agreed to a phone interview. Face-to-face interviews were conducted with the other forty-five participants except for two who were interviewed via Skype. While these data were collected through semi-structured interviews, using the interview protocol as a guide, relevant documents, such as newspaper clippings, internet news and articles, books, and annual reports on the researched companies were also gathered to provide further triangulation (Dexter, 1970). With the permission of the participants, all interviews were voice recorded, and the researcher transcribed them verbatim with all the pauses and local slang used by the participants (Silverman, 2016). One of the interviews was conducted in Chinese. This transcript was translated into English and verified with the participant before being used in the subsequent analysis. The transcripts were sent to all the participants in January 2019, allowing time for them to respond with any changes they felt were needed. Minor amendments were made to transcripts in five cases.

6. Data Analysis

Data analysis makes sense of the data collected and provides order and structure. Such analysis should be a continuous and ongoing process (Marshall and Rossman, 1989). Eisenhardt (1989, p. 539) pointed out that 'analysing data is the heart of building theory from case studies, but it is both the most difficult and the least codified part of the process'. She suggested that case study analysis should include

1. analysing within-case data,
2. searching for cross-case patterns,
3. shaping hypotheses,
4. enfolding literature,
5. reaching closure.

There is a consensus that a clear and transparent description of the analytical processes and procedures used from data collection to analysis is essential for greater validity and reliability (Hutchison et al., 2010). Consequently, the process used is discussed here in some detail.

While there are several ways to analyse text data, such as the data collected in this study, the QSR NVivo and Leximancer programs were used here. The well-known computer-aided qualitative discourse analysis software (CAQDAS) options are useful for the analysis of big text-based data sets (Hutchison et al., 2010). They offer 'visual text analytics' and 'visual data mining', providing better insights into the data's 'patterns of relevance' (Hutchinson et al., 2010). Increasingly, researchers are suggesting that QSR NVivo and Leximancer should be used in a complementary way to explore better qualitative data (Sotiriadou et al., 2014). Leximancer is automated and program-driven and provides an 'impartial analysis' based on the properties of data, which can include interview transcripts, discussion threads, and articles. It brings out essential concepts and themes that are not researcher driven or guided by a conceptual framework (Sotiriadou et al., 2014) and allows voluminous data to be effectively analysed.

QSR NVivo provides a precise identification of concepts and themes that are of interest. However, it requires some manual control of data at points in the analysis (such as coding and query development). This can be a disadvantage as researchers need to intervene by creating the nodes that eventually form the themes and concepts of interest (Wilk et al., 2019). The software identifies the main ideas in the text and suggests how they relate to one another, providing a thematic analysis as the first stage and a relational (or semantic) analysis of the interview data as the second stage.

Researchers agree there are benefits to using both packages and that they can complement each other (e.g. Wilk et al., 2019). Given the exploratory nature of this project, both CAQDAS programs were used as they were seen as providing valuable but potentially different insights into the exploration and understanding of participating companies' internationalisation journeys.

6.1. The Leximancer Analysis

The researcher transcribed the audio recordings, which led to about 150,000 words or about 300 pages in MS Word. Each interview was used as a separate document in the analysis. Subheadings and semicolon punctuation marks were deleted as they can affect the reading of the data. A lexical analysis of the data was initially undertaken in Leximancer. This is

[a] method for transforming lexical co-occurrence information from natural language into semantic patterns in an unsupervised manner. It employs two stages of co-occurrence information extraction – semantic and relational – using a different algorithm for each stage. The algorithms used are statistical, but they employ nonlinear dynamics and machine learning. (Smith and Humphrey, 2006, p. 26)

Leximancer uses blocks of text to identify concepts and themes through an iterative process of seeding word definitions from frequencies and co-occurrences (Sotiriadou et al., 2014). The output provides emergent themes that can be visualised on a map, which is stabilised by removing concepts that are not useful. The map enables an understanding of the narrative interviews as it shows the dominant themes rather than imposing researchers' interpretations of the data. The proximity of themes shows how often they appear in similar conceptual contexts. Thus, when two concepts are distant on the map, it suggests they are not used in the same contexts. The lines or pathways navigate the path in space between concepts and help researchers 'read' the map. The connectivity scores reflect the degree (equivalent to the degree score in network analysis) to which a theme connects to other concepts in the map. Leximancer can group data (e.g. franchisers and franchisees), allowing differences to be examined, and this aspect was used in this study.

The Leximancer-determined theme names were revised to reflect the concepts within them better. The size of the themes is not representative of their importance. Rather, size is indicative of a concept's co-occurrence with other concepts. The themes are heat-mapped from hottest to coolest, where red is the 'hottest' or the most prominent theme. Each concept exerts a pull on the other identified concepts with strength related to their co-occurrence value. A shorter line or spring connection shows a stronger force of attraction between the concepts, suggesting that these concepts co-occur more frequently.

Emergent themes and concepts and their relationships are represented schematically through a concept map, and a quantitative view of those relationships is provided in what is termed an *insight dashboard report*. The concept map gives a conceptual overview of the semantic structure of the online discussions and shows the strength of the association between identified concepts. The Leximancer insight dashboard report provided a quantitative overview of the concept map and a better understanding of the results (Leximancer Manual, 2017). The dashboard is useful for comparison, especially when there are separate groups or categories. In this study, this allowed differences between aspirants, achievers, acquirers, actives, and advisers to be examined.

6.2. The QSR NVivo Analysis

While Leximancer links words to concepts and generates high-level themes, it may not capture the data's richness. Consequently, QSR NVivo (version 12) was used to capture this richness. This software is particularly useful for grounded theory building. It is often used for qualitative coding, which is 'a process by which segments of data are identified as relating to or being an example of a more general idea, instance, theme or category' (Lewins and Silver, 2007, p. 81). Consequently, the data were also examined using NVivo's content analysis procedure, which helps organise and analyse unstructured data by classifying, sorting, and arranging information. This allows an examination of relationships in the data.

The Leximancer analysis output, the research questions, and the conceptual framework provided in chapters 2 and 3 assisted in the concept identification stage (Miles and Huberman, 1994). Distinct events in the data were identified and intensively scrutinised, and meaningful labels were attached (Hutchison et al., 2010). To obtain an initial impression of the data, a word frequency query was used to identify the most frequently occurring words across all the transcripts, which helped identify relevant concepts.

NVivo's main feature is a process called 'coding', which assigns truncated pieces of data to categories and subcategories known as 'nodes'. Nodes and sub-nodes surface, much like a tree structure, that showed relationships and associations to develop themes (Gahan et al., 1998). The coding stage is driven by the researcher as nodes (codes) are created for relevant text by relating them to the concept represented by each node. This researcher-driven coding provided an immediate understanding of what companies were saying about internationalisation and the critical success factors needed to achieve sustainable success when venturing overseas. While time-consuming, the researcher-driven coding process enabled the inclusion of the researcher's insights, allowing an interpretation of meaning to occur at an early stage.

At the open coding stage, phenomena were identified and categorised into preliminary themes with some guidance from prior research (Corbin and Strauss, 1990). The next step (axial coding) enabled the deduction of connections between categories by providing conceptual axes around which critical phenomena revolved (Corbin and Strauss, 1990). This stage allowed the themes to emerge more definitively, and specific themes were condensed into broader themes (Creswell et al., 2007). The last step (selective coding) identified themes (such as 'critical success factors', 'partners', 'products', and 'outlets') as more important and encompassing themes (Corbin and Strauss, 1990). Throughout this process, themes were continually compared with the data (the constant comparison technique) to ensure the best fit was obtained.

6.3. Validity and Reliability of Findings

Eisenhardt (1989) noted that, while the number of cases is often determined by practical considerations such as time and money, the process of gathering data should end when saturation is obtained. Here, incremental learning was minimal in the final interviews, which led to the decision to stop collecting data. The issue of validity in qualitative research relates to the truthfulness of the findings, while reliability refers to the stability of the results (Altheide and Johnson, 1994). For reliability, the challenge is to ensure stability over time and across researchers and research methods (Smith and Robbins, 1984). The present study followed Silverman's (2016) suggestions to ensure and enhance reliability:

1. All face-to-face interviews were recorded.
2. The researcher transcribed all recordings without outsourcing this aspect to a third party. Carefully transcribing these tapes, including the trivial but often crucial pauses and overlaps, added to the data's reliability.
3. The verbatim transcripts were used in the analysis.
4. Coding was done through NVivo, although the researcher was guided by the concepts and themes listed by the Leximancer software.

In qualitative research, validity means truth and relates to the extent to which the results represent the phenomena under study (Hammersley, 1990). To enhance validity in the present study, the researcher used participant validation (Miles and Huberman, 1994; Silverman, 2016). The transcripts were sent to the participants for their validation, and the revised copies were used in the data analysis. Moreover, by using an iterative, replication process, as well as cross-checking, it was expected that the multiple case studies would strengthen the study's internal validity (Yin, 1994). Another safeguard for internal validity is to pretest the interview protocol and audit the transcribed interviews, and the researcher ensured that this process was used here.

The triangulation of data sources also strengthens internal validity, and here, the use of thirty case studies ensured internal validity. A content analysis of the grey literature, such as government agencies and newspaper reports on Singaporean companies that have gone overseas, was also used to improve our understanding of relevant phenomena and strengthen the study's internal validity.

External validity can be an issue due to the small sample size and the fact this was a single-industry study. Another limitation is that the study is contextual with a focus on Singaporean food service companies. However, the multiple cases and the rigour of the analysis with triangulated data sources should strengthen external validity. Nevertheless, the results will be compared with prior research to enhance external validity.

7. Ethical Considerations

The ethical issues that might occur in the present study were considered before the start of the research process, and ethics clearance was obtained from the Human Research Ethics Committee at the University of Western Australia. Policies protecting participants from harmful and adverse consequences were adhered to throughout the research process. Participants were provided with a participant information sheet and signed a consent form before being interviewed. The information sheet was presented to participants who were interviewed by phone or by Skype, and verbal consent was given and audio-taped before the interview began.

Participants were also informed they could withdraw at any time. However, there was no such request in any of the interviews. Participants were also told that, should there be any complaints about how the research was conducted, they could take this up with the researcher, the researcher's supervisor, or the Human Research Ethics Committee at the University of Western Australia. Participants remained anonymous, and their confidentiality had been protected in all reporting. All participants were given a copy of their transcripts, and revisions were made to reflect their views before the data were analysed.

8. Conclusion

The present study used a multiple-case study method to obtain rich qualitative data about the internationalisation experiences and journeys of Singaporean food service companies. The use of a multiple-case study approach, which allows for theoretical replication (i.e. an ability to predict different results for expected reasons) and literal replication (i.e. an ability to predict comparable results), was discussed. Further, the importance of triangulating the data by using various sources of information was outlined. The data collection process was also discussed, as was the use of some CAQDAS programs (Leximancer and QSR NVivo) that assisted in the analysis of the obtained data.

CHAPTER 4

THE ASPIRANTS' MAIDEN VOYAGE

1. *Introduction*

The first group of Singaporean companies examined was internationalisation start-ups, known as aspirants. Section 2 provides some background information about this group while section 3 discusses the interview data and the results obtained from the Leximancer analysis. The narrative provides a general overview of the concepts and the groups of concepts that formed the themes that were relevant to this group. Section 4 presents the findings from the Leximancer analysis, section 5 summarises the findings from the NVivo analysis, and section 6 discusses the findings relevant to the research questions.

2. *Singapore's Aspiring Food Service Companies*

A recent study by QBE Insurance (*Business Times*, 2018) suggested that about 14 per cent of Singaporean SMEs were interested in internationalising. Such organisations are the aspirants that were of interest in this case study. Thus, broadly, any food service company might be classified as an aspirant if it has the intention to venture overseas. However, to be a 'serious aspirant', it would be reasonable to suggest such companies should have more than one outlet in Singapore as this suggests they were interested in growing. In summary, aspirants were companies with more than one outlet that had publicly expressed their intention to venture overseas. They were 'internationally ready' in that they had participated in regional franchise expositions or had a web page offering franchises that suggested they had franchise documentation (e.g. legal agreements and franchise offerings). As there is currently no listing of aspirants in the food service sector, a non-exhaustive list of 180 such companies was compiled. The listing included established and well-known local names (e.g. Swee Heng Bakery, Teck Kee Pau, Akashi Japanese Restaurant, and the Wang Cafe). The data used to examine aspirants came from this list, and the results obtained from this analysis are in the next section.

3. The Leximancer Analysis

There were nine interviews for the aspirant group. Most interviewees (seven) were founders or owners while one was a general manager, and one was a business development manager (Table 4.1).

Table 4.1: The Aspirants

Date	Code	Gender	Age	Education	No. of Staff	SGP	Position
3 Apr 2018	JUC	Male	28	Pre-U	150	13	Director
4 Apr 2018	CHA	Male	51	Grad	150	3	Director
9 Apr 2018	JOE	Male	23	Sec	20	6	Director
9 May 2018	VIT	Male	37	Dip	170	6	MD
28 May 2018	BYN	Male	51	Sec	1,200	10	GM
3 July 2018	WEP	Female	47	Grad	120	4	Founder
17 July 2018	STE	Male	34	Sec	50	2	BD Manager
24 July 2018	JKT	Male	50	Sec	52	7	MD
8 Oct 2018	IAC	Male	40	Grad	55	6	Director

The author interviewed the nine participants face to face using the same set of semi-structured questions. The shortest interview was half an hour, and the longest exceeded an hour. The interviews occurred between April 2018 and October 2018. Responses were transcribed subsequently and stored in separately coded files that were analysed using NVivo and subsequently Leximancer after removing unrelated text, following the procedures described in the earlier chapter.

In the Leximancer analysis, the data were examined in a systemised way (using two-sentence context blocks) to generate concepts. These concepts can be name-like or word-like concepts, which are amalgamated into themes. The concept map identifies emergent themes, showing their connectivity (i.e. the relationships between these themes). Figure 4.1 shows the heat-mapped spheres, each of which represents a theme. Ten themes were found, with the most important being overseas (red amber), outlets (amber), food (green), and partner (yellow green). Quality (blue green), customer (blue), business (light blue), and government (light purple) were less significant themes.

Figure 4.1 shows all the visible concepts within the respective themes that were important to this group of participants. A single concept, labelled in black, is linked to another with a grey line which shows the strength of the association between the two concepts.

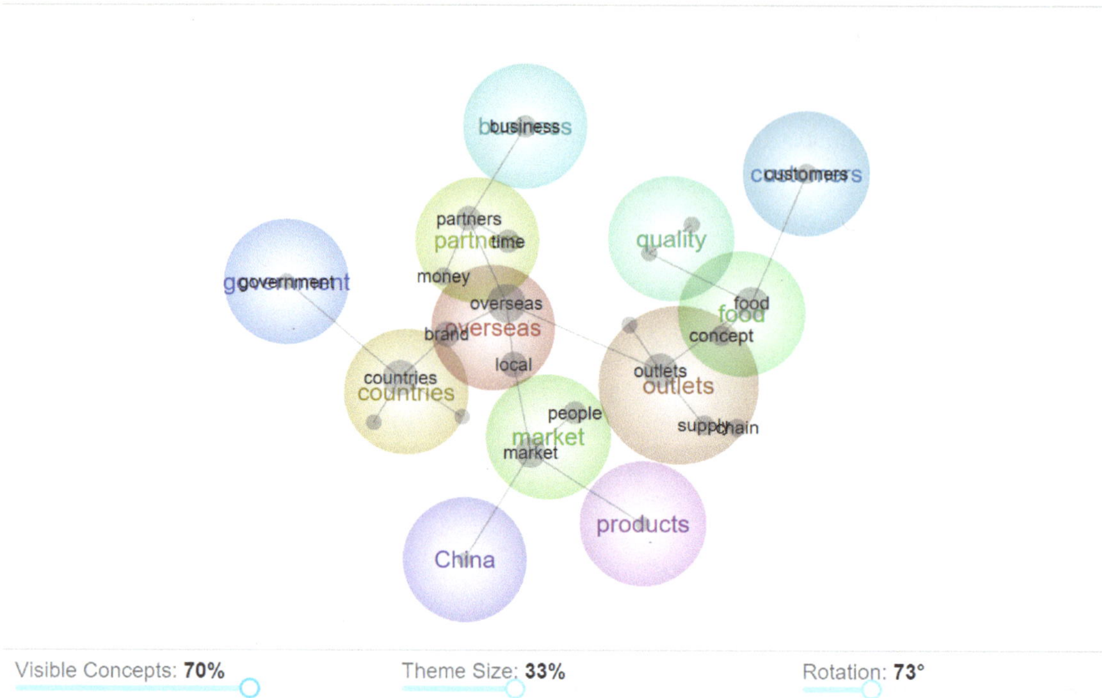

Figure 4.1: A concept map for the aspirants

These contextual associations were validated through the ranked concept relevance list (Table 4.2). Concepts clustered together to form themes, which were depicted in larger types. The concept names were coloured like the theme spheres to show their relative importance. Therefore, in the heat map, the most significant sphere is 'outlets', but the 'hottest' themes are 'overseas' and 'brand'.

Table 4.2: The Ranked Concept List

Ranked Concept List

Name-Like	Count	Relevance
China	25	23%

Word-Like	Count	Relevance
countries	107	100%
outlets	105	98%
overseas	96	90%
food	85	79%
market	74	69%
brand	62	58%
business	60	56%
people	56	52%
time	53	50%
customers	52	49%
partners	49	46%
local	42	39%
government	35	33%
concept	34	32%
supply	27	25%
retail	26	24%
franchising	26	24%
money	25	23%

In a Leximancer analysis, *relevance* is defined as the percentage frequency of text segments that are coded with that concept relative to the frequency of the most frequent concept in the list. Therefore, the most frequent will always be 100 per cent, but this does not mean all text segments contain that concept. Other relative percentages are calculated by dividing a concept's count into the top occurring (100 per cent) relevance concept's count. This measure is an indicator of the relative strength of a concept's frequency of occurrence. In Table 4.2, the list of ranked concept relevance shows the most critical concept for the aspirants is 'countries', followed by 'outlets', 'overseas', 'food', and 'market'.

4. The NVivo Analysis Findings

As this study examined the data using the Leximancer and NVivo software, this section illustrates the NVivo results. Table 4.3 shows the top twenty words, and Figure 4.2 shows the corresponding word cloud of the participants.

Table 4.3: The top twenty relevant words for the aspirants

Word	Length	Count	Weighted Percentage
overseas	8	144	1.04
business	8	122	0.88
food	4	111	0.80
market	6	90	0.65
outlets	7	89	0.64
people	6	89	0.64
brand	5	87	0.63
customers	9	73	0.53
partners	8	67	0.49
family	6	66	0.48
company	7	65	0.47
government	10	60	0.43
partner	7	56	0.41
countries	9	54	0.39
local	5	52	0.38
outlet	6	52	0.38
China	5	51	0.37
concept	7	50	0.36
internationalisation	20	48	0.35
right	5	43	0.31

Figure 4.2: A word cloud of the aspirants

Both the findings from NVivo and Leximancer analysis had similar results (excluding the name-like concept of Singapore, which was the focus of the study). The top ten themes of Leximancer and the top ten words from NVivo software are in Table 4.4.

Table 4.4: The top ten Leximancer themes and NVivo words

Ranking	Leximancer	NVivo	Ranking	Leximancer	NVivo
1	Overseas	Overseas	6	Partners	People
2	Market	Business	7	Business	Brand
3	Outlets	Food	8	Customers	Customers
4	Countries	Market	9	Government	Partners
5	Food	Outlets	10	China	Family

Participants in the aspirants group ranged from having at least two outlets in Singapore to as many as thirty outlets. Many of the aspirants had achieved some success in the domestic market. It is therefore not surprising that internationalising (going overseas) was the central theme for these aspirants. Other related concepts include 'local' and 'brand' and the motivations for going overseas for a local Singapore brand.

5. Cross-Case Analysis for the Aspirants

The Leximancer concept map identified the emergent themes and the connectivity and relationships between these themes across the various categories of participants in internationalisation. It also highlights the importance of the various themes to the groups of participants as the Leximancer analysis analysed groups in separate folders. In Figure 4.3, there are eight heat-mapped spheres, each representing a theme. All concepts and data categories are marked in grey nodes, with a label identifying the concept or the category. The size of the nodes shows the relative strength of the concept or the category, and the groups' positions show the differences in their views. The most prominent theme is 'brand' (red amber), followed by 'partners' (amber), 'support' (yellow green), 'food' (green), 'success' (blue green), 'customers' (blue), 'taste' (blue purple), and lastly 'staff' (purple).

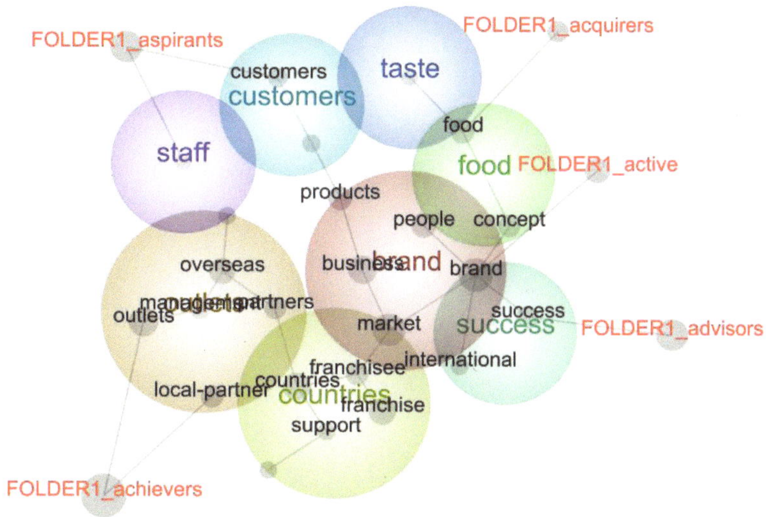

Figure 4.3: A concept map by category

Figure 4.3 shows that the concepts (in black) formed clusters that determined the themes, which appear in the larger type and are coloured the same way as the sphere. As an example, 'brand' is red (the same colour as the sphere) and is the central theme for that sphere. The related concepts in black type are 'people,' 'market,' 'brand' (as a concept), and 'business'. Grey lines linking two concepts suggest a relationship between the concepts while concept proximity shows the strength of the association. Data categories are shown in red (the outlying nodes of the map) (e.g. Folder1_achievers). Concepts and themes closest to a data category are more important to that category and less important to the other categories.

Figure 4.4 shows the dashboard quadrant map generated by the Leximancer analysis. The concepts towards the upper right-hand (magic) quadrant were the most important in the different cases. For the achievers, the most important themes and concepts were 'brand', 'markets', and 'countries', which were in the upper right quadrant. For the advisers, it was 'food'; and for the aspirants, it was going 'overseas'. The dashboard insight report suggested that the cross-case data had 4,090 context blocks made up of 2 sentences in each block, 24 concepts and 5 categories. In the next section, the discussion will focus on the participants' concept prominence .

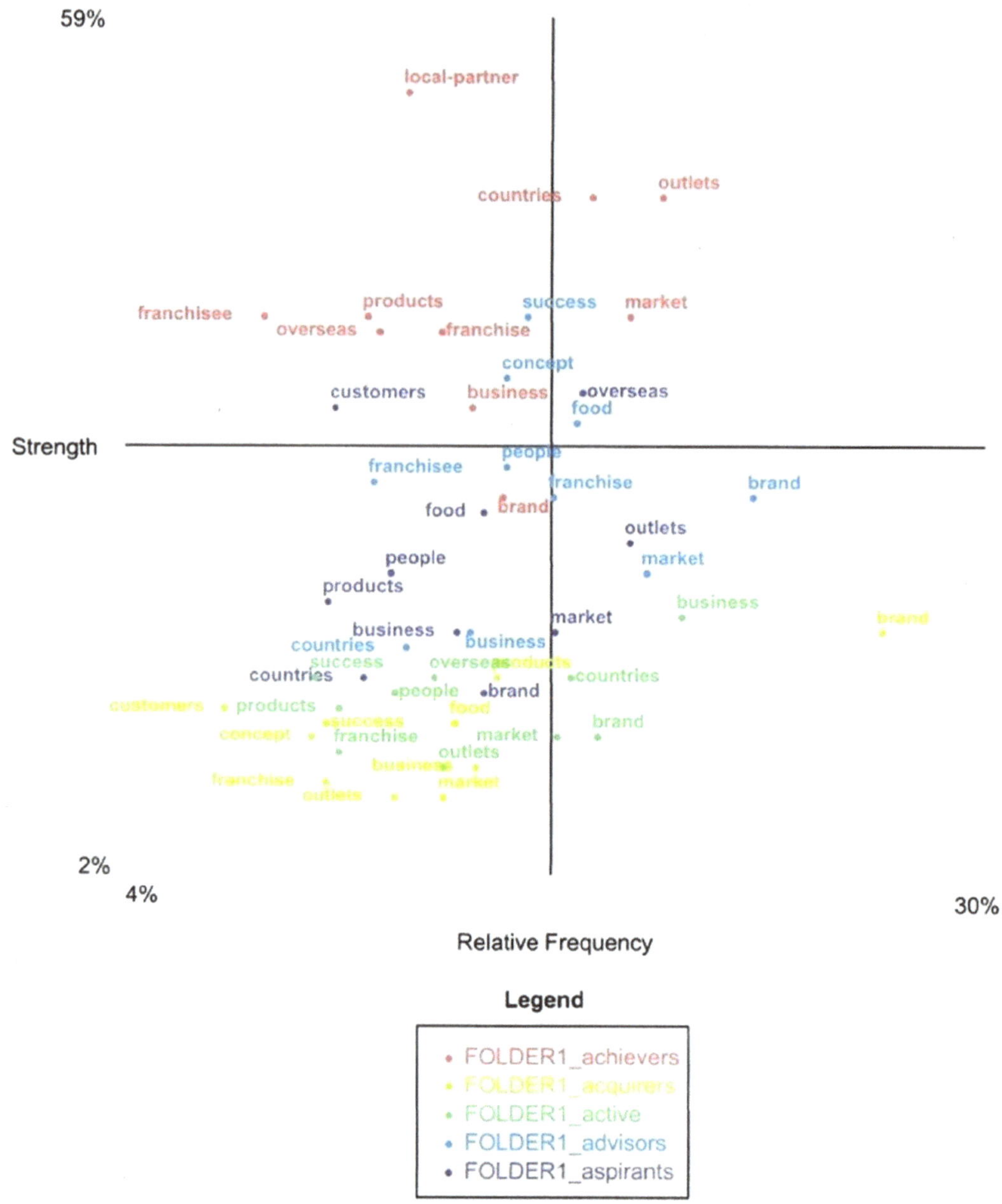

Figure 4.4: The dashboard quadrant map generated by the Leximancer analysis

5.1. Concept Prominence

In a Leximancer analysis, the prominence score combines the strength and frequency scores (Table 4.5), which 'are absolute measures of correlation between category and attribute and can be used to make comparisons over time' (Leximancer, 2018, p. 103). A score higher than 1.0 suggests a co-occurrence happened more often than by chance. The table, which shows the top concepts for each category (i.e. a prominence score of at least 1.0), highlights the relative importance of each concept to the various groups.

Table 4.5: Prominence scores by category

Aspirants	Actives	Achievers	Acquirers	Advisers
Overseas (1.7)	Business (1.5)	The local partner (1.5)	Brand (1.8)	Success (2.0)
Customer (1.7)	Country (1.3)	Country (1.3)	Product (1.5)	Concept (1.7)
Food (1.3)	Success (1.2)	Outlets (1.3)	Customer (1.3)	Food (1.6)
Outlets (1.2)	Overseas (1.2)	Products (1.1)	Success (1.2)	People (1.4)
People (1.1)	People (1.1)	Franchisee (1.1)	Food (1.2)	Franchisee (1.4)
Products (1.0)	Products (1.0)	Market (1.1)	Concept (1.1)	Franchise (1.4)
		Overseas (1.1)		Brand (1.3)

5.2. Compound Concept Prominence

The Leximancer analysis also computes a table of ranked compound concepts by category that reflects the same strength and frequency conditional probabilities. Prominence scores of 3.0 or higher (Table 4.6) suggest that such compound concepts are important to that category. These Leximancer outputs provided the basis for the discussion of the results that are provided in the next section.

Table 4.6: The top-ranking compound concept prominence scores by category

Aspirant Concept Prominence	Active Concept Prominence	Achiever Concept Prominence	Acquirer Concept Prominence	Adviser Concept Prominence
Overseas & Partner (7.2)	Franchise & Team (4.8)	Local Partner & International (3.5)	Customer & Quality (6.2)	Success & International (5.8)
Overseas & Team (6.2)	Overseas & Team (4.5)	Local Partner & Market (3.1)	Product & Taste (5.2)	People & International (5.7)
Food & Taste (5.3)	Overseas & Staff (4.3)	Local Partner & Overseas (3.0)	Brand & Product (4.8)	Franchise & International (5.4)
Customer & Food (5.1)	Overseas & Local Partner (4.2)		Food & Quality (4.6)	Food & Quality (4.7)
Food & Quality (4.2)	Success & International (4.0)		Customer & Staff (4.6)	Concept & Food (4.4)

For the aspirants, the compound concept 'overseas & partners' ranked top in prominence, followed by 'overseas and team' as in Table 4.6.

6. *Why Venture Overseas?*

It is therefore not surprising that going overseas or internationalisation is the top main theme for these aspiring companies. From both the Leximancer analysis and NVivo, the biggest theme and top word is *overseas*. The other related concepts in the Leximancer analysis were 'local' and 'brand', and the cross-analysis highlighted the compound concept of 'overseas and partners' and 'overseas and team' as the most prominent.

The motivations for going overseas for a local Singapore brand were based on the push (internal) and pull (external) factors, and these were varied for the business owners who were interviewed. For many, it was the size of the domestic market of Singapore that drove them to consider internationalisation.

The motivation [for going overseas] for us is a bigger market out of Singapore; the Singapore market is way too small and too competitive, so we spend ten years to create the product, and there is nowhere else to bring it to in Singapore. (WEP, founder)

The other push factor was that business costs such as rentals and labour costs had gone up in Singapore significantly, and recent changes in the foreign worker quotas forced business owners to look further afield.

It is not about being successful domestically that we can go overseas. There are too many changes in the market and economy, costs have gone up, and we need to make changes, and one of the options is to go overseas, and it has come a time for us to consider other areas of growth and to leap out of Singapore. (JKT, managing director of a successful heritage food brand)

Others like JUC, managing director of a new yet successful concept with more than thirteen outlets in Singapore, lamented the excessive cost of doing business in Singapore. He would be attracted to other markets such as Hong Kong where the earnings would be better than in Singapore.

Yet for others like VIT, the managing director of Singapore's heritage food concept, the pull for internationalisation may be more nationalistic with an eye for profitability for its home business.

My dream is to make our food, which is a Singapore heritage food dish, well known out of Singapore, and we hope that we can make this dish in the likes of chilli crab and Hainanese chicken rice. Internationalisation also helped our local business as tourists will come to Singapore one day, and they must have our food just like chicken rice and chilli crab.

Many aspiring companies were hopeful of their internationalisation success, and that was not a flash in the pan; many were looking at sustainable success and not going overseas just for the sake of it.

Going overseas, we must be able to sustain the outlets; otherwise, it will be pointless where we open an outlet and then unable to sustain it, and after five years, for example, we are out of that foreign market. This is surely not what we want. (BYN, general manager of a big F&B group)

Echoing the criterion of sustainability, JUC pointed out that many brands ventured out of Singapore and did not do well, and sustainability was a key issue for all companies including Toast Box (which is a concept of serving local food from the Bread Talk Group) and Ya Kun (another successful Singapore company that sells toasted bread with coconut jam called *kaya*).

7. What Are the Critical Success Factors from the Analyses?

The other keywords that are common from the Leximancer analysis and NVivo are 'market,' 'outlets,' 'food,' 'customers', and 'partners'. The participants recorded that these factors were significant to aspirants venturing overseas. The aspirants intended to venture overseas soon. In Figure 4.4, the themes closer to the aspirants were 'staff,' 'partners', 'overseas', and 'outlets' on one node and 'customers' and 'taste' on the other. In the quadrant map, 'overseas,' 'outlets', and 'markets' were located on the far right of the strength axis. Figure 4.4 suggests the 'Aspirants' are distinct, located on the far left of the map, with prominent concepts being 'customers' and 'staff'.

Aspirants are 'newbies', and rightfully, these companies are concerned about whether customers in foreign countries will like the taste of their food and how they might reach them. They consider the choice of the right market, the right location for their concept, and the right food for that market as keys to their success. The selection of the right local partner is their main concern about venturing overseas. Aspirants regard these two capabilities as vital: being able to identify and select the right partner and then managing these partners.

Over and above the capability of selecting and managing partners, aspirants realised they must prepare a team ('overseas and team, 6.2', in Table 4.6) that had the right 'staff and people' to deal with any overseas initiative. This resource was critical to success. The founders or business owners would kick-start the process, and it would then be the team that supported and managed overseas partners. Aspirants also saw a need to market the food and concept and make them appealing to customers in foreign territories ('customer and food, 5.1'). Marketing was a challenging task as it required them to adapt their marketing strategies. Aspirants needed to adapt their food to suit the local palates without compromising their 'DNA' such that the food lost its soul in foreign soil ('food and taste, 5.3'). The team must have the discernment and skill set to adapt to the new foreign challenges to make the food suitable for local patrons.

Aspirants must also find ways to maintain food quality in foreign countries ('food and quality, 4.2') and to source vital local ingredients. If foreign partners must import ingredients, this will create challenges for both parties. Training is also required before overseas outlets open, and regular retraining is needed to ensure consistent food quality.

8. Conclusion

This chapter focuses on the theoretical analysis of the aspirants, and the ensuing chapter will then elaborate on its critical success factors, strategies, and competencies in venturing overseas.

CHAPTER 5

GETTING IT RIGHT THE FIRST TIME

1. *Introduction*

For the aspirants group, the output findings were described in the previous chapter. This chapter focuses on the critical success factors, competencies, and strategies for any aspiring F&B companies venturing overseas for the first time.

Internationalisation involves stepping out of the comfort of the home country to another foreign host country, and not surprisingly, for the aspirants, the choice of their first overseas outlet will be the key concern and will determine their first internationalisation success and continuing success. As the saying goes, 'Once bitten, twice shy,' so taking the significant first step out of Singapore must be right from the very first instance, and failures will set the company back for a while.

The failure in Vietnam did affect us and our subsequent our internationalisation plan, and it set us back for some time as we had to revisit our plans and examine as to why we did not succeed in Vietnam thus from 2009 to 2014. (TAC, director of a heritage local brand)

2. *Critical Success Factors – Four Basic Rights*

The Leximancer analysis suggested that the main CSFs for the aspirants group's internationalisation were 'overseas', 'team', 'market', 'outlets', 'countries', and 'food', which were also the top five words generated by the NVivo analysis. The concept prominence as well as the compound concept prominence further strengthened the analysis.

Aspirants were not homogeneous in their approach to internationalisation. However, they shared the same concerns about what might constitute success when internationalising. The first group of success factors included more externally related and host-based factors, while the next group was more internal, organisational related, and home based.

2.1. Right Fit

Selecting the right market and country as a first step out of Singapore was a key concern. Choosing the right destination was critical as a failure on a maiden voyage would dampen the spirit of the internationalisation adventure, and it would take time to recover before venturing abroad again. All nine aspirant participants felt that proximity was important when choosing the first destination:

We plan to start in neighbouring countries such as SE Asia as it is nearer to home as we will be able to render faster response and support if required.. These countries are still Asian, and our food would not go too wrong in these countries. (VIT, managing director)

Two of these participants stated that they eventually would look at growing in China but not as their first choice of expansion for the first overseas outlet due to its challenging market conditions.

Our company can go to China, but currently, the thoughts are Japan and Indonesia. Indonesia is preferred because it is close by. (BYN, general manager)

I would choose Chinese-based countries, but I do not think that I would like to go to China because, in China, there are still 'unforeseen traps', and it is not a straightforward country. I would choose Taiwan, Korea, and Hong Kong as the initial stepping stones. (JUC, director)

2.2. Right Food

The right food for the target countries is crucial. What is 'right' is determined by the target customers of the aspiring food service companies. The theme 'customers' ranked amongst the top ten themes and top ten words in the Leximancer analysis and NVivo respectively. Out of Singapore, aspiring food service companies face a different audience whose palates are non-Singaporean, which is a crucial challenge. Food, like any product, must be suitable to the host country's customers, or there will not be a demand, and it will remain a niche that only Singaporeans or those familiar with the brand will patronise. Consumer education is vital in attracting customers:

Every country has its eating habits, and we assess if our food fits the country. If it does not, then it would not be viable to take a franchise. (JKT, managing director)

Unlike physical goods that can be replaced with a newer version, food requires adaptation to suit local tastes. Singapore's aspirants need to know the secret of the adaptation that will cater to the taste of the new locals and not compromise its 'soul' or the DNA of the brand. Often, it is assumed the 80:20 rule will apply (i.e. 80 per cent of the food menu does not need to change, while 20 per cent requires adaptation). So does what is 'core' and 'peripheral' differ from country to country? Troy Franklin, chief operating officer of World Franchise Associates, disagrees with the 80:20 rule, arguing 40 per cent of the menu remains core, 40 per cent requires adaptation, and the remaining 20 per cent requires verification on site to see whether it should remain or requires adaptation. Entrepreneur VIT felt that other than a few essential items, everything else is adaptable.

Authenticity and taste good are not related. It can be authentic, but it may not taste good:

In Sichuan, they like the mala oil, and the food is oily, but in Shanghai, mala oil is unacceptable. The critical point is the localisation of our food to what the locals think tastes good. I think many failed because of this. When we go to Taiwan, they like the herbal taste, and we need to adapt, but bringing the herbal version to Hong Kong might not work. (JKT, managing director)

What constitutes the 'right food' is, therefore, a crucial question. Aspiring companies must ascertain this before they embark on internationalisation.

2.3. Right Location

The choice of the right location was another CSF for this group of aspiring food service companies, which was not surprising as food service delivery is retail. The placement of outlets, one of the top five themes and top five words in both the Leximancer and NVivo analyses, stressed the importance of location in ensuring success. Aspirants were most particular about the location of their first outlet. While location remains important for seasoned companies, such as the BreadTalk Group, opening at the wrong location for a tenth outlet may not be fatal as is likely for aspirants entering foreign territory for the first time:

Having a successful partnership does not guarantee success if the location [of the outlet] is wrong, like in the case of a famous Singapore brand. We are selling food and not in e-commerce [online] business. (JKT, managing director)

Another participant (JUC) suggested that having the best locations would be the factor that determined their success in internationalisation.

2.4. Right Partner

The choice of the partner can make or break any overseas venture. The choice of the entry mode will dictate the need for a partner. If a foreign operation is directly owned, there is no need for a foreign partner, but many aspirants were expecting to franchise or use a combination of franchising and joint venture, necessitating the need for the right partner. BYN, a general manager, observed that for a new brand trying to venture overseas, having the right partner is critical.

It is less risky to use a partner, especially as the right partner will help navigate the challenging landscape of a foreign territory (e.g. dealing with government authorities and landlords).

Having a partner with the retail network and network with the government authorities ensures success. (IAC, director)

Given the need for a partner, the next question was, who is the right partner? JKT (director) summed it up well as he summarised the thoughts of many of the aspirants:

Finding the right partner is our main challenge, a good franchisee that we can work well together [with], trustworthy people, and that can bring about food consistency, which is our main concern.

3. The Five Key 'Knows' – Capabilities and Competencies

This group of success factors is more organisational, internally related, and home based. Bose (2016) suggested that some key internationalisation competencies are capacity, cluster, policy, and innovation. In the NVivo and Leximancer analyses, the aspirants were concerned about themes such as 'business', 'customers', 'the government', 'brand', and 'family' reflecting these aspects.

3.1. Know Your Capacity

Aspirants need to face competition to force them out of their comfort zone. Getting ready for internationalisation presupposes that the company prepares to handle the new challenges of foreign operations. It all starts with the main driver of the company, and in many instances, it is the founder or owner who sets the direction. However, for more established organisations, the senior management team is also likely to be a driver. When asked why it took twenty-six years to be ready for internationalisation, JKT (managing director) commented:

Why twenty-six years? We were not ready in the past, and I am not well educated, and we needed time to understand and learn about our business. We needed to take time to test ourselves [locally], and this is the required time needed for our journey to where we are today.

Going overseas can be a dream and goal for the founder or owner, but it must be supported across the organisation as VIT (managing director) noted.

One of the key capabilities is to be ready for internationalisation, which includes having legal agreements for franchising, licensing, or any form of joint venture as well as the formulation of strategies.

For internationalisation, it is quite straightforward; and if it is franchising, it is about getting this groundwork ready and getting the legal documentation ready. Then we are ready to go. (STE, business development manager)

Another area of concern for aspirants was the assembly of a team to support internationalisation, with 'people' being one of the top words in the NVivo analysis:

We are planning to go overseas and have our worries. It is untried, and we have many questions marks such as logistics. The other issue is the model: whether it is a single, multi, or area franchise. Other questions will be how we send our food over and the suitability of our food and whether the price is right. (VIT, managing director)

3.2. Know Yourself

Sunzi (554 BC to 496 BC) was a revered military philosopher of ancient China and the author of *The Art of War*. While *The Art of War* is still essential reading for military commanders in modern times, Sunzi's ancient wisdom has much relevance for twenty-first-century business leaders. Internationalisation is like warfare, advancing into unknown enemies' territories and conquering the lands. Internationalisation involves winning the hearts and minds of new consumers in new and foreign lands for goods and services.

The starting point in warfare or internationalisation is to 'know yourself'. The business must have unique selling points (USPs) if it is to be attractive in the international arena. For one company, it could be that the heritage food it serves is appealing in another international country; for another, it could be the appeal of the brand. For yet another, it could be the business model. Aspirants have done well in Singapore, and the critical question is whether they can replicate that success in unfamiliar territories:

My understanding is business is about the concept, systems, and people. If it is a Singapore brand, it must make sure the concept and system are proven. I see there are Singaporean companies that are newly established and franchise their business right away before it is proven. (BUR, principal consultant, Indonesia)

One of the critical challenges for aspirants is to be able to produce food of the quality expected by customers in foreign territories. To mitigate the quality issue, many companies export a secret formula sauce in dry or ambient conditions to ensure quality wherever possible. Many aspirants highlighted their concerns in getting the right 'supply':

For Australia, there are strict regulations on imports of items. We prefer that we can prepare our food with the right preparation in Singapore and then export it to Australia. It would be much cheaper rather than having a central kitchen in Australia, which has a high labour cost. Ingredients are our primary concern. (CHA, director)

However, nothing is static, and preferences and consumers' patronage is critical in a world of many choices. Thus, Bose (2016) suggested that 'innovation' was an essential internationalisation capability.

Moving forward, we need to innovate towards healthier food as the world becomes developed. The second innovation is to offer a whole range of halal products for the Middle East and Muslim markets. (WEP, founder)

Other than the food innovation that food service companies undertake to adapt to new and foreign lands, the other is to innovate the brand, which can be virtually unknown as pointed out by JOE, a company director.

Yet another area of innovation is digitalisation and the food delivery mode, which extends the food service business, bringing food to the comforts of the home.

The other area of innovation is digitalisation. We are the market leader offline [i.e. physical outlets], but we want to be the leader online. (JUC, director)

3.3. Know Your 'Enemies'

Knowing oneself without knowing one's enemies is not enough in ensuring success in internationalisation.

If you know the enemy and know yourself, you need not fear the result of a hundred battles. If you know yourself but not the enemy, for every victory gained you will also suffer a defeat. If you know neither the enemy nor yourself, you will succumb in every battle. (Sun, 2004, p. 42)

Once aspirants know their strengths and USPs, it is equally vital for them to know their 'enemies'; and in internationalisation, enemies manifest themselves in the host country's terrains, conditions, challenges, competitive environment, and barriers. Success can only come by overcoming these enemies.

We engage local consultants and our personnel to do a market study before internationalisation. While much information is available through the internet, the local partner will tell us about our principal competitors in each city, the disposable income and these are the details that we cannot get from the internet. (BYN, general manager)

3.4. Know Your Allies

In *The Art of War*, Sunzi also stressed the importance of allies and alliances (Sun, 2004). He advocated seeking alliances with neighbouring princes and the use of local guides to understand the landscape and inherent pitfalls.

Many of the aspirants had opted for franchising or what is commonly known as franchise joint ventures. They must identify suitable overseas 'allies' or partners to be successful. Identifying, understanding, and working with partners was a key theme identified in the NVivo and Leximancer analyses.

For a new brand that is trying to go overseas, to venture, the success rate is not high. Having the right local partner is the key success factor. Ideally, what we are looking for, the local partner should be an F&B player. If it is not an F&B player, it would be very tough. (BYN, general manager)

In the aspirant group, there was little data relating to partners, and this is understandable as they have yet to embark on their internationalisation journeys. However, a few shared their views on how they would like to relate to overseas partners.

The opportunities overseas will be joint ventures, and we have to understand their values, and the values must be aligned such as how they run their own companies, how they treat their staff, suppliers, and customers. (CHA, director)

3.5. Know Your Advocates

In Sunzi's *The Art of War*, knowing your advocates can be a key determinant of success in warfare (Sun, 2004). In this case study, one of the key themes was 'government', and the advocating role of the government in internationalisation was significant. All aspirants praised the Singapore government's efforts to encourage and incentivise them to venture out of Singapore to build an 'extra wing' for the economy. A little help from the government would go a long way in helping aspirants take their first baby step into a new world.

The government can assist us to link up with potential partners, factories, or suppliers or even Singaporean companies over there that can collaborate with us so that we do not have to import too much. (IAC, director)

Another aspirant, JUC, asked for the expansion of current schemes to include the provision of growth capital for internationalisation for food service companies and not just IT or IoT companies.

VIT, a managing director, felt SMEs lack the networks needed for internationalisation (Bose, 2016) and that government help in this area would be of great assistance.

We lack some excellent mentors. SMEs in Singapore may be a bit selfish, and not much sharing happened among Chinese-based companies. The government can initiate this and facilitate more networking and sharing among companies. (IAC, director)

While a government agency does assist by linking potential overseas partners with Singaporean companies, many felt this effort should be a more focused and better-aligned approach:

When there is an interested investor, they come with their agenda, and we will have our agenda. Moreover, the government agency has its own KPI and agenda, so I think for these three parties to have a common agenda is not easy, and this lack of commonness will affect the success of this business matching. (BYN, general manager)

Government agencies are enablers, and aspirants need to know how to tap existing schemes and seek help in their internationalisation efforts. There are many case studies of success stories of companies making inroads in their internationalisation journeys with the aid of government agencies.

4. Road Maps to Success

Bose (2016) suggested four strategies for successful internationalisation (i.e. the choice of mode, destination, timing, and operational strategies). The aspirants had strategies for internationalisation that varied from company to company. Table 5.1 shows the strategies adopted by these participants.

Table 5.1: Strategies for internationalisation for the aspirants

Participant	Timing	Destination	Mode	Operations
JUC	By 2019	Taiwan, Hong Kong, and Malaysia first before the others	JV franchise	Supply chain and staff availability and development
CHA	Not Ready	SE Asia, Australia, China	Prefer JV franchise	Operations issues to be the focus
JOE	By 2019	Asian cities	Franchise	Adaptation for the host countries
VIT	Ready and need help from the government to find partners	Malaysia, Indonesia, Vietnam, the Philippines, and Cambodia	Franchising	Adaptation, the right location, and marketing as keys to success in internationalisation
BYN	Depending on interests from partners	First, SE Asia	No preferred mode	Human resources to help internationalisation
WEP	In talks with potential partners	SE Asia, NE Asia, and the Middle East	Franchising and exporting for retail	Innovations and brand development

Participant	Timing	Destination	Mode	Operations
STE	Owner to decide on venturing abroad	SE Asia, in particular Indonesia and Malaysia	Franchising preferred	Ingredient availability, quality, and brand protection
JKT	Ready with a good partner	Japan and SE Asia	Franchising preferred	Adaptation and innovation as key to success
IAC	Ready	Cosmopolitan capital cities in SE Asia and China	Prefer franchising for the retail food concept	Halal ready for the regional markets

BYN, a general manager, took a more reactive stance towards his business going international, relying on opportunities to present themselves. Another participant, CHA, a director, felt the timing was not quite right yet for his company as operational issues had to be sorted out before venturing overseas:

We have intentions to go overseas with our concept. We must work out certain kinds of processes for our Singapore outlets and ensure that our processes are right and can churn out food quickly and at a higher standard of quality before we go overseas.

For IAC, a director, the company was ready for internationalisation and had at least two options to offer potential overseas partners:

We have two options for internationalisation, the first being our rebranded food concept. The other is the ready-meal market, which has big potential. While Singapore is only 1 million consumers above 65 years old, the ASEAN region has about 80 million above 65 years old, and that is a vast market.

However, another participant (JOE, a director) intended to open his first outlets by 2019:

We do not have any overseas presence now. We hope to start internationalisation in the first half of 2019.

For one other participant (VIT), the key was finding the right partner and the right location and assisting the partner in achieving food consistency and quality to have sustainable growth.

5. Conclusion

This chapter has examined the companies that were aspiring to internationalise. The analysis suggested that these participants had identified some CSFs and that these organisations were 'internationally ready'. A suggested diagnostic assessment tool for aspirants is provided in the appendices.

Being ready and prepared for internationalisation is the first step for an aspirant, and this is fundamental to success. If the first step when starting fails, it will set the company back for some time as was highlighted by many participants.

Four critical success factors (i.e. right destination, food, partner, and location) were vital and included in the diagnostic tool. These identified CSFs suggested the capabilities and competencies needed to prepare for the journey, and five key capabilities were vital. Finally, aspirants must realise that they must map their internationalisation strategies, such as the choice of selected markets, products, and potential outlets, and these strategies would determine success for the target country.

CHAPTER 6

THE TASTE OF THE FIRST FRUITS

1. Introduction

According to the National Business Survey 2017–2018 conducted by the Singapore Business Federation, more Singaporean companies are venturing overseas. In a survey of more than 1,000 Singaporean companies, 8 in 10 said they had expanded overseas (83 per cent), compared with just over half the companies surveyed in the previous year (56 per cent). Many suggested Southeast Asia was becoming increasingly important for the Singapore business community, with 71 per cent currently active in a Southeast Asian country outside Singapore. Of those keen to expand internationally, 69 per cent were planning to increase their Southeast Asian footprint, and the top three countries for companies were all in Southeast Asia (i.e. Myanmar, Vietnam, and Indonesia).

2. Singapore's 'Active' F&B Companies Venturing Overseas

According to the National Business Survey 2017–18, more Singapore companies have ventured overseas. In 2017, more Singapore businesses have expanded overseas. In a survey of more than 1,000 Singapore companies, 8 in 10 Singapore companies said they have expanded overseas in this year's survey (83 per cent), compared to just over half the companies surveyed last year (56 per cent) (n = 1,019 companies).

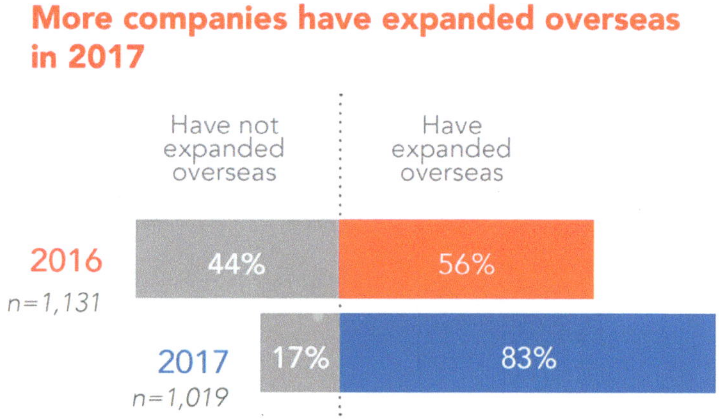

Figure 6.1: More Singapore companies going global

Source: National Business Survey 2017–18, Singapore Business Federation

There has also been a marked increase in Singaporean food service companies venturing overseas (from fewer than ten in 2006 to about eighty-one in 2019) (Asiawide Consulting Directory, 2019). Of these, forty-eight (Table 6.1) had expanded to fewer than three countries. These were termed the *active* group and were the companies of interest in this second case study. Some of them were established and known names (e.g. Swee Heng Bakery, Teck Kee Pau, Akashi Japanese Restaurant, and Wang Cafe), while others are less well known (e.g. 1A Crispy Puffs).

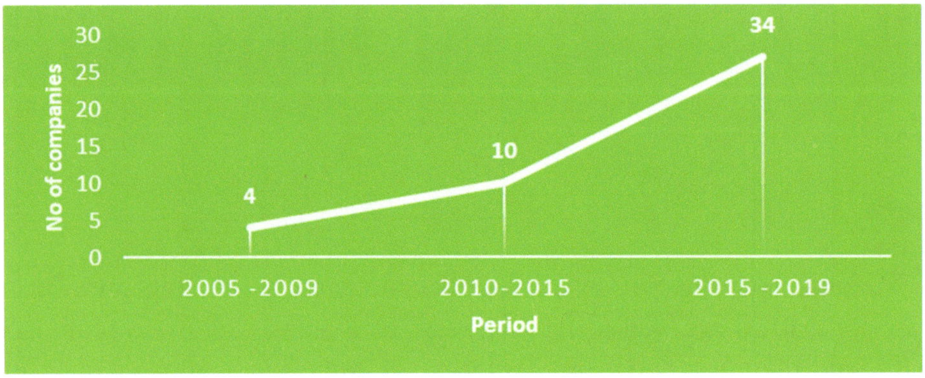

Figure 6.2: The increase in the number of Singapore food service companies venturing overseas from 2006 to 2019

Source: Asiawide Directory and compiled by the author

Table 6.1: The 'active' Singaporean food service companies

	Name of brands	SGP	Int'l	Ttl	# of countries(excl. Singapore)	Established
1	Awfully Chocolate	15	44	59	2	1998
2	TungLok Group	22	13	35	2	2014
3	Twelve Cupcakes	26	8	34	2	2011
4	Mr Bean	64	5	69	2	1995
5	Fragrance	33	5	38	2	1969
6	Geylang Lor 9	1	5	6	2	1996
7	Harry's	20	4	24	2	1992
8	Cavana	3	4	7	2	1982
9	Old Street Bak Kut Teh	16	3	19	2	2010
10	Coffee Club	12	3	15	2	1991
11	1A Crispy Puffs	8	3	11	2	1991
12	Founder Bak Kut Teh	4	3	7	2	1978
13	Ka Soh	2	3	5	2	1960
14	Barcook Bakery	11	2	13	2	2008
15	Pho Street	10	14	24	1	2013

	Name of brands	SGP	Int'l	Ttl	# of countries(excl. Singapore)	Established
16	Les Amis Group	25	10	35	1	1994
17	Snackz It!	11	10	21	1	2005
18	Irvins Salted Egg	8	6	14	1	2016
19	Katrina Group – Bali Thai	36	4	40	1	1995
20	Song Fa	7	4	11	1	1969
21	Thai Village Restaurant	2	4	6	1	1991
22	Astons	36	3	39	1	2005
23	Soup Restaurant	14	3	17	1	1991
24	Chop House	3	3	6	1	2004
25	Cedele	27	2	29	1	1997
26	Ming Fa	13	2	15	1	1946
27	Lixin Teochew	12	2	14	1	1968
28	Seoul Yummy	8	2	10	1	2004
29	Janice Wong	3	2	5	1	2011
30	Chicken Up	3	2	5	1	2010
31	LiHO	84	1	85	1	2007
32	Jollibean Express	25	1	26	1	1995
33	TCC Cafe	16	1	17	1	2003
34	Joe & Dough	15	11	4	1	2009
35	Dian Xiao Er	12	1	13	1	2008
36	PS.Cafe	9	1	10	1	1999
37	Curry Times	8	1	9	1	2015
38	Munch	6	1	7	1	2005
39	Baker & Cook/Plank	5	1	6	1	2013
40	Rong Hua Bak Kut Teh	4	1	5	1	2014
41	Xiao Bar Wang	4	1	5	1	2009
42	Brewerkz/Cafe Iguana	4	1	5	1	1997
43	Ponggol Nasi Lemak	3	1	4	1	1979
44	Maki-San	3	1	4	1	2012
45	Toss & Turn	2	1	3	1	2012
46	Small Potatoes	2	1	3	1	2015
47	VeganBurg	1	1	2	1	2010
48	Roost	1	1	2	1	2003

Source: Compiled by the author

Many participants cited Southeast Asia as becoming increasingly important for the Singapore business community, with 71 percent of companies currently active in a Southeast Asia country outside of Singapore. Of those keen to expand, 69 percent were planning to expand their Southeast Asia footprint.

The top three countries that companies were most enthusiastic about growth prospects were in Southeast Asia: Myanmar (27 per cent), Vietnam (25 per cent) and Indonesia (21 per cent).

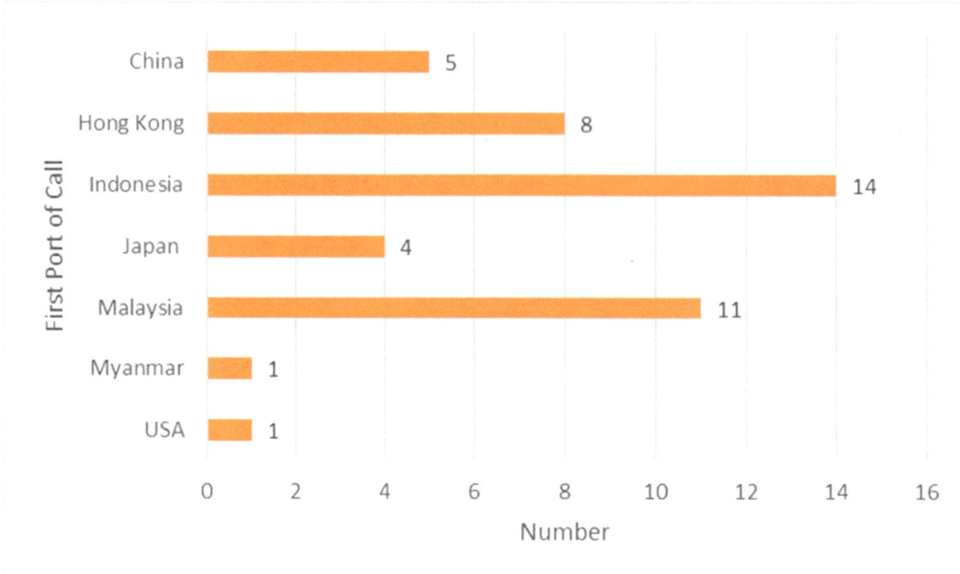

Figure 6.3: The first port of call for the actives

While the first case study examined aspiring Singapore food service companies that were keen on venturing overseas, this case study examined companies that had expanded into one or two countries and were actively looking to expand their overseas presence (i.e. the actives).

Following the same structure used in the earlier aspirants study, this chapter begins with an introduction while section 2 discusses the Leximancer analysis that provides a general overview of the concepts and the groups of concepts that formed the themes that were relevant to this group. Section 3 presents the findings obtained from the Leximancer analysis. Section 4 summarises the findings from the NVivo analysis while section 5 relates the results to the study's research questions.

3. The Leximancer Analysis

Seven interviews were conducted within the actives group, with all but one having just begun their overseas journey. All the interviews were with founders or key staff within their respective businesses. Participants in the active group had at least one outlet in one or two overseas countries and had achieved some success in their domestic market (i.e. in Singapore) before taking their first steps overseas. Table 6.2 provides a profile of the companies and the participants who were interviewed.

Table 6.2: Profiles of the actives

Date	Code	Gender	Age	Edu	# Staff	SGP	Overseas Outlets	Position
28-Dec-17	ADW	Male	45	Grad	30	4	1	MD
9-Feb-18	EAN	Male	48	Sec	60	3	1	Director
7-Mar-18	SSN	Male	38	Sec	105	12	3	MD
18-May-18	ALT	Male	55	Grad	90	1	1	CEO
6-Jun-18	TAC	Male	33	Grad	150	33	5	Director
14-Jun-18	FRL	Male	39	Grad	140	8	1	MD
24-Jul-18	ATS	Male	46	Sec	500	36	2	CEO

The author interviewed the seven participants face to face using the same set of semi-structured questions. The shortest interview was about thirty-eight minutes, and the longest exceeded seventy minutes. The interviews occurred between December 2017 and July 2018. Responses were transcribed and stored in separately coded files that were analysed using NVivo and Leximancer after removing unrelated text, following the procedures described in chapter 4.

In the Leximancer analysis, the data were examined in a systemised way (using two-sentence context blocks) to generate concepts. These concepts can be name-like or word-like concepts, which were amalgamated into themes. The concept map identifies emerging themes, showing their connectivity (i.e. the relationships between the themes).

Figure 6.1 shows the heat-mapped spheres, each of which represents a theme. There were ten critical themes, with the most prominent being ‘business’ (red), ‘local partner’ (yellow orange), ‘brand’ (yellow green), ‘outlets’ (green), ‘market’ (light green), and ‘staff’ (blue green). The less critical themes were ‘time’ (blue), ‘team’ (blue violet), and ‘management’ (purple).

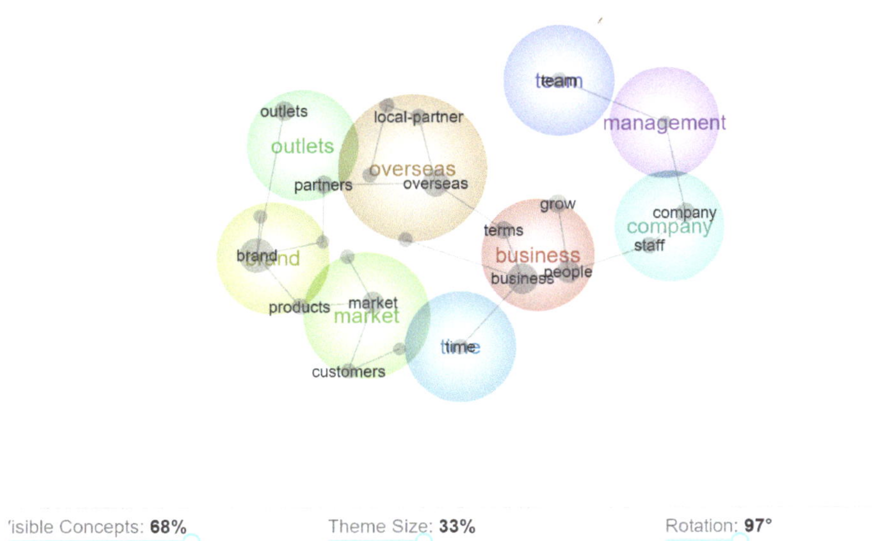

Figure 6.4: A concept map for the actives

These contextual associations were validated through the ranked concept relevance list (Table 6.3). Concepts clustered together to form themes, which are depicted in larger types. The concept names are coloured like the theme spheres to show their relative importance. Thus, in the heat map, the most significant sphere was 'overseas', but the 'hottest' in the red was 'business', which was the most important theme for the actives. For the active companies, concepts such as 'business', 'people', 'terms', and 'grow' were significant and discussed in more detail in later sections.

Table 6.3: The ranked concept list

Ranked Concept List

Name-Like	Count	Relevance
Singapore	69	78%
Indonesia	23	26%

Word-Like	Count	Relevance
business	89	100%
overseas	55	62%
people	51	57%
market	50	56%
company	48	54%
brand	47	53%
look	42	47%
countries	37	42%
different	36	40%
time	35	39%
take	33	37%
staff	32	36%
terms	31	35%
grow	30	34%
team	30	34%
work	29	33%
outlets	29	33%

As was noted in chapter 4, in a Leximancer analysis, *relevance* is defined as the percentage frequency of text segments that are coded with that concept relative to the frequency of the most frequent concept in the list. Therefore, the most frequent will always be 100 per cent, which does not mean all text segments contained that concept. Other relative percentages are calculated by dividing a concept's count into the top occurring (100 per cent) relevance concept's count. Thus, this measure is an indicator of the relative strength of a concept's frequency of occurrence. Table 6.3 suggests the most critical concept for the actives was 'brand', followed by 'business', 'overseas', 'outlets', 'people', 'market', and 'partners', and these themes will be discussed in the subsequent sections.

4. The NVivo Analysis Findings

As this study used Leximancer and NVivo software to analyse the data, the top twenty words for this group of participants are shown in Table 6.4, and the corresponding word cloud is depicted in Figure 6.5.

Table 6.4: The top twenty relevant words for the actives

Word	Length	Count	Weighted Percentage
good	4	240	1.47
business	8	161	1.42
brand	5	149	1.23
take	4	348	1.17
Singapore	9	109	1.12
market	6	110	1.04
company	7	101	1.03
local	5	120	0.92
partner	7	84	0.86
countries	9	90	0.86
outlets	7	92	0.80
products	8	88	0.69
overseas	8	62	0.64
people	6	62	0.62
success	7	66	0.61
management	10	94	0.58
family	6	64	0.56
terms	5	51	0.44
franchise	9	42	0.43
government	10	66	0.42

Figure 6.5: A word cloud for the actives

The NVivo results were like the Leximancer results (excluding the name-like concept of Singapore, which was the focus country in this study). The top ten Leximancer themes and the top ten NVivo words were as follows:

Table 6.5: The top ten Leximancer themes and NVivo words

Ranking	Leximancer	NVivo	Ranking	Leximancer	NVivo
1	Brand	Good	6	Markets	Local
2	Business	Business	7	Company	Partner
3	Overseas	Brand	8	Partners	Countries
4	Outlet	Market	9	Time	Outlets
5	People	Outlets	10	Staff	Products

5. *Cross-Case Analysis*

The cross-case analysis identified the emergent themes and the connectivity and relationships between these themes across the various categories of participants in internationalisation. This section provides an overview of the Leximancer concept map that was used to identify the emergent themes and the connectivity and relationships between these themes. It also highlights the importance of the various themes to the groups of participants as the Leximancer analysis enables groups to be examined when included in separate folders.

As can be seen in Figure 9.1, there are eight heat-mapped spheres, each representing a theme. All concepts and data categories are marked in grey nodes, with a label identifying the concept or the category. The size of the nodes shows the relative strength of the concept or the category, and the groups' positions show the differences in their views. The most prominent theme is 'brand' (red amber), followed by 'partners' (amber), 'support' (yellow green), 'food' (green), 'success' (blue green), 'customers' (blue), 'taste' (blue purple), and lastly 'staff' (purple).

Figure 6.6: A concept map by category

Figure 6.6 shows that the concepts (in black) formed clusters that determined the themes, which appear in the larger type and are coloured the same way as the sphere. As an example, 'brand' is red (the same colour as the sphere) and is the central theme for that sphere. The related concepts in black type are 'people', 'market', 'brand' (as a concept), and 'business'. Grey lines linking two concepts suggest a relationship between the concepts while concept proximity shows the strength of the association. Data categories are shown in red (the outlying nodes of the map) (e.g. Folderl_achievers). Concepts and themes closest to a data category are more important to that category and less important to the other categories.

The dashboard insight report suggested that the cross-case data had 4,090 context blocks made up of 2 sentences in each block, 24 concepts, and 5 categories. In the next section, the discussion will focus on the participants' perceptions of the concepts'prominence.

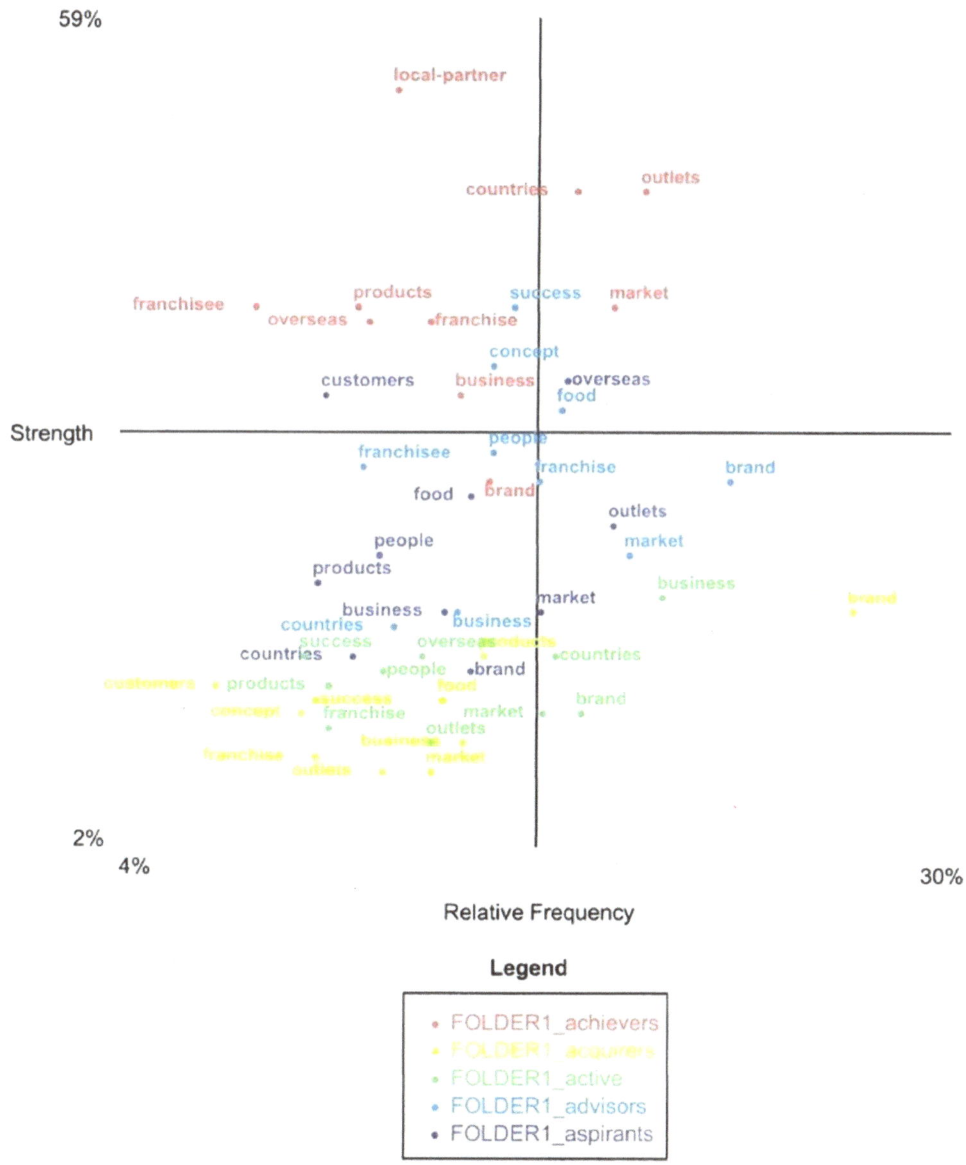

Figure 6.7: The dashboard quadrant map generated by the Leximancer analysis

It also highlights the importance of the various themes to the groups of participants as the Leximancer analysis analysed groups in separate folders. Figure 6.7 shows the dashboard quadrant map generated by the Leximancer analysis. The concepts towards the upper right-hand (magic) quadrant were the most important in the different cases. For the achievers, the most important themes and concepts were 'brand', 'markets', and 'countries', which were in the right upper quadrant. For the advisers, it was 'food'; and for the 'aspirants', it was going 'overseas.' For the actives, the important themes were 'food', 'concept', 'brand', 'people', and 'market'.

5.1. Concept Prominence

In a Leximancer analysis, the prominence score combines the strength and frequency scores (Table 6.6), which 'are absolute measures of correlation between category and attribute and can be used to make comparisons over time' (Leximancer, 2018, p. 103). A score higher than 1.0 suggests a co-occurrence happened more often than by chance. The table, which shows the top concepts for each category (i.e. a prominence score of at least 1.0), highlights the relative importance of each concept to the various groups.

Table 6.6: Prominence scores by category

Aspirants	Actives	Achievers	Acquirers	Advisers
Overseas (1.7)	Business (1.5)	The local partner (1.5)	Brand (1.8)	Success (2.0)
Customer (1.7)	Country (1.3)	Country (1.3)	Product (1.5)	Concept (1.7)
Food (1.3)	Success (1.2)	Outlets (1.3)	Customer (1.3)	Food (1.6)
Outlets (1.2)	Overseas (1.2)	Products (1.1)	Success (1.2)	People (1.4)
People (1.1)	People (1.1)	Franchisee (1.1)	Food (1.2)	Franchisee (1.4)
Products (1.0)	Products (1.0)	Market (1.1)	Concept (1.1)	Franchise (1.4)
		Overseas (1.1)		Brand (1.3)

The actives have had the first taste of internationalisation, and this has had an impact on how they might progress. If there was little success, their drive to internationalise further was dampened, and they reflected on prevailing gaps and tried to correct them before expanding. This group has had some success ('Success and International' prominence score of 4.0) and seeks more success as is evident in the importance attached to the 'success', 'markets', 'country', and 'overseas' concepts.

Another CSF was 'business' (with a prominence score of 1.5). Related concepts were 'staff', 'people', and 'partners', which were crucial to success. 'Actives' had real cases to see whether there were gaps in their management, human resource processes, or partner relationships. Other CSFs were like the aspirants (i.e. 'food', 'products', and 'taste'). With some internationalising experience, the actives believed their food concept must be suitable for overseas markets and the taste acceptable to locals, which guided their choice of future overseas markets.

5.2. Compound Concept Prominence

The Leximancer analysis also computes a table of ranked compound concepts by category that reflects the same strength and frequency conditional probabilities. Prominence scores of 3.0 or higher (Table 6.7) suggest that such compound concepts are important to that category. These Leximancer outputs provide the basis for the discussion of the results that are provided in the next section.

Table 6.7: The top-ranking compound concept prominence scores by category

Aspirant Concept Prominence	Active Concept Prominence	Achiever Concept Prominence	Acquirer Concept Prominence	Adviser Concept Prominence
Overseas & Partner (7.2)	Franchise & Team (4.8)	Local Partner & International (3.5)	Customer & Quality (6.2)	Success & International (5.8)
Overseas & Team (6.2)	Overseas & Team (4.5)	Local Partner & Market (3.1)	Product & Taste (5.2)	People and International (5.7)
Food & Taste (5.3)	Overseas & Staff (4.3)	Local Partner & Overseas (3.0)	Brand & Product (4.8)	Franchise & International (5.4)
Customer & Food (5.1)	Overseas & Local Partner (4.2)		Food & Quality (4.6)	Food & Quality (4.7)
Food & Quality (4.2)	Success & International (4.0)		Customer & Staff (4.6)	Concept & Food (4.4)

The actives have ventured overseas in at least one country and subsequently expanded into another country. In Table 6.7, the themes important to the actives were 'food', 'taste', 'success', 'brand', 'people', 'markets', and 'concept,' which was the most important. The actives shared the prominence accorded to 'food' and 'taste' with the acquirers and 'brand', 'concept', 'people', and 'success' with the advisers. The actives and acquirers shared the importance accorded to the right food concept and taste for success in internationalisation. Like the advisers, the actives believed other keys to success were the 'brand', 'market selection', 'people', and 'concept'. In terms of prominence scores, 'business' scored the highest (1.5) while other concepts were 'country' (1.3), 'success' (1.2), 'overseas' (1.2), 'people' (1.1), and 'products' (1.0).

Beyond the capability to choose their next market, the actives felt they needed to develop teams as this was a limiting factor for international growth. This can be seen in the high prominence scores for the compound concepts 'franchise and team' (4.8), 'overseas and team' (4.5), and 'overseas and staff' (4.3). Some related concepts with 'overseas' were 'brand', 'concept', and 'training and audit', suggesting the actives felt they needed to be capable of managing and protecting their brand in overseas markets. They also needed to train overseas franchisees and conduct periodic audits.

Typically, for the aspirants, the founder or owner had taken charge of this phase as it was the first port of entry. However, as internationalisation increased in importance, there was recognition of a need to hire people to assist in business development and negotiation. While the aspirants could only speculate about the challenges of managing overseas partners, the actives had genuine experience in collaborating with local partners in foreign territories. Thus, 'overseas and local partner' had a high prominence score

(4.2). The experience that actives had gained provided a scorecard of positives and problems in managing local overseas partners. The actives recognised they needed to deepen this capability and manage local partners with diverse cultural backgrounds if they were to make further progress. Therefore, the actives felt that success rested on the right choice of markets and countries and the development of its team so they could better manage overseas partners.

6. Conclusion

This chapter focuses on the theoretical analysis of the actives, and the ensuing chapter will then elaborate on its critical success factors for the active Singapore F&B companies, strategies, and competencies in venturing overseas.

CHAPTER 7

CAN INITIAL SUCCESS BEGET FURTHER SUCCESS?

1. Introduction

The first taste of internationalisation can be both sweet and stressful or challenging. It is sweet in terms of the initial success in getting into the international arena, reaping some recognition and reward for the brand and company, but stressful in dealing with potential partners before the signing of the agreement and then subsequently collaborate with partners who were not staff of the company and who are from a different nationality and culture. Yet the actives took on the route of internationalisation as, hopefully, the benefits outweigh the costs of venturing beyond Singapore.

Having made an initial attempt at venturing overseas, these active companies remained focused as they strived for more success in their overseas ventures. They have experienced the challenges of entering a foreign market and dealings with foreign partners. These lessons and experiences will be valuable as active Singapore F&B companies take on their next internationalisation move and plot their next 'destination'.

2. Critical Success Factors – Four More Rights

The aspirants group (discussed in chapter 5) focused on the four basic 'rights' (i.e. right fit, right food, right location, and right partner). While the actives did not discount the importance of these four basic rights, they considered four other rights as being paramount in furthering their internationalisation effort (i.e. right appeal and offering, right alignment, right team, and right foundation). The group's CSFs were once again a mix of internal (organisation specific) and external (host country) factors, and they are discussed in subsequent sections.

2.1. Right Appeal and Offering

To venture overseas, Singaporean companies must have the right appeal to foreign customers and potential partners. The brand is a CSF in driving success in a new foreign market.

Our outlet in Johor is doing very well, and that is because of the proximity to Singapore. Even before we were there, our brand is known; and once we enter the market, the results were great. (ATS, CEO)

Brand appeal is the right CSF in getting into a foreign market. The right appeal in branding also builds trust, retains customers, and ensures international success as seen in the track records of American brands such as McDonald's, Subway, and Starbucks, according to EAN, a company director. EAN added that having a strong brand appeal ensures sustainability and prevents brand hijacking (Choo, 2005), which occurs when a foreign partner abandons the brand and opts for an alternative brand or creates its brand.

That is the reason why we thought the best way is to have strong branding, and when you have it, it is a deterrent to switching brands.

Venturing overseas starts with the right appeal of the brand and food concept. The latter is the crux of why some concepts are sought after and succeed in the international arena, while others fail.

The other aspect of right appeal is offering the right terms regardless of the market entry mode (i.e. franchise or joint venture). The financial returns must make sense to the acquirers of the brand:

The obstacle is the franchisor asking for exorbitant pricing, and then it is a little difficult. Everything is based on the right price; in Chinese, *Yi fan chien Yi fan wuo.* The high franchise fee is one common mistake. (HRL, acquirers of several Singapore brands)

A seasoned local consultant in Indonesia, BRU concurred that the master franchise fee of Singapore concepts is as high as a global US brand, and that will affect the viability of any local taking up the brand.

Consequently, actives saw having the right appeal in terms of branding and the food concept as being critical when entering a foreign market. Acquirers of a brand look at the cost of acquisition, and thus, attractive terms are needed to seal the deal and ensure the Singapore brand can expand into a foreign country.

2.2. Right Alignment

The NVivo and Leximancer analyses suggested the other CSF was finding a 'good' 'partner'. Interestingly:

The related words for 'Good' in NVivo are beneficial, dependable, effective, full, good, healthy, honest, just, near, practical, respect, right, secure, serious, sizeable, skill, sound, and well.

These words refer to the attributes and qualities of foreign partners. They also refer to their conduct and attitudes towards the business or the owners of the brand. Therefore, finding the right partner is an essential CSF when internationalising. The actives have had some experience dealing with such partners, which explains the importance they attach to the right alignment of values and the need for positive working relationships.

Apart from the alignment of business expectations, FRL, a managing director, suggested that corporate and personal values alignment helps working relationships and overseas development. This alignment of values applies to both the company and its partners if it is to be effective, especially in the case of an overseas joint venture.

ATS, a managing director, suggested a need for hands-on alignment at the beginning of the relationship but that this can change when the network becomes stable:

We require them to be hands-on, but later when the franchise is stable and successful, it can be left to the management team and the system.

Thus, having the right alignment for both the company and its overseas partners is a CSF.

2.3. Right Team

As many of the actives were beginning their internationalisation journeys, they experienced challenges in putting a team together to support their international growth. For the aspirants, internationalisation tended to be spearheaded and pioneered by the founder or the owners of the Singaporean companies as STE, a business development head, noted:

The question [to internationalise] is whether the boss wants to do it and it is not a waste of his time.

However, when they have become actives and international activities pick up, having the right team is crucial if internationalisation is to become a reality and to be sustainable in the longer term. The active companies realised they had to rely on their staff as they internationalised:

The other critical success factor is that we must constantly build our people, follow up with our practices to suit modern lifestyles, and we must upgrade ourselves. All these will flow to the other specific areas. (ATS, managing director)

Our management team has often aspired to go international, and it is part of our instinctual drive towards this; the only question is how to do that and whether we dare to execute this. (SSN, managing director)

2.4. Right Foundation

Just like the aspirants in the previous chapter, the actives realised the right foundation was a CSF in furthering the growth of their brands overseas. By the right foundation, participants were referring to the right systems, which could be logistics and training, operation flows, R & D, and the management of their food concept as observed by ADW, a managing director.

For ALT, a CEO, the right foundation referred to both front- and back-end systems:

So the partnership is significant in terms of that they will take care of the front, the physical store and the operations, while we focus on the back end.

Not having the right foundation can result in failures for some of the participants as highlighted by SSN, managing director, since their failure in Vietnam in 2009 was due to the brand not being properly developed, inconsistent quality, and our management system not being developed and thus resulting in that failure.

TAC, a director, shared a similar experience from when his company had to retreat from Vietnam in 2015, which he attributed to not having sound systems:

In the 2015/16 financial year, we were in deficit; and the next year, we turned profits and so took time to understand the local cultures and have to build the systems for the business.

The actives that have realised the importance of having the right foundation will ensure that international progress is successful and sustainable.

3. The Four Pillars (Key Competencies and Capabilities)

The actives have just started their internationalisation journey and have realised there are some key competencies and capabilities that they need to possess to further succeed on the international stage. The NVivo and Leximancer analyses suggested that the actives felt that an ability to deal with partners, forge deals, and overcome differences were key competencies as was an ability to build their brands in international markets. They also felt team development was crucial for further internationalisation. These aspects are discussed in subsequent sections.

3.1. Build the Brand

While the actives' brands are established in Singapore, they are, nonetheless, young on the international stage. Consequently, the actives are fully aware that they have to build the brand in these new markets. Getting a brand overseas is the first step, and obtaining the capabilities needed to build a brand so it is recognised regionally and globally will be a challenge. The actives have had to invest in building their brands and in developing these capabilities, a view shared by many and particularly by ADW, a managing director.

Another managing director, agreed that not having a properly developed brand affected its venture overseas in 2009 and set the company back five years:

The acceptance of our brand and our products is the critical success factor for us in internationalisation. We started venturing overseas much earlier than in 2014 with Vietnam in 2009. At that time, we failed as we were not very experienced, and our brand lacked development. When we were there, we were considered premium, but our brand was not strong enough. (SSN, managing director)

We do not have a number in mind or a target of how many outlets to define success because we are young as a brand. Once a brand goes international, it boils down to exposure, and you will have franchisees from other countries keen to accept the brand. The [international] expansion will be faster. Our objective is to bring the brand overseas, expand it, and not so much as making profits of that yet; we just want our brand to go overseas. (ADW, managing director)

SSN, managing director, concurred that a not properly developed brand affected its venture overseas in 2009 and set the company back for a further five years.

The acceptance of our brand and our products is the key success factor for us in internationalisation. We started venturing overseas much earlier than 2014 with Vietnam in 2009. At that time, we failed as we were not very experienced, and our brand has not been properly developed. When we were there, we were considered premium, but our brand was not strong enough.

Many F&B companies would like to bring their culture to another country. However, that country may not accept the culture. To be successful, the overseas brand must be accepted and be part of the local culture without losing its soul. That is a better chance of success.

Taking a brand overseas or enhancing it demands a concerted effort as it must stay relevant to the markets both domestically and internationally. What constitutes the brand rests with consensus amongst the owners, which can be a challenge amongst family-owned SMEs.

We have too many family members who are involved, and it is difficult to come to a consensus on taking the brand overseas. What happened was it was only two years ago that, as the family members are getting older and older, we discussed the plans for our business whether to continue as it is or to sell it off. So being conservative people, they would not want to let it go, and so we thought that we had to look for alternatives to continue this business.

In the modern age, the competency in managing a brand has expanded from the traditional medium to other platforms like social media. Active companies must engage these modern media to take advantage of these to develop, enhance, and project brands to a wider and newer audience.

We must invest more and even in branding. We are more in social media to reach out to the young and the old; it is still via advertisement and TV, and we asked our staff to reach out to the customers and offer samples to try, and when they like it, they will buy it. (TAC, director)

The biggest lesson that we learned from the US giants, for example, McDonald's, is about branding. Branding is their biggest asset, and we hope to be able to reach that level one day. It taught us about branding, and it is worth it more than anything. If we do the branding well, the kind of trust and approval from the customers is priceless. We are at this stage where we would like to use social media to promote our brands, and that is the fastest. (EAN, director)

The actives recognised that building and supporting the brand in foreign markets was a critical competency. Such companies need a capable brand and marketing manager as overseas partners look at the brand's owners for directions in handling and marketing the brand in their market which will appeal to a new set of customers in host countries.

3.2. Build the Framework with Overseas Partners

The active companies were working with their first or second set of overseas partners and had first-hand dealings with them. Consequently, they could appreciate the challenges they might face. The NVivo analysis found words like *deal*, *contracts*, *engage*, *involve*, *accept*, *conduct*, *train*, and the like, and these suggested the need for competence in dealing, relating, and engaging with overseas partners. Singaporean companies must have a leader who will take charge of internationalisation if they are to expand further afield.

Dealings with overseas partners start with the first contact and the signing of a contract. For many, having a good contract that protects the company is a crucial safeguard. A good agreement spells out the boundaries that determine how the two organisations relate to each other within the venture. It is a long-term project that lasts if the contract is in force.

TAC, a company director, advocated flexibility and achieved a win-win strategy with overseas partners. While conflicts can happen regardless of how the business is doing, EAN hoped to solve them amicably without affecting the business and the brand:

If there are conflicts, we have to sit down and discuss and come up with agreed terms and try ways to stop the conflicts from escalating.

Like EAN, ADW, a managing director, hoped to resolve issues with overseas partners amicably and only look towards legal recourse as a last resort:

The terms and conditions are all in the contract, but then again, they [franchisees] are overseas and the question of whether the contract is enforceable. Enforcing a contract could trigger immediate termination, and that is drastic.

Thus, competency and capability in managing overseas partners are of paramount importance as the actives seek to further their growth internationally.

3.3. Build the Foundation

Another critical competency highlighted by the actives was ensuring the foundation remained strong and able to handle international growth.

So I think domestic success is important before going overseas. The fundamental reason for going out of Singapore is that we have a formidable team in Singapore. The base must be strong, and we do not have to worry about Singapore's operations and that we have excess capacity to build and expand regionally and globally. (FRL, managing director)

As the actives took on the international stage, gaps and challenges within the organisation surfaced that required them to enhance their capabilities. Noticeable gaps were in training overseas partners and foreign staff, logistics, the export of critical ingredients, and learning how to replicate signature offerings on foreign soil. ADW, a managing director, reiterated that this is a key requirement for internationalisation.

Another key challenge for a new active company is the supply of critical ingredients to foreign countries that have strict import regulations as noted by ALS, a chief executive officer. Developing an effective supply chain is an essential, critical competency for internationalising companies wishing to maintain the quality and consistency of their products.

It was also clear that the actives realised they needed to train foreign staff with different cultural backgrounds and values as FRL, a managing director, noted:

In Singapore, we are more productive, and one staff can handle many tasks but not in Indonesia. In terms of customers' expectations, customers are more patient in Indonesia. As the staff cost is reasonable, and so we can put in more people over there.

If these Singaporean companies have foreign workers in Singapore, such issues will be more easily addressed. ALS, a managing director, noted that his Filipino or Indonesian staff working in Singapore could be sent as trainers to the Philippines or Indonesia respectively. Alternatively, sending local well-trained Singaporean employees to foreign territories would give them some good exposure. Without such resources, SSN, a managing director, believed that the actives would need to consider how training is to be provided as they plan their expansion overseas, and setting up an academy would help.

The right foundation is a critical competency that actives need to build as they prepare to deepen their internationalisation experience.

3.4. Build the Team

Yet another critical competency that the actives highlighted was their staff and team:

The base must be strong, and we do not have to worry about Singapore's operations and that we have excess capacity to build and expand regionally and globally. (FRL, managing director)

Internationalisation starts with one person's dream and aspiration, and that is usually the founder or CEO. To sustain this, however, activities must go beyond their dreams. Every staff member on the international development team is vital:

To succeed overseas, I decided to invest in the talent pool. I have the limits of knowledge, and to break through, I must borrow the strengths of others. (ATS, CEO)

TAC, director, noted that the times have changed and that having the right team will make a difference in internationalisation.

My dad is a top-down leader, and he cares for everyone, and everyone just waited for him to make the decision. But now it is not this way; although management still gives instructions, we must listen to the staff's ideas and views and digest and take everyone as a stakeholder. And when the company is doing well, all will be rewarded. So we value them in all aspects, and everyone works for the money, but they will also see how the company values them.

We must learn from big US corporations like McDonald's; they are big corporations and, which are particularly good in inculcating culture, developed system and staff development, which are what we try to follow if we want to venture overseas.

In conclusion, active participants recognised that building these four competency pillars was critical for any fledging company intending to move internationally.

4. Road Maps to Continuing Success

It was apparent that the actives had internationalisation strategies that differed from those used by the aspirants. Following Bose's (2016) four strategies model (i.e. mode, destination, timing, and operation strategies), the apparent active strategies are shown in Table 7.1.

Table 7.1: Strategies for the actives

Participant	Timing	Current Destination	Future Plans	Mode	Operations
ADW	2018	The Philippines	Five outlets in five countries, no specific countries	Prefer franchising	• Adaptation of the standard contract for different countries • Rebranding from a Chinese concept to a modern concept
EAN	2018	Indonesia	Southeast Asia	Prefer franchising	• Focusing on branding • Supplying key ingredients for overseas outlets by using the 'retort process' method or producing on site in overseas locations; developing a multi-brand for the future
ALT	2019	China	Five outlets in five countries, other cities in China, Japan, Australia, London, Indonesia, Philippines	Franchising	• Developing a paste at ambient temperature for overseas outlets so food consistency can be achieved and reducing the cost of equipment for overseas operations

Participant	Timing	Current Destination	Future Plans	Mode	Operations
FRL	2019	Indonesia	Vietnam, Malaysia, and other Southeast Asian countries	Joint venture preferred for Indonesia and Vietnam; for others, franchising	• Building a stable team for further internationalisation • Focusing on a few markets given the limited resources • Searching for good partners • Being a multi-brand entity in the future.
ATS	2016 2018	Myanmar Malaysia	Southeast Asia	Franchising preferred	• Building a new central kitchen to supply key ingredients to overseas franchisees • Investing in a talent pool to fuel international development • Need to innovate on food, customers' experience.
TAC	2009	Malaysia	Hong Kong, Korea, and China	Joint venture or franchising preferred	• Building a strong team for further internationalisation

4.1. Market Entry Mode

Almost all participants (six out of seven) preferred franchising as their entry mode:

We are looking only into franchising as it is easier to manage that way; joint venture will be a bit challenging as we will have a team over there. (ADW, managing director)

EAN, a director, suggested franchising as a preferred market entry strategy in many countries. Moreover, local laws tend to protect the rights of residents disproportionately over foreign franchisers in the event of any disputes.

For FRL, a managing director who opted for a joint venture in Indonesia and potentially in Vietnam and Malaysia, the market entry mode choice was coincidental:

Strangely, it was not intentional that these countries were joint ventures to deal with franchise regulations. I did not think about that, and it was a blessing in disguise.

4.2. Operational Decisions in Internationalisation

Ibeh (2003) identified several factors that drive positive international business performance. These include decision-makers' previous experience, international contacts and orientation, firm-specific competencies relating to planning, the adoption of innovative technologies, foreign market information search, and managing channel relationships. These were evident in the actives' responses.

After their initial internationalisation experience, ADW, a managing director, felt there was a need to make their existing contract more aligned for its future expansion:

The terms and conditions are all in the contract, but then again, they [franchisees] are overseas, and sometimes the contract does not apply in that country, so we have to look into this in future.

Another strategic, operational decision many participants made was in marketing and branding:

We will strengthen our brand. The concept design can be continuously changed (e.g. Putien, the Michelin star [restaurant]). They were previously a very Chinese concept. Our brand needs to change from a Chinese concept to a modern concept. (ADW, managing director)

5. Conclusion

This chapter began with a background discussion of the active companies that had started their internationalisation journey, with most venturing into at least one other country. These companies had started their internationalisation voyage, but they had noticed some gaps and challenges in their journey.

In addition to the four 'rights' mentioned by the aspirants (i.e. right fit, right location, right partner, and right food), the actives added five pillars (i.e. right appeal, right offering, right alignment, right team, and right foundation) that they felt formed the basis for a successful internationalisation journey. While the aspirants need knowledge about how to internationalise, for the active companies, the motto was not 'Know' as they have passed that stage. Their motto is to 'build' as they need to strengthen their capacities and capabilities.

For their onward journey, aspirants need to build (1) the brand, (2) a framework within which they work with their overseas partners, (3) a team, and (4) the foundations of their concept and business. These pillars were critical to the actives' further international growth.

Having stepped out of Singapore, the actives also realised there were gaps in their resources and that new capabilities are needed if they wish to deepen their internationalisation roots. Such new capabilities include branding, marketing, R & D, logistics, and providing appropriate support for new overseas partners.

With so many unknowns and challenges, the actives preferred franchising as a market entry mode. Dealing with franchise regulations and uncertainty with other countries' legal frameworks were cited as reasons for these preferences. Besides that, the need for local knowledge was critical in venturing out of Singapore.

It was also clear that the actives preferred proximity. They are likely to consider all the ASEAN nations for their first stop. This finding supports the Uppsala model that suggests that geographical, administrative, psychic, and cultural distance play important roles. Thus, closer ASEAN countries offer the least risk of failure. Many actives opted for regional countries due to the compatibility of food preferences, customers' awareness of their food concept, and their understanding of regional markets as preferred international destinations. In the next chapter, the focus shifts to the achievers and how they expanded and grew in overseas markets, and this analysis will provide information about any differences between the various groups.

CHAPTER 8

THE BEST IS YET TO BE

1. Introduction – Singapore Food Service SMEs Going Places

In an 11 April 2017 report in the *Business Times*, Mr Tan Chor Sen, OCBC Bank executive vice-president, stated that while Singapore SMEs traditionally have ventured abroad, very few are from the consumer sector like food and beverage. He noted that while this is not seen five or ten years ago, many are now from the food service sector, especially in Malaysia, Indonesia, China, Hong Kong, and Myanmar (https://www.asiaone.com/business/singapore-smes-going-places).

Some of the notable Singapore brands which have ventured overseas are BreadTalk, Ya Kun, Sushi Tei, and Bee Cheng Hiang. Tan further pointed out that if an F&B company was able to succeed in Singapore with its high cost of rent and labour, 'you can survive anywhere else'.

IE Singapore, the government agency then that partners with local firms to venture overseas, helped secure more than 450 deals around the world last year, the bulk of them in China and Southeast Asia. In 2016, some 37,000 local companies of all sizes and across sectors – 80 per cent of them SMEs – benefited in one way or another from the statutory board's broad-based assistance, said the agency's chief executive Lee Ark Boon in a recent report (https://ie.enterprisesg.gov.sg/Venture-Overseas).

Overseas expansion, according to Lee, remains challenging as 'the region is not homogenous like the European Union and the rules and regulations in each country out of Singapore are different'. The other issues will be funding and managing people. Companies have difficulties locating good staff and also sending staff from Singapore.

Overseas expansion is not a bed of roses; many succeed and others fail. Lee noted that

I see the same people fail and start up again. Generally, by the first three years, 30 per cent of the initial cohort will wind up and by the 5th year, 50 per cent are gone. Failure is not a stigma, because the returns can be very great.

Therefore, for all Singapore companies which have ventured overseas, the outcome could be for the better or worse, and the best is yet to be.

The first set of case studies was on those Singaporean companies in the food service sector which were labelled as aspirants, starting on their internationalisation journey. After this, the focus was on actives, referring to companies that had managed to expand overseas into one or two overseas markets in their early stages of internationalisation. This chapter will adopt the same format used in describing the other two groups in the achievers group of case studies.

Chapter 4 discussed aspirants (companies just starting their internationalisation journey), while chapter 5 discussed actives (companies that had expanded into one or two overseas markets and were in their early stages of internationalisation). This chapter discusses achievers (companies that are successful and have a presence in at least three countries overseas). Section 2 provides some background information on Singaporean companies that have made significant progress internationally while sections 3 and 4 discuss the achievers' interview data and the Leximancer and NVivo analyses. Section 5 highlights the cross-case analysis.

2. *Singapore's F&B Achievers*

As was noted in earlier chapters, there is no list of Singaporean F&B companies that are making significant progress in venturing overseas. Consequently, a list was compiled from personal networks and publicly available information (Table 8.1).

Singapore's top F&B achievers have expanded rapidly overseas. While sales revenue and contribution from sales from overseas outlets data are not readily available, it is reasonable to suggest the importance of internationalisation to achievers. However, the journey to becoming an achiever is not the same for every company. Nevertheless, this study aims to understand the factors that have contributed to the success of this group as these factors will also be important to aspirants and actives.

Table 8.1: The top achievers in Singaporean food service sector

Concept	SGP	Int'l	Ttl	No of countries	First int'l	First overseas	FO/TO	Average
				(excl. Singapore)	outlet	outlet	%	per country
BreadTalk	116	717	833	16	2003	Indonesia	86	45
Bee Cheng Hiang	45	250	295	10	1995	Malaysia	85	25
Roti Mum	1	249	250	7	2006	Indonesia	100	36
Shihlin	12	174	186	4	2005	Malaysia	94	44
Pezzo	32	91	123	6	2014	Malaysia	74	15
Killiney	29	80	109	7	2001	Malaysia	73	11
Sushi Tei	13	68	81	7	1998	Indonesia	84	10
Seoul Garden/BREEKS!	13	67	80	5	2006	Malaysia	84	13
Ya Kun	57	52	109	8	2001	Indonesia	48	7
TWG Tea	11	50	61	14	2012	Japan	82	4
Awfully Chocolate	15	44	59	2	2007	China	75	22
Paradise	24	38	62	10	2011	Indonesia	61	4

Concept	SGP	Int'l	Ttl	No of countries (excl. Singapore)	First int'l outlet	First overseas outlet	FO/TO %	Average per country
Putien	12	37	49	5	2006	Indonesia	76	7
Crystal Jade	40	36	76	10	1996	Vietnam	47	8
SaladStop!	18	32	50	4	2014	Philippines	64	8
Fish & Co.	13	29	42	9	2003	Malaysia	69	3
Sakae Sushi	10	28	38	2	2001	Indonesia	74	14
Pastamania	23	27	50	12	2013	Malaysia	54	2
Each-a-Cup	33	25	58	3	2011	Malaysia	43	8
Pontian Wanton Mee	50	24	74	1	2010	Malaysia	32	24
Wee Nam Kee	8	16	24	3	2011	Philippines	67	5
4Fingers	14	15	29	5	2015	Malaysia	52	3
Food Republic	15	14	29	6	2008	HK	48	2
Pho Street	10	14	24	1	2015	Malaysia	58	14
TungLok Group	22	13	35	2	1993	Indonesia	37	7
Brotzeit	5	13	18	8	2010	Malaysia	72	2
Xiao Ban	3	13	16	3	2015	Vietnam	81	4
Old Chang Kee	90	12	102	3	2005	Malaysia	12	4
Hong Kong Sheng Kee	20	12	32	3	2011	Malaysia	38	4
Les Amis Brands/ NamNam/Pepperoni	25	10	35	1	2013	HK	29	10
Jumbo Group	12	10	22	3	2013	China	45	3
Snackz It!	11	10	21	1	2010	China	48	10
Twelve Cupcakes	26	8	34	2	2015	Indonesia	24	2
Imperial Treasure	15	8	23	3	2012	China	35	3
Irvins Salted Egg	8	6	14	1	2017	Philippines	43	6
Mr Bean	64	5	69	2	2010	Japan	7	3
Fragrance	33	5	38	2	2005	Malaysia	13	3
Umisushi	18	5	23	3	2013	Indonesia	22	2
BreadTalk	116	717	833	16	2003	Indonesia	86	45
Geylang Lor 9	1	5	6	2	2015	Malaysia	83	3
Bali Thai	36	4	40	1	2009	China	10	4
Harry's	20	4	24	2	2010	Indonesia	17	2
Song Fa	7	4	11	1	2016	Indonesia	36	4
Cavana	3	4	7	2	2006	Indonesia	57	2
Thai Village	2	4	6	1	2014	China	67	4
Astons	36	3	39	1	2015	Myanmar	8	3
Koo Kee Yong Tow Foo	28	3	31	3	2015	China	10	1
Old Street Bak Kut Teh	16	3	19	2	2018	Indonesia	16	2
Soup Restaurant	14	3	17	1	2014	Malaysia	18	3

Concept	SGP	Int'l	Ttl	No of countries	First int'l	First overseas	FO/TO	Average
Coffee Club	12	3	15	2	2014	Malaysia	20	2
Boon Tong Kee	8	3	11	3	2012	Philippines	27	1
1A Crispy Puffs	8	3	11	2	2014	Indonesia	27	2
Fatboy's/Burger Bar	5	3	8	3	2015	Malaysia	38	1
Hawker Chan	4	3	7	3	2017	Australia	43	1
Bak Kut Teh	4	3	7	2	2016	Indonesia	43	2
Si Chuan Dou Hua	3	3	6	3	2014	Myanmar	50	1

Source: Compiled by the author

The number of top achievers over the decades is shown in Figure 8.1. From the table, it is clear that the last decades produced twenty-five out of forty (62.5 per cent) of the current listing of top achievers in Singapore versus the earlier decades. This could be attributed to a host of external pull and internal push factors confronting Singapore companies. The fact remains that with the escalating cost of labour and rentals in Singapore, more and more Singapore companies are looking further afield to the region for growth and sustainability of their business as noted by Mr Tan of OCBC Bank (https://www.asiaone.com/business/singapore-smes-going-places).

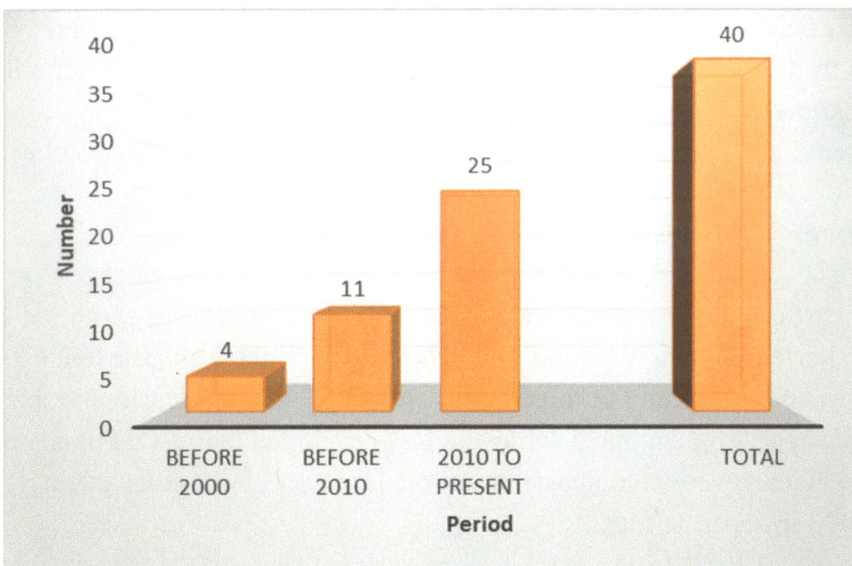

Figure 8.1: The number of top achievers over the decades

This can also be seen in the number of foreign outlets vis-à-vis domestic outlets. In Figure 8.2, for the top achievers group, the percentage of foreign outlets remained relatively high.

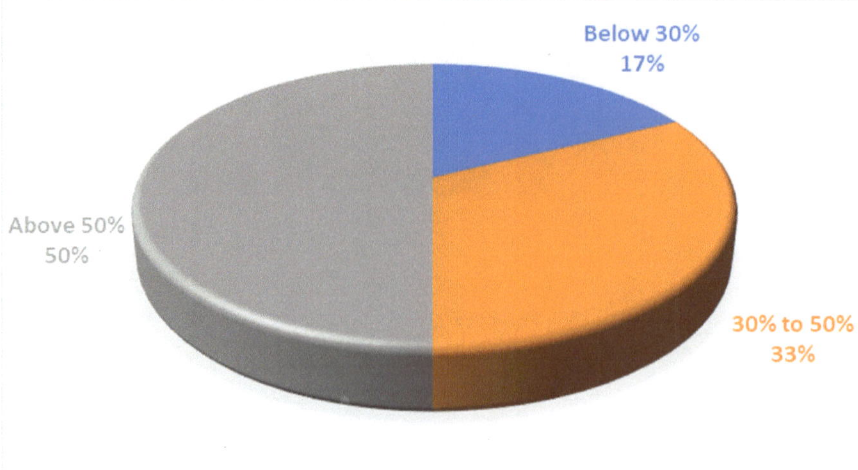

Figure 8.2: The percentage of foreign outlets

It showed that Singapore's top achievers were growing rapidly overseas. While data sales revenue and contribution from sales from overseas outlets were not readily available and difficult to solicit, it is reasonable to say that the importance of internationalisation for the top achievers amongst Singapore companies in the food service sector cannot be understated.

The journey towards becoming an achiever will not be the same for every company. Nevertheless, this present study aims to draw upon the experiences of these achievers from the enquiry on the fourteen participants and what matters to them in their journey to achieving success. It will also have implications for budding actives and aspirants in the planning of their internationalisation road maps.

3. The Leximancer Analysis

Fourteen achiever participants were interviewed face to face using the same set of semi-structured questions, with the shortest interview lasting about thirty-five minutes and the longest exceeding an hour. Unlike the aspirants and actives, all but three of the achievers were professional managers who oversaw internationalisation, suggesting that most achievers had developed teams that handled overseas ventures (Table 8.2). The interviews were conducted between March and December 2018. The interviews were transcribed and stored in separate files.

Table 8.2: The achievers

Date	Code	Gender	Age	Edu	No. of Staff	SGP	Overseas Outlets	Position
7 Mar 18	NIC	Male	44	Sec	50	4	3	MD
1-Apr-18	ASL	Male	55	Grad	200	13	67	CEO
5-Apr-18	LIA	Male	55	Grad	60	8	16	Director
12-Apr-18	DDD	Female	33	Grad	5,000	116	717	BDM
13-Apr-18	CHI	Male	53	Grad	3,000	12	10	GM
21 May 18	SON	Male	40	Grad	1,200	90	12	CFO
21 May 18	PTT	Male	31	Grad	50	3	13	ED
30 May 18	EIL	Female	41	Grad	600	64	5	BDM
6 Jun 18	DBA	Male	37	Grad	350	18	32	MD
12 Jun 18	EES	Female	29	Grad	240	14	15	AFM
12 Sep 18	MAN	Male	45	Grad	200	5	13	VP
25 Sep 18	SOO	Male	55	Grad	100	32	91	Head
5 Dec 18	JAG	Female	28	Grad	600	13	68	ABDM

The obtained data were processed with NVivo and Leximancer using the procedures described earlier, and the findings are discussed in subsequent sections.

Figure 8.3 shows the Leximancer concept map with all the visible concepts within the obtained themes that are important to the achievers. A single concept labelled in black is linked to another with a grey line. The linkage shows the strength of the association between the two concepts. These contextual associations are further examined through the ranked concept relevance list (Table 8.3).

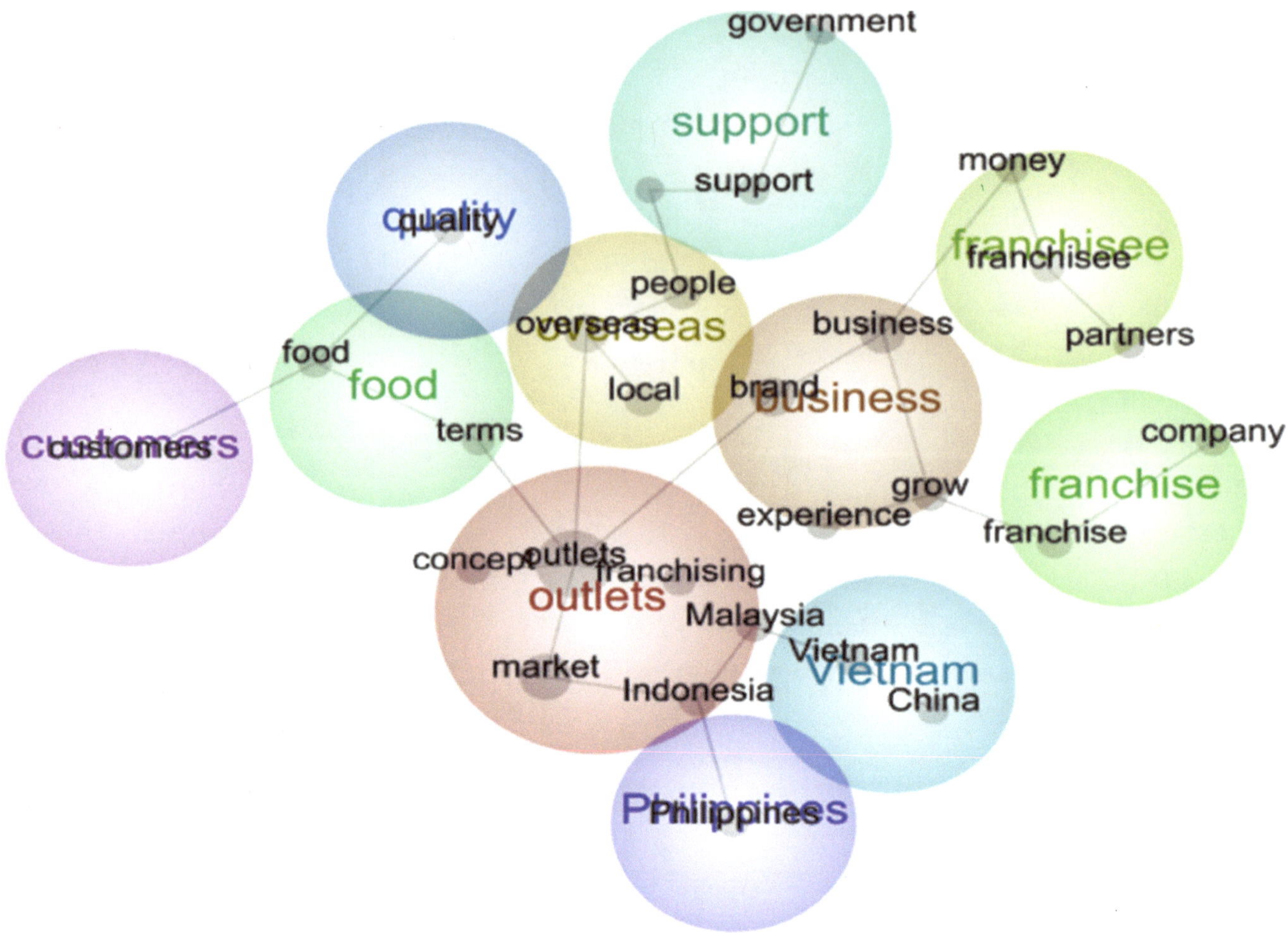

Figure 8.3: A concept map for the achievers

These concepts clustered together to form a theme that appears in a larger type (Figure 8.3). The concept names are coloured like the theme spheres to show their importance. Concept proximity shows the strength of the association between the two concepts. Figure 8.3 suggests that the largest and 'hottest' theme is 'outlets' (red amber), followed by 'brand' (amber), 'franchisee and partners' (yellow green), and 'local' (green). The less important themes were 'food' (blue), 'franchise' (light blue), and 'government and support' (purple).

Table 8.3: The ranked concept list

Ranked Concept List		
Name-Like	**Count**	**Relevance**
	58	14%
Indonesia	58	14%
China	49	12%
Vietnam	46	11%
Philippines	41	10%
Word-Like	**Count**	**Relevance**
outlets	415	100%
market	188	45%
business	131	32%
overseas	115	28%
brand	113	27%
people	80	19%
franchise	72	17%
food	71	17%
local	69	17%
company	67	16%
grow	62	15%
franchisee	61	15%
concept	57	14%
terms	53	13%
customers	52	13%
money	46	11%
partners	46	11%
franchising	45	11%
government	44	11%

In the Leximancer analysis, *relevance* is defined as the percentage frequency of text segments coded with that concept relative to the frequency of the most frequent concept in the list. Consequently, the most frequent will always be 100 per cent, which does not mean all text segments contain that concept. Other relative percentages are calculated by dividing a concept's count into the top occurring relevance concept's count. Thus, this measure is an indicator of the relative strength of a concept's frequency of occurrence.

In Table 8.3, Malaysia and Indonesia were significant to the achievers' international expansion. The list of ranked concept relevance suggests that the most critical concept for the achievers were 'outlets,' followed by 'market', 'business', 'overseas', 'brand', 'people', and 'franchise.' These themes are discussed in subsequent sections.

4. *The NVivo Analysis Findings*

This study used both Leximancer and NVivo to analyse the data. Here, the top twenty words for the achievers are shown in Table 8.4, and the corresponding word cloud can be seen in Figure 8.4.

Figure 8.4: A word cloud for the achievers

Table 8.4: The top twenty relevant words for the achievers

Word	Length	Count	Weighted Percentage
local	5	381	1.47
market	6	307	1.33
outlets	7	329	1.31
partner	7	242	1.11
brand	5	305	1.11
countries	9	249	1.06
franchise	9	178	0.82
products	8	178	0.74
overseas	8	142	0.65
support	4	205	0.65
conflict	9	130	0.57
franchisee	10	114	0.52
people	6	104	0.45
management	10	156	0.45
Malaysia	8	94	0.43
success	7	103	0.41
customers	9	85	0.39
government	10	145	0.37
concept	7	101	0.36
terms	5	95	0.35

The NVivo findings were, once again, not dissimilar (excluding the name-like concept of Singapore, which was the focus of the study) to the findings obtained from Leximancer. The top ten Leximancer themes and the top ten NVivo words are shown in Table 8.5. The subsequent section elaborates on the connections and relatedness of the themes and concepts from both sets of analyses.

Table 8.5: The top ten Leximancer themes and NVivo words

Ranking	Leximancer	NVivo	Ranking	Leximancer	NVivo
1	Outlets	Local	6	People	Countries
2	Market	Market	7	Franchise	Franchise
3	Business	Outlets	8	Food	Products
4	Overseas	Partners	9	Local	Overseas
5	Brand	Brand	10	Company	Support

5. *The Cross-Case Analysis*

The cross-case analysis identified the emergent themes and the connectivity and relationships between these themes across the various categories of participants in internationalisation. This section provides an overview of the Leximancer concept map used to identify the emergent themes and the connectivity and relationships between these themes. It also highlights the importance of the various themes to the groups of participants as the Leximancer analysis enables groups to be examined when included in separate folders.

As can be seen in Figure 8.5, there are eight heat-mapped spheres, each representing a theme. All concepts and data categories are marked in grey nodes, with a label identifying the concept or the category. The size of the nodes shows the relative strength of the concept or the category, and the groups' positions show the differences in their views. The most prominent theme is 'brand' (red amber), followed by 'partners' (amber), 'support' (yellow green), 'food' (green), 'success' (blue green), 'customers' (blue), 'taste' (blue purple), and lastly 'staff' (purple).

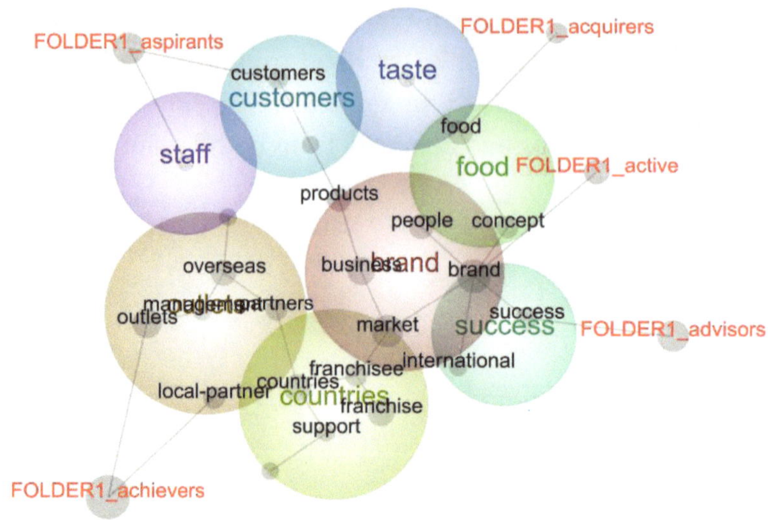

Figure 8.5: A concept map by category

Figure 8.5 shows that the concepts (in black) formed clusters that determined the themes, which appear in a larger type and are coloured the same way as the sphere. As an example, 'brand' is red (the same colour as the sphere) and is the central theme for that sphere. The related concepts in black type are 'people,' 'market,' 'brand' (as a concept), and 'business'. Grey lines linking two concepts suggest a relationship between the concepts while concept proximity shows the strength of the association. Data categories are shown in red (the outlying nodes of the map) (e.g. Folderl_achievers). Concepts and themes closest to a data category are more important to that category and less important to the other categories.

Figure 8.6 shows the dashboard quadrant map generated by the Leximancer analysis. The concepts towards the upper right-hand (magic) quadrant were the most important in the different cases. For the achievers, the most important themes and concepts were 'brand', 'markets', and 'countries', which were in the upper right quadrant. For the advisers, it was 'food'; and for the aspirants, it was going 'overseas'. The dashboard insight report suggested that the cross-case data had 4,090 context blocks made up of 2 sentences in each block, 24 concepts, and 5 categories. In the next section, the discussion will focus on the participants' perceptions of the concepts' prominence.

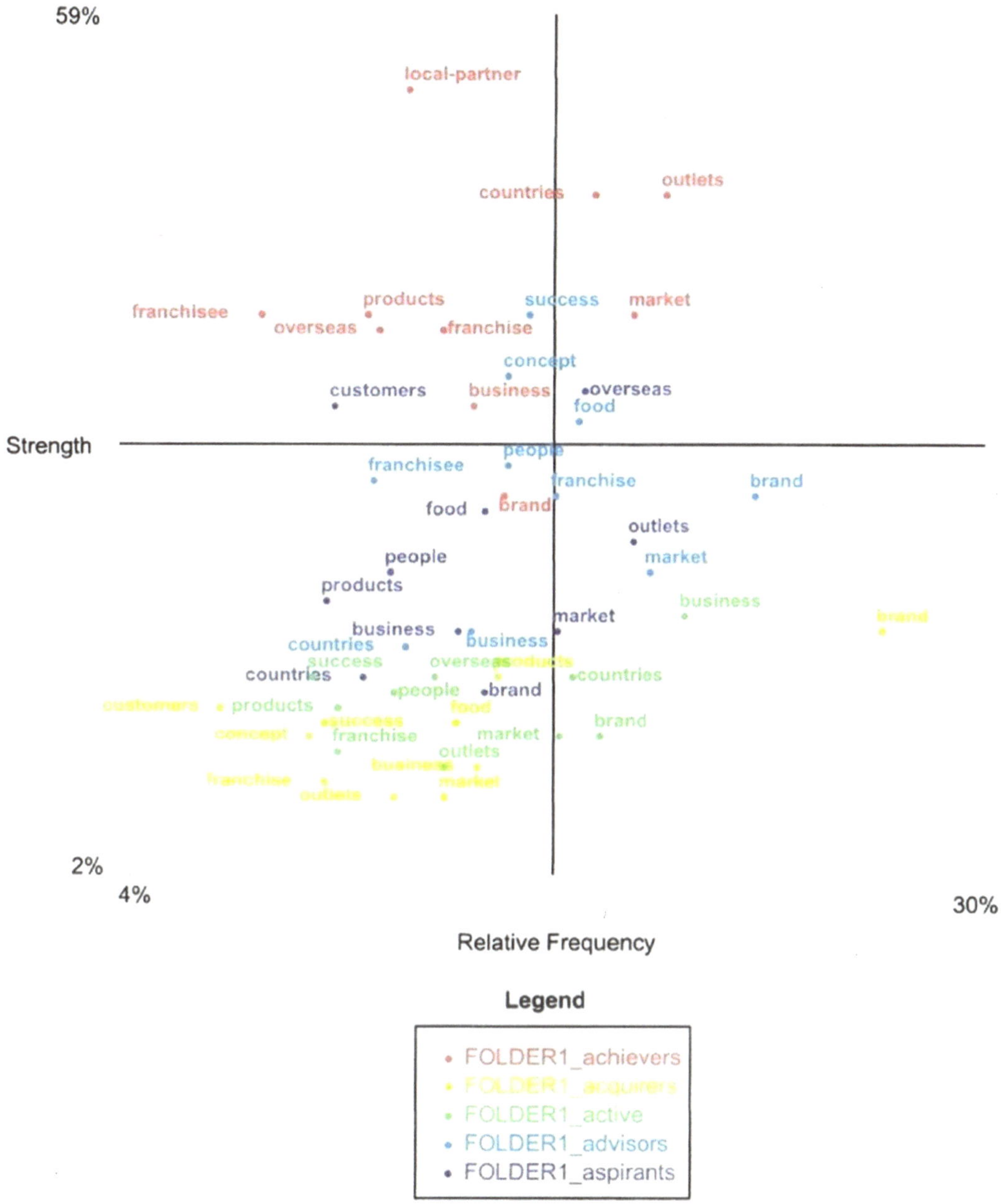

Figure 8.6: The dashboard quadrant map generated by the Leximancer analysis

5.1. Concept Importance

In a Leximancer analysis, the prominence score combines the strength and frequency scores (Table 8.6), which 'are absolute measures of correlation between category and attribute and can be used to make comparisons over time' (Leximancer, 2018, p. 103). A score higher than 1.0 suggests a co-occurrence happened more often than by chance. The table, which shows the top concepts for each category (i.e. a prominence score of at least 1.0), highlights the relative importance of each concept to the various groups.

Table 8.6: Prominence scores by category

Aspirants	Actives	Achievers	Acquirers	Advisers
Overseas (1.7)	Business (1.5)	The local partner (1.5)	Brand (1.8)	Success (2.0)
Customer (1.7)	Country (1.3)	Country (1.3)	Product (1.5)	Concept (1.7)
Food (1.3)	Success (1.2)	Outlets (1.3)	Customer (1.3)	Food (1.6)
Outlets (1.2)	Overseas (1.2)	Products (1.1)	Success (1.2)	People (1.4)
People (1.1)	People (1.1)	Franchisee (1.1)	Food (1.2)	Franchisee (1.4)
Products (1.0)	Products (1.0)	Market (1.1)	Concept (1.1)	Franchise (1.4)
		Overseas (1.1)		Brand (1.3)

The achievers have overseas outlets in three or more countries and have experienced success in internationalisation. In Figure 8.5, the themes important to the achievers were 'managing partners', 'local partners', 'overseas', 'outlets', 'franchise', 'franchisee', and 'support' as one important node, and the other would be 'staff'. The achievers were in the bottom left-hand corner and, like the aspirants, different as a category, with little in common with the other groups. The key concepts were 'local partner' and 'outlets', which is where the achievers concentrate as they seek to expand their international operations. The other concepts achievers focused on were 'support' and 'franchise'. The closest concept they shared with the aspirants was 'staff', with both groups recognising that having the right staff was critical.

The achievers have achieved international success, but many are looking for further success, which explains why 'outlets' and 'countries' (with a prominence score of 1.3) and 'overseas' (with a prominence score of 1.1) are important. Achievers want to extend their network, irrespective of the number of overseas markets they have. Their internationalisation efforts are ongoing as they are seeking new markets. They realise they need to strengthen and deepen their networks in each country in which they have a presence, which explains the emphasis on 'outlets' (prominence score of 1.3). The development of these networks is dependent on their strategies and management structure, which means the achievers see a need to expand the size and capabilities of their international development team.

With outlets in several countries, the achievers focus on supporting their franchisees, which explains why 'local partners' (a prominence score of 1.5) and 'franchisee' (a prominence score of 1.1) are important themes.

5.2.1. Compound Concept Prominence

The Leximancer analysis also computes a table of ranked compound concepts by category that reflects the same strength and frequency conditional probabilities. Prominence scores of 3.0 or higher (Table 8.7) suggest that such compound concepts are important to that category. These Leximancer outputs provide the basis for the discussion of the results that are provided in the next section.

The achievers recognise a need to develop capabilities in providing appropriate support to overseas franchisees if they are to achieve continuing success and mitigate threats to their franchiser-franchisee relationships, such as disputes, terminations, and brand hijacking. The capabilities needed to manage relationships with local partners are vital to maintaining networks. However, extensive networks in different countries mean the achievers' governance structures are different from those used by the actives, which is not surprising given the different spans of control. These governance differences are reflected in the prominence scores of some ranked compound concepts (i.e., 'local partner and international' [3.5], 'local partner and market' [3.1], and 'local partner and overseas' [3.0]).

Table 8.7: The top-ranking compound concept prominence scores by category

Aspirant Concept Prominence	Active Concept Prominence	Achiever Concept Prominence	Acquirer Concept Prominence	Adviser Concept Prominence
Overseas & Partner (7.2)	Franchise & Team (4.8)	Local Partner & International (3.5)	Customer & Quality (6.2)	Success & International (5.8)
Overseas & Team (6.2)	Overseas & Team (4.5)	Local Partner & Market (3.1)	Product & Taste (5.2)	People and International (5.7)
Food & Taste (5.3)	Overseas & Staff (4.3)	Local Partner & Overseas (3.0)	Brand & Product (4.8)	Franchise & International (5.4)
Customer & Food (5.1)	Overseas & Local Partner (4.2)		Food & Quality (4.6)	Food & Quality (4.7)
Food & Quality (4.2)	Success & International (4.0)		Customer & Staff (4.6)	Concept & Food (4.4)

The achievers must deal with local partners in different countries and markets that have diverse situations and challenges. Each market is different and requires a different mindset. The achievers felt the need for a global mindset if they were to manage complex, extensive international networks of overseas franchisees or partners effectively.

The other capability that achievers need is managing markets (with a prominence score of 1.1). Each market has a distinct set of local requirements, and the achievers must be able to adapt to local tastes while still retaining their DNA (the soul of their overall concept and brand). Food taste and suitability are significant issues for the achievers, especially when dealing with an extensive international network of outlets, such as those managed by BreadTalk Group, Ya Kun, Sushi Tei, and SaladStop!.

6. Conclusion

This chapter began with a background of the achievers. After the NVivo, Leximancer, and cross-case analyses, the results were examined and discussed. This sets the stage for us to look at the critical success factors, competencies, and capabilities needed for the achievers to progress and take on the global stage in the subsequent chapters.

CHAPTER 9

SAVOURING THE FRUIT OF SUCCESS

1. Introduction

Chapter 8 covers the analysis based on Leximancer analysis and NVivo software for the achievers group as well as the cross-case analysis. In this chapter, the critical success factors for the achievers group will be discussed.

The author defines *achievers* as successful companies which have a presence in at least three countries overseas. These Singapore F&B companies had their maiden international experience for their first country in the past and replicated that success in another country and subsequently went on to achieve further success in the third country and beyond. The key question is how these successful Singapore F&B companies replicate their successes. What were their critical success factors, and were there any moderating factors governing or affecting their path to further success? These achievers have replicated their successes and savoured the taste of success in their respective countries, and the question remains whether they will be able to further their success in the countries that they have had a presence in or go on to achieve further success in yet another new country. Does success in one country beget success in another? This chapter sets out to address these pertinent issues.

2. The Secrets of Success

The 'secrets' of success for the achievers and, conversely, the factors for failures will be keys in this study as many SMEs, both aspirants and actives, want to emulate the success and avoid any pitfalls. They are, therefore, models and important case studies for all Singapore companies.

In a *Straits Times* report on 4 October 2018, Singapore companies are looking at going global (https://www.straitstimes.com/business/economy/singapore-companies-on-global-acquisition-spree-value-of-overseas-deals-more-than).

'We're certainly seeing a desire among Singapore Inc companies to globalize,' said David Biller, Citigroup Inc's head of Southeast Asia corporate and investment banking. 'Many of the next-generation leadership teams in these organizations are helmed by executives with multinational experience and they bring a focus on cross-border growth.'

Pankaj Goel, the co-head of Southeast Asia investment banking and capital markets at Credit Suisse Group, in the same report said that

[a]chieving organic growth in a relatively small market like Singapore is difficult, and building capabilities and scale will be increasingly important for corporates to stay relevant globally.

Achievers have gained significant success in regional markets. Many of these companies have an overseas presence in ASEAN, and only a few of them like BreadTalk, SaladStop!, and Pezzo have ventured beyond Southeast Asia to China, the Middle East, and North Asia like Japan and South Korea.

According to a Bloomberg report on 5 October 2018, the Singapore government has always wanted to develop their local companies to go global as follows.

'The Singapore government has been encouraging companies for years to expand abroad to develop the country's profile,' said CMC's Lizza. 'GIC and Temasek have been at the forefront of it.'

Temasek spokesperson Stephen Forshaw said the group's portfolio companies were independently managed and 'Temasek doesn't direct their business decisions.'

'Of course, over many years, some of these companies have grown organically into regional and global businesses, and in cases, acquisitions have naturally followed,' he said. (https://www.connectedtoindia.com/singapore-companies-doubling-up-on-overseas-acquisitions-this-year-bloomberg-report-4636.html)

The global challenge is also a dream for many achieving Singapore food service companies and has attained regional success in venturing overseas.

Every Singapore company will love to have a footprint in the USA, Europe, or Australia, but be realistic by just having one outlet over there, which we might not be able to support regularly, and there will be too many variations. We are focusing on the growth of our brand globally. (CHI, general manager)

My dream is to be able to have our heritage brand in many countries and our brand becomes global. (NIC, managing director)

The question remains how the achievers can push through with greater success in the next phase of their development to become a global brand and company. What, then, are these critical success factors for the next stage of their internationalisation journey?

3. Four Global Perspectives

The 'secrets' of success for the achievers and, conversely, the factors for failure are crucial to many SMEs (i.e. aspirants and actives). Consequently, they are important models and valuable case studies for all Singaporean companies.

About half of the forty Singaporean achievers have ventured into three countries (Figure 9.1). Six achievers have a presence in ten countries. They had achieved success in Southeast Asia and wanted to expand beyond Australia, India, the Middle East, and North Asia. Examples include BreadTalk, which has outlets in the Middle East and India; SaladStop!, which has expanded to Japan and Spain; and Pezzo, which is operating in the Middle East. The critical challenge facing many achievers trying to achieve global status is venturing into Europe and the Americas.

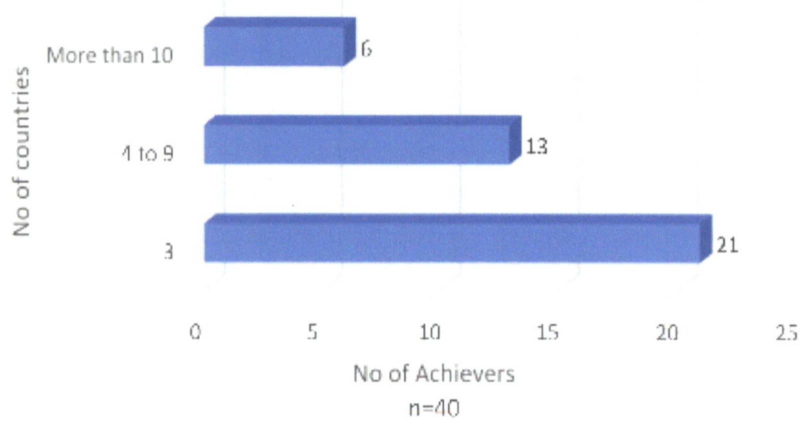

Figure 9.1: Overseas ventures in various countries by achievers

Every Singaporean company will love to have a footprint in the US or Europe or Australia, but be realistic by just having one outlet over there, which we might not be able to support regularly, and there will be too many variations. (CHI, general manager)

The "dream" question remains, however, how the achievers can push through to even greater success in the next phase of their development as they attempt to become global brands. What are the critical success factors for the next stage of their internationalisation journey? The interviews suggested several such factors (i.e. global aspirations, global branding, having a global mindset, and global support). These are discussed in subsequent sections.

3.1. Global Aspirations

The achievers had made substantial progress in internationalisation and could have been content with what they had achieved, or they might wish to forge ahead. Many like CHI, a general manager, echoed that the CSF for becoming a global success is to have such an aspiration and be willing to put in the effort needed to build a global brand and presence. Without such an aspiration, progress is unlikely.

The primary motivation for going global is to increase brand value and revenue from overseas operations, noted SON, a chief financial officer.

In a *Business Times* report on 10 December 2018, CEO Henry Chu of the BreadTalk Group, the biggest franchiser in Singapore, suggested that he would like to take the group to Europe and the United States (Lee, 2018).

'The US is a big country, there's spending power, and it is easy to do business there, so we see it as an opportunity. We are already very well-represented in Asia, so for us to move to the next level, we must venture into areas we have not been to,' says Mr Chu.

'For the US, we just need to decide how we want to operate it, be it through a joint venture partner, a franchise or other means, to make this business successful.'

For yet another achiever, the company had a good chance to be a global company in the next few years as it was already at the gateways to the key markets of Europe and the United States:

In five years, we would have been a global company; with India getting on board, we would cover much of Asia, and we are just short of Vietnam. For the US, it is possible, but I would say that let us go global with three blocks, ASEAN especially the Philippines as a block, the Indian subcontinent, and the Middle East. What happens is that the Middle East and the Philippines are gateways to Europe and the US, respectively. When we are there, any US companies will look at the Philippines and see it with their own eyes, and so will the European companies with the Middle East. (SOO, head of franchise)

Aspiring to be a global brand is a CSF for many of the world's food service giants, and local brands must have that same grit and determination if they are to move further up the internationalisation ladder.

3.2. Global Branding

Attaining achiever status does not mean branding takes a back seat. Many participants, including ASL, a chief executive officer, stressed that to have further growth and become a global company, further investments in branding are a key CSF.

Many participants, including EIL, a business development manager, saw adaptive branding on a global stage as critical for international success. While keeping a standard branding, many achievers tweaked branding to suit foreign markets:

In Indonesia, we tend to be a little higher end. In Spain, we are a bit more lifestyle. We have nice seats with a patio, and with the climate and lifestyle, other design changes as well. (DBA, managing director)

Thus, participants agreed that appropriate branding strategies were vital for the continued growth of their brand and that their brand had to be relevant and localised to target countries to ensure it appealed to different audiences and target markets.

3.3. Global Adaptation

As Singaporean companies expand overseas, adaptation is inevitable, and managing this basis is also seen as a CSF. Such adaptation also sets the stage for global expansion as eating habits and dining preferences differ from country to country. Areas of adaptation for food service companies include taste, price, and operational procedures as pointed out by ASL, a managing director.

Taste is one area that we adapt; the taste in some countries is different from Singapore, and we must change. Certain percentages we allowed to change, and certain things are not allowed to change. There is feedback for certain things to be spicier, and we can be spicier.

The pricing strategy is the other area that we adapt to. We must make sure that the product is priced to be accepted by the locals. Yet another area is that certain operational procedures must be changed because the staff mentality is different. There is a requirement for us to understand these differences. We must try to understand their requirements, and there is no such thing as we can transpose Singapore's standards on the foreign markets.

Once a Singaporean company steps out of regional markets towards North Asia and the Middle East, there is a need to adapt to weather and seasonality:

In all markets, we adapt based on seasonality. We introduce warm items to the menu as we have stores in winter countries. In the beginning, it is important to make the brand look international, and then we must localise the brand. (DBA, managing director)

Halal certification is a definite requirement given the significant number of Muslim patrons in a target country:

We must adapt, and in some countries such as Malaysia and Indonesia, our concept must be halal. In others, for example, Vietnam, we use their local produce in our menu. (JAG, assistant business development manager)

The key is to achieve the right balance in adaptation without losing the soul or DNA of the food concept. LIA, a managing director, noted that there were customers who commented that if they were looking at local food, they would not be walking into his Singapore concept stores overseas.

Adaptation is therefore a CSF. However, the main question is, what should be adapted, and how should such changes be implemented to obtain a positive response from the local customers? Ultimately, as participants noted, it is not a 'cut and paste' approach out of Singapore, and achievers must wrestle with these issues as they expand beyond the comfort zones of Southeast Asia, where eating and dining habits are like those in Singapore.

3.4. Global Support

Global support is yet another key CSF noted by the achievers'. LIA, a managing director, summed up that if the company cannot support its overseas franchisee, it should not go international.

Achievers faced the issue of global support as their networks extended beyond Southeast Asia. Such extensions meant they had to support far-off areas in North Asia, the Middle East, India, and Europe, where country, cultural, and time differences have implications about the type of support to partners worldwide.

As DDD, a business development manager, noted, when his company expanded to the Middle East, support was lacking and not up to the mark. However, the company rectified that in subsequent years.

The Middle Eastern people like to buy in bulk, and we customise gift boxes so they can buy ten to twenty products at one go.

The level of support given to overseas partners varied from country to country. According to DBA, a managing director, the key message to overseas partners was that they would be well supported. Achievers had to work with their overseas partners and vary their approaches to suit local working cultures:

Things can be bureaucratic, especially in Japan, and we must learn to deal with that. For a young brand like ours, this is a mismatch. However, when we go to Indonesia, we must be humble but 'politely' forceful as we must instil standards. Some are open relationships, and others are more hierarchical. (DBA, managing director)

As such support comes with a cost, as mentioned by DBA, many companies chose to enter countries closer to Singapore.

Beyond Southeast Asia, achievers need to consider global support if they are to become a global brand, and this is critical to achieving global success. Consequently, careful planning is needed before expanding into outer frontiers such as the United States and Europe if such expansion is to be financially feasible. Failure to provide adequate global support can lead to dire consequences.

Every Singaporean company will love to have a footprint in the US or Europe or Australia, but be realistic by just having one outlet over there, which we might not be able to support regularly. (CHI, general manager)

If the overseas partner is a big company, surely, it looks nice, sure, and we can grow fast and be in many locations. To be fair, the question is whether we can support them. If overnight we are all over the world just because we are with a big company that puts us in many locations, the key question is whether we can provide the support to ensure product quality. It will be good for the brand, and if we cannot support them, then we may suffer over time. (LIA, managing director)

4. Conclusion

In summary, achievers in this study considered the four global perspectives, namely, global aspirations, global branding, global adaptations, and global support, as critical success factors. The proper management of these critical success factors differentiates them from a regional player to becoming a global brand.

Beyond these factors, what other key competencies as well as capabilities do achievers need to have to become a worldwide brand? These attributes and qualities will be discussed in the next chapter.

CHAPTER 10

STRIVING TO BE A GLOBAL F&B COMPANY

1. *Introduction*

The critical success factors for the achievers were covered in the previous chapter. Singapore F&B companies have a different level of success in the international arena. Many have ventured to ASEAN and East Asia (China, Japan, and Korea), and few have made headway to the Middle East, Europe, the Americas, and Australia.

The next phase of development will be becoming a global F&B company, and several companies such as BreadTalk, Jumbo, TungLok Group, Paradise Group, and Bee Cheng Hiang endeavour to move into the global stage. To be a global company, what key competencies and capabilities must Singapore F&B companies possess to advance into the world stage? This chapter discusses these issues from the participants' points of view.

2. *The Global Mindset – Five Core Competencies: Five Rs*

In striving to become global brands, Singaporean food service companies recognised the need to have a global mindset. Ranker et al. (2014, p. 23) suggested that a 'global mindset' was 'an orientation of openness towards other cultures, other people, and other ways of doing things' or an 'ability to step outside one's base culture to understand that there is no universally correct way to do things'. He argued that leaders of global organisations need to adapt and use appropriate styles to get the job done and suggested that such styles depend on the target country, the culture, and the people with whom they are interacting. The attributes of a global mindset include

1. an openness to learning,
2. an ability to adapt to new cultures,
3. an ability to manage different cultures,
4. recognising there is no one correct way,
5. being interested,
6. proactively using diversity,
7. not being bound by local customs.

Javidan and Walker (2012, p. 38) stated that a global mindset consists in three different dimensions: (1) intellectual capital, (2) psychological capital; and (3) social capital.

In stepping up to become global brands, Singaporean companies also need the five Rs, which are the competencies and capabilities that participants felt are required for global expansion.

1. Restructure their network
2. Renovate or re-innovate their brand and concept
3. Realign their support for overseas partners
4. Re-adapt their concept and food in foreign markets
5. Rekindle with overseas partners

The following sections will discuss these competencies and capabilities.

2.1. Restructure Networks

The Leximancer analysis suggested that 'outlets' was an important theme, and the NVivo analysis found that *outlet* was the third most frequently used word.

From the directory compiled by the author, fifteen of the participants (blue bars) had started internationalisation more than ten years ago, and four of these companies (orange bars) were interviewed for this study. Three more companies would be reaching their tenth year of internationalisation next year, and two of them were part of this study.

Figure 10.1 showed the number of companies and the year when they had their first overseas outlet (series 1) and the number of companies that were interviewed for this present study (series 2).

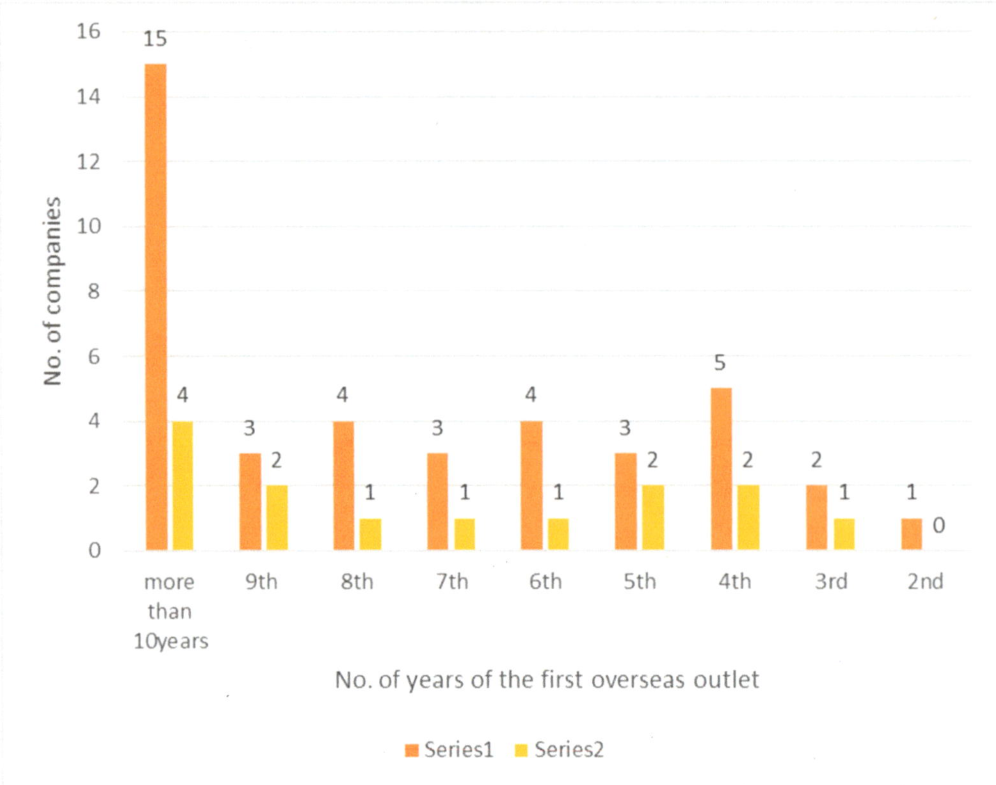

Figure 10.1: Number of companies and number of years of their first overseas outlet

With a larger network of outlets, it is obvious that the achievers are preoccupied with their network of overseas outlets. The performance of these outlets would affect their earnings and increase brand equity. Given that, achievers must possess the global mindset in approaching the restructuring of their networks and be prepared to change as they entered a different phase to be a global company. What may work in one country may not do so well in yet another, and this understanding and capability of instituting the restructuring can be challenging and disastrous if not overseen correctly.

Typically, unless terminated prematurely, restructuring can only be executed when the current agreement lapses, usually after ten years, and the companies can hit the reset buttons and amend their existing network arrangement.

There was no tipping point or any indicator that we based on for internationalisation. Just going overseas was the motto of the current management. We take the view that if things do not work well, be prepared to change. (EES, assistant franchise manager)

DDD, business development manager, highlighted that significant changes were happening in her company after thirteen years to grow in the next phase.

During the last two years, there have been many changes to use all its current expertise and capabilities to grow to an even bigger organisation. So previously during the last thirteen years, it had focused on doing a franchise business. It has grown into taking on more creative, complex business structures such as joint-venture franchises with different stakeholdings depending on the appetite and risk for each of the brands. The whole philosophy changed when our new group CEO came on board in 2017.

Different business models were considered for existing networks across foreign markets as noted by ASL, CEO, and it made sense in hindsight not to give out master franchises in some countries.

In Malaysia, we tend to do well as we compete amongst ourselves by having our franchisees and ourselves competing to open at prime locations. When we went to Malaysia, we are just thinking of just giving out a franchise, and the partner does not want a master franchise but only a single franchise. So it was that way.

But when we went to other countries, they took the master franchise. We realised later that it is better not to give master franchise. If they do not grow, we cannot grow, whereas in Malaysia, the franchisee did not want a master franchise; and when the business turned out to be better, other people want to come in and compete with him. It is much better.

For the rest, we could not do joint venture as, in the beginning, we signed master franchise, and so we cannot pursue this mode. We must wait for these agreements to lapse.

Achievers learned from their initial experience in internationalisation that will influence the restructuring of their expansion models when the current arrangement is due for renewal.

But there was a lot to learn for franchising. The Philippines was my learning ground. I gave the master franchise for the whole of the Philippines. I knew the pros and cons of giving the master franchise to someone who was to oversee the whole country.

Of course, right now, I will not give the master franchise to one party just like Indonesia, for example. If I gave the master franchise to someone for the whole of Indonesia, I am at his mercy.If I see a market that he could do and the guy is not ready, then I have to wait, and the opportunity is gone or lost. Or the franchisee himself is not capable to take it to greater heights. (LIA, director)

Therefore, achievers, while setting their sights on gaining more ground on the international stage, need to have the knowledge and capabilities to restructure their existing networks to reap further benefits while they seek new territories. The restructuring can only happen when the agreement lapses which is typically after 10 years as noted by EES, an assistant franchise manager.

DDD, a business development manager, noted significant changes were happening in her company after 13 years with a new Group CEO in 2017. The company has grown to take on more creative, complex joint ventures and an increased appetite for risk with each of its brands.

In summary, "Achievers", while wishing to expand on the international stage, need to have the know-how and ability to restructure existing networks if they are to succeed in new territories.

2.2. Realign Support Structure

The achievers identified global support as a CSF, and to succeed in this, they needed to deliver effective support structures for their overseas networks. The governance structures of increasingly extensive overseas networks require not only a global mindset but also the ability to manage partners from different cultural backgrounds and experiences within foreign macro-environments as noted by ASL, a managing director. Many participants, such as DBA, suggested that support costs were crucial.

The main downside would be the resources required to be put in as the fees can be a mismatch, and if they just open one, the amount of effort is not commensurate. We must add people to support the new country. Our team has grown a lot, and we must bring in more people, and the costs may exceed the revenue derived from franchising. (DBA, managing director)

Every Singapore company will love to have a footprint in the USA, Europe, or Australia, but be realistic by just having one outlet over there, which we might not be able to support regularly, and there will be many other support issues. (CHI, general manager)

For China, it will require a lot of resources such as management and capital. (PTT, executive director)

In that way, it is a bit easier; but for us, an SME, we do not have someone who specialises in managing overseas local partners, and that is a resource issue as this person has other responsibilities quite unlike multinationals, where they will have that person to just focus on relationship management. (MAN, vice-president)

As growing SMEs, many achievers felt they had difficulties with elaborate governing structures. The risk of not having good governance structures was evident as a lack of compliance might result in the pre-termination of franchise agreements. EES, an assistant franchise manager, shared her experience of terminating franchise agreements in Indonesia and the Philippines due to non-compliance.

They are on a single-unit basis for five years, and we opened in 2012 in Jakarta before, and at the peak, there were three outlets. What happened was non-compliance as we had to shut the outlets subsequently under the new management. The new management cleaned up the franchisees.

Indeed, a lack of a good governance structure deters many companies from taking on more countries, noted SOO, a head of the franchise.

We are required to build the support for the organisation to move forward. I told the owners that we have to establishregional offices to support our international growth, satellite offices, and we must have a man on the ground to be successful.

Thus, having the capability to realign support for overseas partners was critical for these achievers as they strove to be global brands and companies.

The key question is whether we can provide the support to ensure product quality and our overseas partners succeed. It will be good for the brand, and if not, we may suffer over time. Support [for franchisee] is especially important, and if you are not ready, do not go international. (LIA, managing director)

This capability requires a global mindset to build bridges across diverse cultures, backgrounds, and experiences. It manages the expectation of how the brand and concept will fare in the respective foreign territories. Achievers, in short, need to have that capability to have a breakthrough in globalisation.

2.3. Rebrand

Many participants have recognised the need to re-examine their branding strategies in foreign markets, with some highlighting a need to rebrand in such markets if they are to be more successful. Such strategies also include packaging, said DDD, an assistant business development manager.

We will drive some inspiration from other companies and brands such as the Japanese, which tend to put lots of emphasis on the packaging. That is one area that we must improve, and with the right packaging, we can strengthen our branding. Once taken out of our stores, it will attract attention, and it will be a statement for the brand.

For DBA, branding also includes more than the packaging; it covers the source of food and the supply chain.

The next phase is about digging deeper into our supply chain to strengthen our brand. It will mean not just a local and environment-friendly supply chain but packaging as well. The packaging must be eco-friendly. This is a huge part of our branding, and the trend in Singapore is towards that, and the government is promoting this.

For many of the achievers, rebranding will improve globalisation:

We must build more branding campaigns in international markets that will build more brand awareness. The principal motivation for internationalisation is to enhance brand presence, and that will allow us to scale in overseas market. (ESL, business development manager)

The innovation of the brand for the achievers is a continuous process that needs to be undertaken to ensure that the brand and concept remain relevant to the locals in each country. Many will fully agree with ASL, a CEO, that to be a global company, branding for globalisation is key.

When we grow bigger, we can do a more global brand building; we invest more.

Branding and rebranding are ongoing exercises that are critically important for the aspirants, actives, and achievers as they face challenges in remaining relevant to locals in foreign territories if they are to secure their patronage.

2.4. Readapt the Food, Service, and Products

Achievers also need to adapt to each of their foreign markets. While adaptation in the earlier section has covered seasonal, religious, and local palates, flexibility and ingenuity in coming up with food variations is a competency that supports global success. As noted by DBA, a managing director, even big companies such as McDonald's struggle to do this well, even though scalability is not an issue for such food giants. The critical challenge is to adapt the food 'without losing its soul or the DNA', said DBA, a managing director.

In 2009, we are moved and driven by market opportunities. We saw an obvious requirement for healthy eating as we grew; we have customers asking more questions about where our food comes from. We then go into our supply chain; we start to have more vegans coming to our outlets. Our menu continues to evolve, and so for us, the journey for us is always to keep up with the markets. This is to ensure that we adapt to every market, and the menu in various markets changes to suit.

NIC, managing director of another successful local heritage brand, concurred that not meeting the taste of local customers and satisfying their palates could spell disaster:

We want to open in South China in Guangzhou. Shenzhen has an influx of people from Sichuan with a strong taste, and our food may not be very suitable for them. Din Tai Fung has only five tables, while Crystal Jade is fully packed. The difference is due to a matter of taste. If you do not adapt, it is a problem; the question is whether you can still have the usual Din Tai Fung and created a new menu for the locals.

Adaptation and re-adaptation must occur in internationalisation according to EES, assistant franchise manager, to avoid stagnation. This is the 'disease' of achievers, and once successful, there is a tendency to rest on our laurels and ride on our current success. Not seeking continuous disruption in the food as in re-adaptation could spell dire consequences for successful companies.

We must innovate, the menu has been stagnant for a long time, and we are launching a new product next month. We are launching a new product item, but the brand in terms of innovation is not so much. We are more focused on business and unit economics to drive the business. We do not look at the seasonality of products, which is a boon and bane.

In summary, achievers should heed DDD, a business development manager who argued that there must be a strategy and plan and discipline:

It is good to have a strategy and to restart relooking at how we do things and be disciplined. So we must have a strategic approach and be very clear in what we intend to achieve in each of these countries.

2.5. Rekindle Working Relationships with Overseas Partners

Compared with the aspirants and actives, the achievers had a more significant opportunity in potential conflicts with their overseas partners given their extensive international coverage. Having the right global mindset and applying the right disposition when relating to overseas partners is a vital capability whether it is of the CEO, the business development manager, the franchise manager, or the support team.

A key challenge is when conflicts occur. ASL, a CEO, suggested that trust and effective communication were crucial in resolving issues such as the illegal use of brands and not following procedures in opening new outlets.

Trust is something that both sides must respect. We grow in respect, and business can create tension, and if we do not think win-win, then there will be challenges. We must communicate with partners as they also have other businesses, and after a while, they do not focus on our brand, and we must keep a tab on them. Our team and I track all our partners, and we try to visit our partners as frequently as we can.

Overall, it has been beneficial for internationalisation. The greatest mistake is where, when we grow overseas at the beginning, we did not have enough communication with our local partners and assigned resources, which resulted in some difficulties. We did not regularly keep track and visit the grounds more frequently.

When conflict and a lack of compliance occurred, the franchise agreement was the pillar to fall back on. EES, an assistant franchise manager, commented that there was always a need to seek compromise and that terminating a contract was a last resort.

Another more established company had a reporting system that governed its extensive network. The company also helped prevent any lapses through regular contact sessions with its overseas partners:

For existing partners, we have a franchise coordinator [FC] who holds two or up to three countries. They have responsibilities over those countries, and they know the owners personally. They always call on them and meet them to keep the relationship healthy. (DDD, business development manager)

Other than trust and effective communication, participants felt values needed to align to reduce potential conflicts, said JAT, an executive director.

MAN, a vice-president, suggested that Singaporean companies must try to understand local partners. Rather than auditing and taking punitive action, there were differences in the way the achievers managed relationships with local partners. He believed there is an Asian model and a way of dealing and relating with foreign partners which differs from the Western approach.

When we do an audit, I would like my staff to tell me three good things that the overseas local partners have done. They must have done three good things, and the truth is that it is easy to finger-point and hard to see the good side of things. On overseas audits, we do not want to have the franchisee think that it is me again coming here to find fault. They would dread having this audit. We want to encourage them and help them to succeed, and this mindset is important.

Other than trust and effective communication, JAT, executive director, stressed that if the values of the local partner were aligned with the company, potential conflicts could be reduced.

We would like the local partners overseas to share the same values and align with us. For those company-owned, we passed on the values. For joint-venture partners, different countries would have diverse ways and styles of management, but we still want these proven methods and values to be passed on such as incentive schemes.

Besides having a compromise and trying to understand the local partner rather than audit and take punitive action, would there be a difference in the Asian model of internationalisation concerning managing the relationship between the local partners and the company? NIC, managing director, agreed that the process was not to finger-point but to look for lapses and seek rectification.

For franchising, when there is a conflict, it is logically meant to go through the process, and it is not about pointing the finger at who is wrong and who is right. It is about fixing the issue, and if everybody is working for the brand, there would not be much [to worry about].

LIA, director of a successful Singapore heritage brand, concurred that 'give and take' is a good policy in international franchising for him and his company:

'Give in and give way' is the policy. To give in is not in submission and for things that cannot be done like how it is n Singapore; it may not work in your local context, and it does in theirs. Give in, in that sense and do not insist it is done in your way. Give way; give a little allowance, a little discount as you cannot expect a hundred per cent even in a local sense. I have outlets that are very tough to maintain the same quality throughout and with individual chefs, so give way to that little bit of differences.

Therefore, the capability to collaborate with overseas partners cannot be understated. As the company progressed to become an achiever, it had to deal with diverse overseas partners who had different aspirations, cultural backgrounds, and expectations on how the brand should be conducted and done in each territory.

3. Global Success Maps

The achievers were not a homogeneous group. Some had more than ten years of experience and extensive coverage in Asia and were beginning to expand to First World countries (e.g. the United States and Europe). Others were gaining more ground through further regionalisation. Thus, their success maps for the next five years differed in terms of the choice of mode, destination, timing, and operation strategies (Bose, 2016) (Table 10.1).

Table 10.1: Strategies for the achievers

Participant	First overseas outlet	Destinations	Mode	Operations
NIC	2016	Taiwan, China, Japan, and Australia	Prefers franchising as it is easy to expand, capital-light, and overseas partners provide local management and knowledge No need to dedicate too many resources	• Supply chain expertise to supply overseas outlets • R & D for the proprietary sauce in ambient condition • Rebranding needed for the next phase of internationalisation • Intellectual property issues in Japan and Indonesia • Staff training and retraining of overseas franchisees needed
ASL	2006	Deepening penetration in existing markets, new focus on the Middle East	Prefer JVs and fully owned outlets	• Branding for globalisation • Reporting structure for overseas franchises • Better communication with overseas partners • Re-adaptation of food in various markets

Participant	First overseas outlet	Destinations	Mode	Operations
LIA	2011	UK, Europe, and the US	Franchising preferred as owners felt JV and partnerships were sensitive and difficult to handle Franchising seen as less risky and open to JVs if partners are right	• R & D for the proprietary sauce in ambient conditions to support overseas operations and maintain food quality • Marketing expertise in promoting the brand and food overseas • Building a team to support international growth
DDD	2000	Improve the performance of outlets in various countries. Find new overseas partners in US, Japan, and Europe	JV and even wholly owned outlets Multiple brands and even acquisition	• Find new overseas partners • Continue to strengthen the existing brand • Focus on R & D to deliver adaptation for diverse markets like the Middle East • Build new leaders amongst the loyal staff • Strategic planning required for future expansion into a new market

Participant	First overseas outlet	Destinations	Mode	Operations
SON	2005	Expand beyond the UK to Europe and SE Asian countries	Open to JV or franchising options JV for Malaysia and Indonesia and wholly owned outlets in Australia	• R & D and central production to support overseas operations • Dealing with import restrictions and product quality issues • Selection of overseas partners beyond friends and related parties critical for expansion
PTT	2015	Other SE Asian countries, Hong Kong, China	Started with wholly owned outlets in Vietnam Franchising in other SE Asian countries	• Ability to adapt to the local taste • Innovation in using technology, such as vending machines, for products. • Ability to scale overseas operations and systems. • R & D needed to support overseas expansion and supply key ingredients in ambient conditions • Marketing as the other key capability needed for overseas expansion

Participant	First overseas outlet	Destinations	Mode	Operations
EIL	2010	SE Asia and open to other countries	Franchising preferred in the existing markets Open to JVs	• Import restrictions, meaning there is a need to source local suppliers • Language as an issue: need staff who can speak the local language • Handling various partners in different countries
DBA	2014	Focus on China and Europe in future	Franchising and JVs if the partner is right	• Supply chain management as key • Branding as an eco-friendly and healthy food option crucial • Developing the staff needed to manage the network
EES	2009	SE Asia, China, Japan, and the US	Started with wholly owned outlets in Malaysia. Franchising preferred for non-key territories like Thailand; will eventually be franchised in the long run due to the need for local knowledge	• Developing the capability to deal with overseas partners • Registration of intellectual property issues in China • R & D of more sauces and supply of proprietary sauces • Menu innovation crucial • Rebranding necessary

Participant	First overseas outlet	Destinations	Mode	Operations
JAT	2011	Other SE Asian countries, Australia, and China	Started with wholly owned stores in Malaysia and Indonesia Franchising preferred outside capital cities	• Adaptation of concept to suit the eating habits of various countries • Building a team to support further internationalisation
MAN	2010	Strengthen presence in the US Focus on China, Japan, and Korea	Franchising preferred as it is capital-light, and the brand is already in the country Open to JV for Japan and Korea	• Registration of intellectual property in target markets • R & D to achieve adaptation for the overseas market • Adaptation in the overseas market to be successful
JAG	1998	China and South Korea	Franchising preferred due to the need for local knowledge	• Adaptation as key in all markets • Local knowledge essential. • Capability to manage local overseas partners

Participant	First overseas outlet	Destinations	Mode	Operations
SOO	2014	The US and Europe	Prefer franchising for speed in expansion overseas and not having to deal with too many franchisees other than the master franchisee in each country	• Support capability and capacity to meet the extensive overseas network • Reconciliation of the various models between a total kiosk concept and a QSR and developing operational procedures to support both • Ability to deal with logistics and supply chain issues • Overcoming import restrictions in various countries

4. Conclusion

This chapter provided a background of the achievers and discussed the results from the NVivo and Leximancer analyses. Participants suggested there were four CSFs to attaining success on the global stage:

1. Having global aspirations
2. Having a structure that provided global support for a global network
3. Projecting a global brand message and offers
4. Adapting to different markets and eating habits

The analysis suggested that having a global mindset is critical to companies seeking to move forward with the five Rs (restructure, revitalise, realign, rebrand, and re-adapt). Participants suggested they had to restructure their networks, often with new partners that could support the brand's success. Another important initiative was to realign support capabilities and provide a more robust and cohesive working relationship with overseas partners. They also needed to rebrand, which required internal or external assistance in projecting a new global brand image that transcends not just the menu but also decor, customers' experiences, pricing, and the like. Finally, they need to re-adapt on an ongoing basis if they are to stay relevant in all their markets and to work, deal with, motivate, and reconcile conflicts with overseas partners if they are to ensure the stability of their overseas networks.

The path towards becoming a global brand is varied, but the CSFs, capabilities, and strategies identified in this chapter will help aspiring and active companies prepare for their onward journey and provide answers to the research questions asked in this study. For these achievers, the word that symbolises their effort towards further success and globalisation is *prune*. Achievers have had to look at everything that they do and prune the weeds that might suffocate their success. Thus, with a global mindset, achievers need to focus on the five Rs:

1. Restructure the network.
2. Realign support for network partners.
3. Rebrand.
4. Re-adapt food, service, and other products.
5. Rekindle relationships with network partners.

These capabilities are the pillars that are critical to furthering growth through internationalisation.

The way the achievers managed differences and conflicts suggests the emergence of an Asian style of internationalisation. While the contract remains the bedrock, these achievers were mindful of enforceability and saw legal recourse as a last resort. They preferred discussion and the realignment of expectations as a way of gaining trust and respect from partners.

While many achievers started with franchising, they looked at other options when time contracts were renewed. Many opted for a master franchising model but also considered other modes, such as multi-unit franchising and joint ventures. A hybrid form, called the joint-venture franchise, is gaining popularity amongst achievers. Here, franchisers convert part or whole of the franchise fee into shares in a JV company that later owns and opens the first outlet as proof of concept. Subsequently, the JV company gives out franchises. Some Singaporean achievers preferred to open outlets in Europe and the United States through joint ventures or even through wholly owned outlets.

CHAPTER 11

PICKING THE RIGHT CHERRY

1. Introduction

According to the *Cambridge English Dictionary*, an *acquirer* is an individual or company that buys another company. Thus, an acquirer in the context of this study could be a company or individual who buys a brand or concept for development in their country from a Singaporean food service company. This case study sought to understand the critical success factors acquirers looked for and whether these factors corresponded to what the internationalising companies deemed necessary.

There are few insights or published materials about the critical factors acquirers look for when buying a brand. One example was reported in the *Wall Street Journal* on 2 May 2014. A major global luxury conglomerate (LVMH), through its owned private equity firm (L Capital), acquired a 90 per cent stake in one of Singapore's famous Chinese restaurant chains (Crystal Jade). One rationale for the purchase was its strong brand and presence in China, while another was the owner's plan to cash out and retire as he was 65 years old. However, financial considerations were the main driver.

Other than the listed companies which had to issue a press statement for such acquisition or report in the media, many of the SMEs' brand owners, as well as acquirers, do not publish any statements; and thus, there is virtually a lack of information about why the acquirer decided to take on a Singapore brand or any. Yet this knowledge is vital for Singapore companies that wish to venture overseas as this study attempts to provide some insights into how the acquirers consider critical success factors in selecting and acquiring a Singapore brand.

This chapter will follow the same format used in the preceding case studies. In section 2, the interview data and the results obtained from the Leximancer analysis are discussed. Section 3 presents the findings from the cross-case analysis while section 4 concludes the chapter.

2. Acquirers of Singapore F&B Brands

Two acquirers were interviewed on the telephone, and five were interviewed face to face using the same set of semi-structured questions in the previous case studies. The shortest interview lasted slightly more than thirty minutes, and the longest lasted about fifty minutes. All the interviewees were owners or owner-managers of adopted Singapore F&B brands in their countries (Table 11.1).

Table 11.1: The acquirers

Date	Code	Gender	Age	Education	Year	No. of Outlets	Country	Position
22 Feb. 2018	ROS	Male	51	Grad	2014	2	Indonesia	CEO
11 May 2018	HRU	Male	49	Grad	2004	40	Indonesia	MD
3 Jul. 2018	BUD	Male	51	Grad	2002	25	Indonesia	Director
10 Jul. 2018	FRE	Male	35	Grad	2010	6	Philippines	MD
7 Aug. 2018	JIA	Female	42	Grad	2019	1	Australia	Owner
18 Aug. 2018	ALE	Male	25	Sec	2014	3	Malaysia	Director
12 Sep. 2018	MOG	Male	33	Grad	2015	4	Indonesia	Head

The interviews were conducted between February and September 2018, and five of the seven interviews were conducted in the participants' countries, with the author travelling to these countries for this purpose. The interviews were transcribed and stored in separate files that were analysed using Leximancer and NVivo.

3. The Leximancer Analysis

Figure 11.1 shows the visible concepts within the respective themes that were important to this group of participants. These contextual associations were validated with the ranked concept relevance list (Table 11.2).

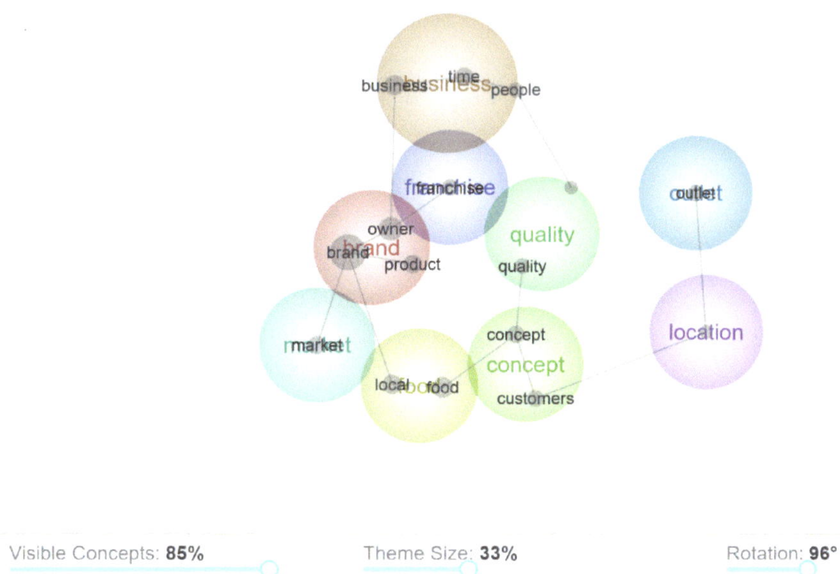

Figure 11.1: A concept map for the acquirers

The concepts cluster to form themes that appear in a larger type in Figure 11.1. The concept names are coloured, like the theme spheres, to show their importance. Concept proximity shows the strength of the association between the two concepts. In the heat map (Figure 11.1), the largest sphere is 'business', but the 'hottest' theme is 'brand' (red amber), followed by 'business' (amber), 'concept' (green), and 'food' (yellow green). The less important themes are 'market' (green blue), 'outlet' (light blue), and 'location' (purple).

Table 11.2: The ranked concepts list

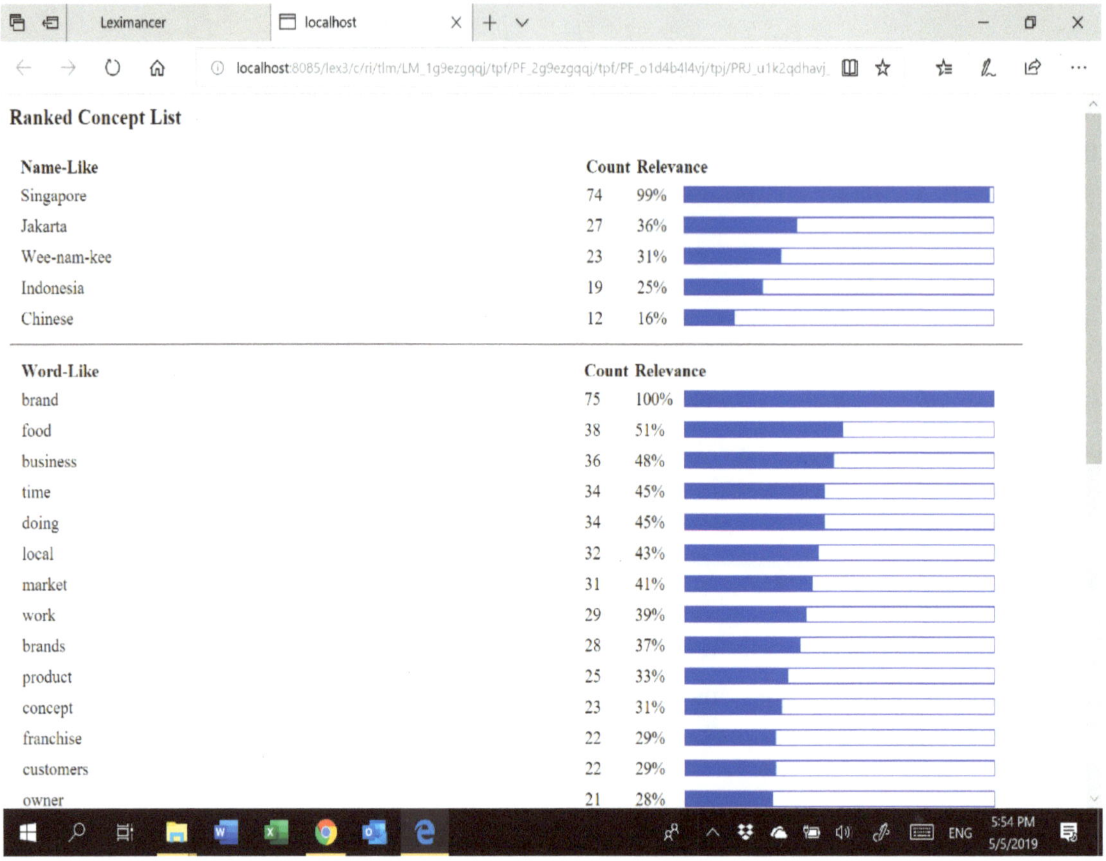

Ranked Concept List

Name-Like	Count	Relevance
Singapore	74	99%
Jakarta	27	36%
Wee-nam-kee	23	31%
Indonesia	19	25%
Chinese	12	16%

Word-Like	Count	Relevance
brand	75	100%
food	38	51%
business	36	48%
time	34	45%
doing	34	45%
local	32	43%
market	31	41%
work	29	39%
brands	28	37%
product	25	33%
concept	23	31%
franchise	22	29%
customers	22	29%
owner	21	28%

In a Leximancer analysis, *relevance* is defined as the percentage frequency of text segments that are coded with that concept relative to the frequency of the most common concept in the list. It is an indicator of the relative strength of a concept's frequency of occurrence. In Table 11.2, the list of ranked concept relevance suggests that the most critical concept for the acquirers is 'brand', followed by 'business', 'owner', 'food', 'time', 'outlet', and 'local', and these themes are discussed in subsequent sections.

4. The NVivo Analysis Findings

As this study used both Leximancer and NVivo to analyse the data, the top twenty words for the acquirers are shown in Table 11.3, and the corresponding word cloud can be seen in Figure 11.2.

Table 11.3: The Top 20 relevant words for the 'Acquirers'

Word	Length	Count	Weighted Percentage
brand	5	186	2.78
Singapore	9	128	2.16
operations	4	139	1.32
locations	5	102	1.25
consumers	4	173	1.06
product	7	56	0.89
outlet	6	58	0.83
food	4	47	0.79
owner's openness	5	45	0.76
affordable	4	57	0.73
franchise	9	41	0.69
success	7	39	0.59
concept	7	35	0.53
people	6	31	0.52
competition	11	25	0.41
import	9	31	0.41
support	4	59	0.41
partners	8	21	0.35
terms	5	29	0.35

Figure 11.2: A word cloud for the acquirers

The findings from NVivo were not dissimilar to those obtained in the Leximancer analysis (excluding the name-like concept of Singapore, which was the focus of the present study). The top ten Leximancer themes and the top ten words from the NVivo analysis (Table 11.4) were used as the foundation for the discussion of these results contained in subsequent sections.

Table 11.4: The top ten Leximancer themes and NVivo's top ten words

Ranking	Leximancer	NVivo	Ranking	Leximancer	NVivo
1	Brand	Brand	6	Outlet	Product
2	Business	Singapore	7	Local	Outlet
3	Owner	Operations	8	Market	Food
4	Food	Location	9	Location	Owner's openness
5	Time	Consumer	10	Product	Affordable

5. *The Cross-Case Analysis*

This section provides an overview of the Leximancer concept map that was used to identify the emergent themes and the connectivity and relationships between these themes across cases. It also highlights the importance of the various themes to the groups of participants as the Leximancer analysis enables groups to be examined when included in separate folders.

As can be seen in Figure 11.1, there are eight heat-mapped spheres, each representing a theme. All concepts and data categories are marked in grey nodes, with a label identifying the concept or the category. The size of the nodes shows the relative strength of the concept or the category, and the groups' positions show the differences in their views. The most prominent theme is 'brand' (red amber), followed by 'partners' (amber), 'support' (yellow green), 'food' (green), 'success' (blue green), 'customers' (blue), 'taste' (blue purple), and lastly 'staff' (purple).

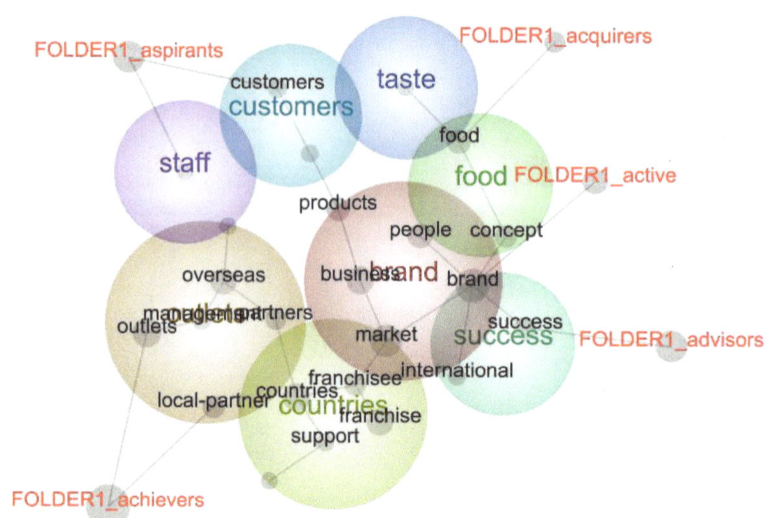

Figure 11.3: A concept map by category

Figure 11.3 shows that the concepts (in black) formed clusters that determined the themes, which appear in a larger type and are coloured the same way as the sphere. As an example, ‘brand’ is red (the same colour as the sphere) and is the central theme for that sphere. The related concepts in black type are ‘people,’ ‘market,’ ‘brand’ (as a concept), and ‘business’. Grey lines linking two concepts suggest a relationship between the concepts while concept proximity shows the strength of the association. Data categories are shown in red (the outlying nodes of the map) (e.g. Folderl_achievers). Concepts and themes closest to a data category are more important to that category and less important to the other categories.

Figure 11.4 shows the dashboard quadrant map generated by the Leximancer analysis. The concepts towards the upper right-hand (magic) quadrant were the most important in the different cases. For the achievers, the most important themes and concepts were ‘brand’, ‘markets’, and ‘countries’, which were in the upper right quadrant. For the advisers, it was ‘food’; and for the aspirants, it was going ‘overseas’. The dashboard insight report suggested the cross-case data had 4,090 context blocks made up of 2 sentences in each block, 24 concepts, and 5 categories. In the next section, the discussion will focus on the participants’ perceptions of the concepts’ prominence.

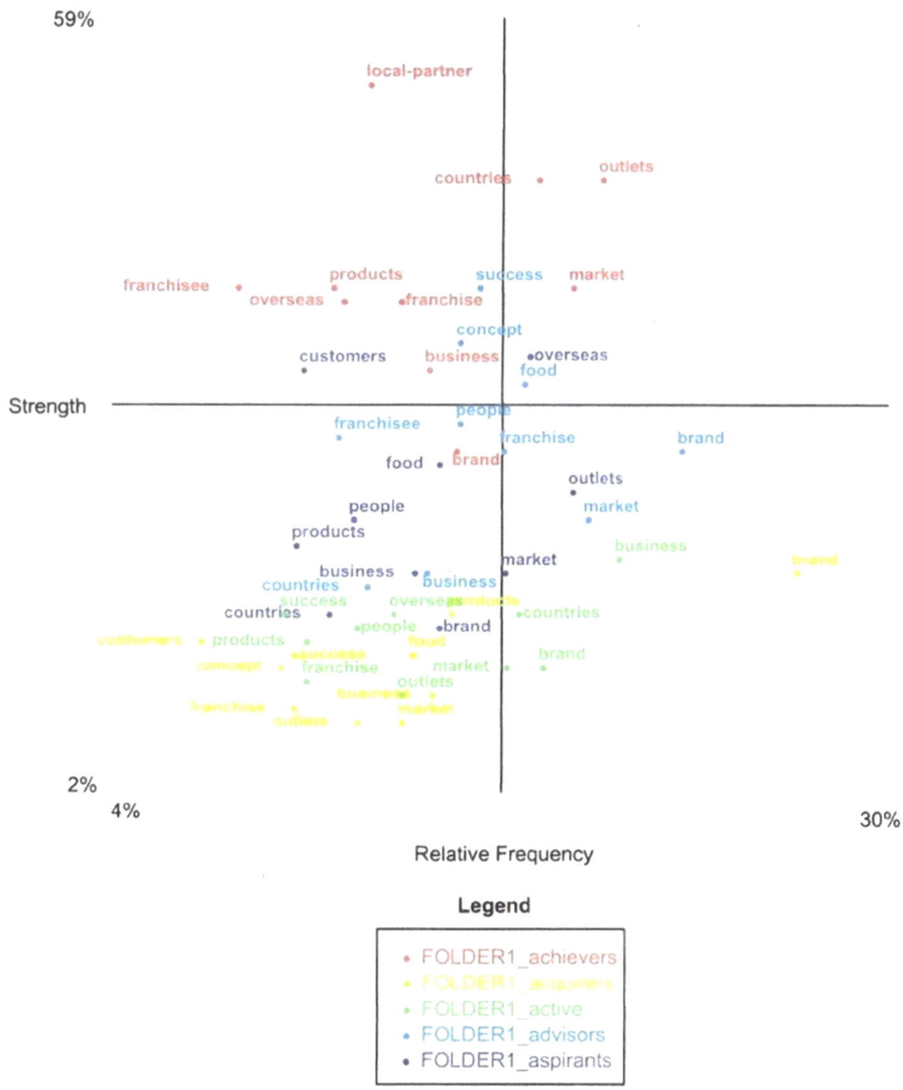

Figure 11.4: The dashboard quadrant map generated by the Leximancer analysis

5.1. Concept Prominence

In a Leximancer analysis, the prominence score combines the strength and frequency scores (Table 11.5), which 'are absolute measures of correlation between category and attribute and can be used to make comparisons over time' (Leximancer, 2018, p. 103). A score higher than 1.0 suggests a co-occurrence happened more often than by chance. The table, which shows the top concepts for each category (i.e. a prominence score of at least 1.0), highlights the relative importance of each concept to the various groups.

Table 11.5: Prominence scores by category

Aspirants	Actives	Achievers	Acquirers	Advisers
Overseas (1.7)	Business (1.5)	The local partner (1.5)	Brand (1.8)	Success (2.0)
Customer (1.7)	Country (1.3)	Country (1.3)	Product (1.5)	Concept (1.7)
Food (1.3)	Success (1.2)	Outlets (1.3)	Customer (1.3)	Food (1.6)
Outlets (1.2)	Overseas (1.2)	Products (1.1)	Success (1.2)	People (1.4)
People (1.1)	People (1.1)	Franchisee (1.1)	Food (1.2)	Franchisee (1.4)
Products (1.0)	Products (1.0)	Market (1.1)	Concept (1.1)	Franchise (1.4)
		Overseas (1.1)		Brand (1.3)

The Leximancer analysis also computes a table of ranked compound concepts by category that reflects the same strength and frequency conditional probabilities. Prominence scores of 3.0 or higher (Table 11.6) suggest that such compound concepts are important to that category. These Leximancer outputs provided the basis for the discussion of the results that are provided in the next section.

Table 11.6: The top-ranking compound concept prominence scores by category

Aspirant Concept Prominence	Active Concept Prominence	Achiever Concept Prominence	Acquirer Concept Prominence	Adviser Concept Prominence
Overseas & Partner (7.2)	Franchise & Team (4.8)	Local Partner & International (3.5)	Customer & Quality (6.2)	Success & International (5.8)
Overseas & Team (6.2)	Overseas & Team (4.5)	Local Partner & Market (3.1)	Product & Taste (5.2)	People and International (5.7)
Food & Taste (5.3)	Overseas & Staff (4.3)	Local Partner & Overseas (3.0)	Brand & Product (4.8)	Franchise & International (5.4)
Customer & Food (5.1)	Overseas & Local Partner (4.2)		Food & Quality (4.6)	Food & Quality (4.7)
Food & Quality (4.2)	Success & International (4.0)		Customer & Staff (4.6)	Concept & Food (4.4)

5.2. Compound Concept Prominence

The acquirers are non-Singaporean companies or individuals who acquired a Singaporean food and beverage brand for their country. In Figure 11.5, the themes important to the acquirers were 'taste', 'customers,' 'food', and 'brand', which they shared with the actives. The acquirers were particularly concerned that the taste was suitable for their target customers as this was critical. Besides having a suitable taste, the acquirers were concerned with getting the right brand for their markets. The acquirers' views about CSFs had implications for Singaporean brands and companies as without acquirers, international expansion would be impossible for most.

For this group, the right appeal is crucial as the brand (with a prominence score of 1.8) affects significantly those deciding to acquire a Singaporean brand. Therefore, Singaporean companies must ensure brand development and enhancement strategies appeal to overseas buyers. This competency goes beyond having a beautiful logo as it includes the concept, decor, image, collateral, brand positioning, and promise. The right brand appeal is a prerequisite for any Singaporean food and beverage company intending to expand overseas.

Other key concepts are 'food' (1.2), 'product' (1.5), and 'food concept' (1.1). The food must appeal to local overseas palates and might require some adaptation to succeed. Acquirers acquire a brand to earn profits, which explains why 'success' had a prominence score of 1.2. Thus, they need locals to accept Singaporean food. They buy brands they believe will provide suitable products for local customers, which is why 'brand and product' (4.8) has a high prominence score. Thus, Singaporean companies need to ensure that the delivery of their products is congruent with their brands' promises.

Acquirers also seek tasty food quality, and many opt for a brand that delivers consistent food quality and right-tasting products. ('Food and quality' has a prominence score of 4.8, and 'product and taste' has a score of 5.2.) They believe their customers look for decent quality ('customer and quality', 6.2), which means a Singaporean brand must consistently deliver decent food quality if it is to expand its international network successfully. Another important compound concept was 'customer and staff' (4.6). The importance of quality customer service is crucial to ensure the continuing success of any international food and beverage company.

6. Conclusion

The chapter covers the theoretical findings and analysis of the acquirers group using NVivo and Leximancer analyses. The participants uncovered the key themes and concepts. The cross-case analysis further strengthens the results and provides insights into the key compound concept prominence, which needs to be discussed in the next chapter. The next chapter will highlight the key reasons why acquirers will be interested in acquiring the Singapore F&B brands for their countries. It will shed light on why acquirers think that their investments should be sound and risks mitigated by 'importing a foreign brand' into their homeland and making it a success.

CHAPTER 12

WHY BUY SINGAPORE F&B BRANDS

1. Introduction

In the previous chapter, the theoretical framework and findings highlighted the concepts and factors that were important for acquirers adopting Singapore F&B brands. The NVivo and Leximancer software provided the analysis. The cross-group analysis further concretised the relevance and prominence of these concepts as well as the compound concept.

In this chapter, the important question of why foreign buyers will acquire Singapore F&B brands will be addressed. What are their considerations in adopting the local brands?

2. The 'Seven Secrets'

The acquirers are companies or individuals who had acquired a Singapore brand as a local partner or franchisee in their respective foreign markets. The research study focused on what acquirers considered the critical success factors in purchasing the Singaporean brand.

The 'seven secrets' of success' for the acquirers and, conversely, the factors for failures will be key to this study as they serve as invaluable lessons for many Singapore F&B companies with international ambitions. They are known as the seven Ss namely, suitable brand; suitable owner and owner's openness; suitable business; suitable concept, taste, and products; suitable adaptation; suitable terms; and suitable location.

2.1. Suitable Brand

The brand was critical when acquirers were deciding whether to take up a food service concept and import it to the home country. Indeed, according to MOG, head of an Indonesian F&B group, familiarity was the primary motivation for acquiring the brand:

We chose this brand because we know it for a long time. If we Indonesians come to Singapore and always go for the brand and it has become comfort food, it would work in Indonesia.'

For BUD, a company director, not only was the Singaporean brand he acquired a familiar brand but it also had emotional and sentimental aspects as his late mother loved the Singapore brand.

HRU, the managing director of an Indonesian company with a portfolio of Singaporean brands, said the fact that he had lived and studied in Singapore and was familiar with the brands helped. Not only was he familiar with the brand but the brand also had to be a champion in its category and an industry standard before it was chosen.

We are from Singapore and familiar with the brand. We did not look at other brands. When we are back in Singapore, we will only try this brand and compared it with different other brands in the same category. We just feel that this brand is incredibly special and different, and their menu is different and nice.

The brand must be familiar, said JIA, a business owner, and it must also be able to fill the gaps in her home country, Australia. FRE, a managing director, concurred with JIA's comments, suggesting locals quickly understood the brands he acquired in his country as they had been successful in Singapore.

RSO, a general manager who acquired a heritage Singaporean brand for Indonesia, noted that brand recognition is crucial, and even not having a halal certification was not an issue given the large Chinese population in Jakarta.

The benefit of acquiring this brand is that we can gain customers quickly with the brand as it is a foreign brand. For us, in Jakarta, we prefer to try new concepts from other countries such as Taiwan and Singapore instead of our local brands. There is no local version of this brand except in the local neighbourhood but not in the shopping malls.

FRE, a managing director, argued that the Singaporean brand had to have a unique selling proposition if overseas partners are to acquire the brand rather than creating their own. The Singaporean brand must be able to compete with other international brands but also with self-created concepts in host countries:

The brand must have USPs and [be] differentiated from what is available in foreign markets. It must be something new and something people are looking out for but not available yet. The brand owners must be concerned as to why people would franchise your brand versus creating a brand on their own.

Further, even if the brand is known, ALE, a company director, emphasised that there is a need to promote it to locals.

When we started, the challenge was that the locals were not familiar with our brand, and so we gave free samples. We must practice this in a new market, and that is an effective way to attract them, and if it is good, they will come in.

In summary, the acquirers felt choosing a suitable brand was critical to their success.

2.2. Suitable Owner and Owner's Openness

Besides the brand, the analysis suggested that owner's openness or finding a suitable owner respectively was critical to the success of a concept in a host country:

The brand owner is a consideration. We have the flexibility to develop out of the standard menu, and the brand owner allowed it. The brand owner allowed us to adapt the food to local tastes. (MOG, head of business development)

The acquirers, whether overseas franchisees or joint-venture partners, felt it was essential to have strong communication and a good working relationship with the owners to ensure success in their local markets as highlighted by RSO, a general manager of an acquired Singapore brand in Indonesia, as well as BUD, a director.

The communication between franchisor and franchisee is also key to the success of the brand in the foreign market. There is a requirement for more communication and analysis of the product performance, and that will spur the development of other menu items for the local market. We would not like the brand owner to be 'too pushy', for example, to emphasise that it is working well in Singapore, and so it will work just as well as in Jakarta. The local partner knows the market better, and the brand owner should listen and communicate. (BUD, director)

HRU, a managing director of an Indonesian company with many Singaporean brands, highlighted the need for the right chemistry between the owners and his team and an alignment of vision and values for the brand and the business.

While it does not mean that what the principal believes is wrong but what I believe is right, it is just chemistry; and without the right chemistry, there will be a lot of future problems. As we progress in business, there will be increased problems, and how do we solve these problems if the wavelengths differ? If language is different, we will be 'wasting time' rather than looking at solutions and improving, and that is the key.

He also noted that the right chemistry will determine the road ahead for both parties, and that is vital in ensuring success when the rubber meets the road:

On and off, there will be conflicts, and that is why chemistry is essential before we start the relationship. Humans are just like rubber bands, and if it stretches beyond the limit, they will snap, and that is the end of it. I believe in courtship time, discussion with the franchisors, honesty, the truthfulness must be there. If that is not even present, then I think the courtship is too short.

In summary, finding the right owner is an important first step, after which the right chemistry is needed to counteract any problems along the way.

2.3. Suitable Business and Operations

Another CSF that acquirers consider is the suitability of the business and its operations. Of particular concern are the importing of key ingredients and the availability of substitute ingredients locally, as pointed out by AMO, a head of business development. In many countries, such ingredients will be subject to import quotas and other restrictions, including high tariffs.

Beyond the chemistry of the owner and the acquirer, BUD, a director, reiterated that both management teams must be able to work to produce a sustainable result. Another key area was the transfer of knowledge and assistance to 'clone' or replicate a successful formula and product consistency in the home country:

The difficulties are maintaining product consistency and creating the product as the chef is only trained for three weeks. The Singapore chef is only in Jakarta for a month, and the challenge is to ensure consistency when he leaves. (AMO, head of business development)

The brand is as good as it is being run and managed. A good brand will be ruined if the management is terrible, and conversely, a not-so-famous brand is good if it is well run and managed. For HRE, a managing director, handling the operations well and establishing the right foundation is key to success:

Singapore brands are easier to be accepted in Indonesia, but again, operations are another matter, and the key success factor is how you run the business. It is easier to be accepted due to the proximity and the number of visitors that come in and out of Singapore, and thus, acknowledging the brand is therefore easier. In contrast, not knowing the brand versus the fact that you have seen it will make it easier. The acceptability is higher.

I believe in the foundation to be successful. How do you support and ensure consistency? These are the building blocks. If the foundation is not strong and everything that we pile on top are the services, then everything on top will fail. This applies to any brand and anywhere. The concept also must be right for the market.

BUD, a director, agreed and rejected a Singaporean brand as there was no one to drive the project.

We rejected the famous Singapore heritage brand as there is no one keen to run the operations. We like the product and the brand, and when it comes to who runs the operations, none of my friends is keen to operate. We must have someone keen to spearhead this. The possibility of being successful rests on someone keen to take responsibility for running this. The investment is not too high, but we must have someone among my friends who have the desire and commitment to doing it.

Apart from good chemistry, HRE, a managing director, recognised the need for the owner's support for the concept and the business to ensure quality and consistency:

By support, I mean recipes which are given, but I will focus on pre- and post-support. If I am opening the overseas outlet on my own, then what sort of resources do I have to make it work? It cannot be, as it is a franchise, let them do everything on their own and not care too much about how well they are doing. We cannot have the attitude that just lets them do it on their own and we do not audit, check, or monitor random checks, and all these are particularly important.

A brand can only be consistent if the principal is doing the right thing. The franchisee is equally important, but who knows the brand better than the brand owner? It is the responsibility of the brand owner to monitor, control, and secure the consistency; otherwise, it is a matter of time before deviations happen that will affect the brand.

Finally, there must be congruency between the owners' expectations and the acquirer's views right from the beginning as highlighted by JIA, an owner based in Australia.

2.4. Suitable Concept, Taste, and Products

The suitability of the concept, taste, and product is a fundamental issue for any acquirer. Even if a brand is attractive, if the food and concept are not suitable, success in the host country is unlikely, said HRE, a managing director:

If you asked me why I choose a brand, I would rather start with why that product. The heritage Singapore brand that we acquired is special, and in Indonesia, none specialised in this style.

When I have presented the opportunity, if there is no one doing this, then it is an opportunity. Although Indonesia is a Muslim market, there is a significant Chinese population. We can be a market leader for this product, and in terms of this brand, I met the owner. The owners are my partner's classmates, and I looked at how they operate the business; there is good SOP, and in terms of branding, they are doing a lot of work briefing their brand, and it has been a growing brand in Singapore.

Singapore's heritage brand is comfort food for us, and we can make it halal in Indonesia. It is already famous in Singapore and can also be famous for Indonesians.

Other participants also emphasised the importance of taste and the consistency of the food products:

Critical success factors are consistency, the location, and the brand, and everything boils down to consistency. Besides, the product must be good, taste good, and the price is acceptable. Many factors determine success. The product must be right, and that is the most significant part that determines success. (RSO, general manager)

The suitability of food and concept will differ between home and host countries as noted by BUD, a director, when he looked at how suitable Singapore food might be in a vast country like Indonesia and the differences in taste preferences between those who live in Jakarta and the people in Medan or Borneo.

The acquirer recognised that the suitability of the food concept, taste, and products was a CSF. They suggested these factors heavily affected their decisions to acquire brands and products.

2.5. Suitable Adaptation

The adaptation of food is another way to increase the relevancy of that food in a host country, and participants recognised that most concepts needed some adaptation to succeed in a new market:

Whatever the brand from Japan or anywhere else, they must change the taste to suit local Indonesians. When we talk about changes, we are talking about tampering with the saltiness or the spice level to suit the locals. (AMO, head of business development)

Even if there is little adaptation in terms of taste, adaptation could be needed due to eating habits being governed by religious beliefs, as well for as different populations in specific locations as in a vast country like Australia, said JIA, a business owner. A good summary of this vital area of suitable adaptation was highlighted by HRE, a managing director:

Singapore brands must think like the locals. The product may be selling well in Singapore, but will it do well in Indonesia or anywhere else? Your design of furniture is another area of adaptation; while in Singapore, you may not require bench seats, just use hard seats. In Singapore, you have a lot of walking crowds along with streets and shophouses but not in other countries.

Participants felt the right approach for suitable adaptation was to do market studies and to work with owners to make informed and wise decisions to ensure success in a host country. In summary, Singapore F&B companies must do their due diligence before any overseas market entry.

Look first, study first, and learn first, and then we meet your local partners, and you will talk intelligently. It is not easy as every country is quite different.

We cannot rely on the overseas local partners to do the work as, sometimes, they might be doing the wrong thing unknowingly; thus, it has to be a two-pronged approach, and I always believe if you dare to collect money [franchise fees], you better perform, meaning support to the maximum. You cannot just collect the money and then say to the partner that 'you are on your own and just figure out what to do on your own. RSO, a general manager.

2.6. Suitable Terms

When the food is suitable, the brand is right, and the chemistry with owners is good, another potential obstacle is the commercial terms agreed between the owner and the acquirer.

The obstacle could be the franchisor asking for exorbitant pricing, and then it is a little tricky. Everything is based on the right price; in Chinese, 一分钱，一分货 (*yì fēn qián, yì fēn huò*), which means you get what you pay for. A high franchise fee is one common mistake. (HRE, managing director)

A famous Singapore brand approached us, and they wanted to take over the franchise. They are overly aggressive in terms of the target and numbers [expected by the franchiser]. So we were not happy with the numbers. It is a 'number' issue while market acceptance is all right and doing all right and not phenomenal. The numbers offered by our group were not accepted as what they wanted was too exorbitant.

To be more attractive, Singapore's companies should consider lower initial franchise fees than what they expect because, for Indonesia, Singapore's franchise is quite expensive. (FRE, managing director)

The financial consideration and what constitutes the right price (i.e. franchise fee and royalties) must be carefully weighed by Singapore F&B companies in venturing overseas. Such matters may make or break negotiations between acquirers and brand owners. Other non-financial considerations such as character, integrity, track record, and the development plan proposed by the acquirers need to be factored into the consideration besides just financial consideration. LIA, a managing director, sums up his views of what constitutes the right price for any overseas venture.

What matters in internationalisation is not just dollars and sense but whether the Singapore brand is sustainable in foreign territory. What is the point of getting a high franchise fee if the brand could not survive beyond a few years? I believe in a reasonable price for the territory, and the local partner is credible and protects my brand and grows it with more outlets.

2.7. Suitable Location

Food service delivery is a retail business, and a suitable location is vital to the success of a brand and a concept. Many participants noted that having the wrong location often spells disaster even for well-known and reputable brands:

When we started this famous Singapore brand in 2014, it was in a location at Shah Alam, Malaysia. We chose there because of the population, but the location was not good. We then moved to the mall after we waited for a long time for this location. We did much better than the previous location. (ALE, director)

The decline could be due to poor location and the quality issue at this Singapore brand's outlet. We just must be careful and find the location to be profitable. (BUD, director)

The seven secrets discussed in this section were CSFs that acquirers considered when assessing Singaporean brands and food concepts for their territories. These are vital in ensuring success for an acquired business as they ensure the Singaporean brand remains sustainable in their countries.

3. Road Maps for the Acquirers

The acquirers were not homogeneous in the strategies they chose to develop Singaporean brands. Thus, their road maps for the next five years differed in terms of the choice of mode, destination, timing, and operation strategies (Table 12.1).

Table 12.1: The acquirers' road maps

Participant	Year of first outlet	Destination in the next 5 years	Mode	Operations
AMO	2015	More locations in Jakarta	Wholly owned outlets No intent to sub-franchise	• Food innovations needed to attract customers amid greater competition; G2G support for payment of royalties • Maintaining consistency in food quality

Participant	Year of first outlet	Destination in the next 5 years	Mode	Operations
ALE	2014	Third outlet to open in the first quarter of 2019 Franchising of outlets in another part of the country	Started as a joint venture Wholly owned outlets for the first phase and sub-franchising for other parts of the country	• Develop the brand with a more franchised outlet • Introduction of new products • Established a new central kitchen to support growth
BUD	2011	Organic growth for the future, with its current 25 outlets across the country	Started as a franchise and all outlets, except one, wholly owned Franchising for the outlying areas in the country	• Improve current operations with a focus on people management and customer service
HRE	2004	Organic growth of the various brands in the portfolio Grow our current self-developed brand Develop your brand shortly	Mainly joint ventures with owners	• Continue to build a team of loyal staff • Develop critical skills of existing staff so that productivity levels will be enhanced

Participant	Year of first outlet	Destination in the next 5 years	Mode	Operations
JIA	2019	Grow organically in existing territory	Multi-unit franchise	• Develop a team of capable staff for current operations and future expansion • Adapt to locals' requirements in terms of taste and concept. • After the maiden store, look for other suitable locations
FRE	2010	Grow organically in the country	Took on the master franchise for the country	• Food innovations for a close to 10-year-old brand to stay relevant in the market • Supply of key ingredients
ROS	2014	Develop more outlets in the other parts of the country including Surabaya, Medan, and Bali	Multi-unit franchise	• Ensure consistent food quality and supply of key ingredients. • Develop a capable team

4. Conclusion

This chapter began with a discussion of the backgrounds of the acquirers of Singaporean brands in the food service sector. Seven overseas partners were interviewed about the CSFs they considered when acquiring brands. The results from NVivo and Leximancer analyses were then discussed, which suggested that the participants shared seven CSFs:

1. Having a suitable brand
2. Finding a suitable owner
3. Ensuring the food had a suitable concept, taste, and products
4. Having a suitable business and operation
5. Finding suitable adaptations
6. Negotiating suitable terms
7. Having suitable locations

For the acquirers questioned in this study, the suitability of the food concept, taste, and products is the most important CSF. Singaporean companies need to take heed of this and should conduct market studies to examine these issues and, if need be, adapt the food to suit local tastes. It is also clear that acquiring terms must be attractive and that owners need to ensure they do not price themselves out of the market. The right terms are particularly important for the aspirants taking their first steps out of Singapore. Given this situation, such companies might need to agree to preferential rates if they feel an overseas partner is a right candidate for their international expansion.

Table 7.5 listed the road maps the different acquirers have for the next five years. For Singaporean companies, whether aspirants, actives, or achievers, the acquirers' feedback provides useful information for the subsequent development of their internationalising strategies. The acquirers are the Singaporean companies' customers, and they need to be treated in that way. By understanding what is important to potential acquirers, Singaporean companies can find suitable overseas partners and ensure sustained success along their internationalisation journey.

Many of these acquirers have enjoyed success by acquiring Singapore brands. They act as ambassadors for these Singaporean brands, and their decision to acquire more will depend on the seven Ss. The path towards becoming a successful regional or global brand is having an intimate knowledge of the needs of overseas acquirers and their customers and having a strong collaborative relationship with these partners.

CHAPTER 13

THE WISDOM OF THE WISE

1. Introduction

Brown (2018) defines an *adviser* as 'a person lawfully tasked and employed to provide expert advice and counsel through the establishment or continuance of interpersonal relationships founded on mutual trust and respect'. For some reading this, that definition may seem obvious; for others, it may seem almost counter-intuitive. However, this definition is used here to contact such people.

Eleven advisers from various countries were interviewed to gather their views on the internationalisation of Singaporean companies. These advisers were experts and established franchise consultants in their home countries as they assisted foreign companies seeking to bring their concept and brand into the country. Many of these companies had sought help, strategic input, and assistance in franchise documentation from such advisers.

Fletcher and Harris (2011) noted that smaller firms might not have relevant experience or useful networks when attempting to internationalise. Such SMEs often relied on government advisers, market brokers, or consultants for their experience and expertise. Advisers provide useful services to businesses, particularly SMEs, as they have access to key contacts and information as they interact with local business owners, government officials, and potential acquirers. Their contribution, viewpoints, and feedback on various aspects of internationalisation are likely to be useful to Singaporean companies planning to internationalise, which led to the decision to include them in the present research project in the ways discussed in subsequent sections.

2. The Advisers

Three participants were interviewed by telephone or a Skype conference call while the remaining eight participants were interviewed face to face in their home countries using the same set of semi-structured questions. The shortest interview was just over ten minutes, and the longest was about an hour. All but two of the interviewees were owners of their consulting companies. The interviews were conducted between March and August 2018, and the author travelled to Australia, Thailand, Malaysia, Indonesia, and South Korea to undertake the interviews, which were transcribed and stored in separate files (Table 13.1).

Table 13.1: The advisers

Date	Code	Gender	Age	Edu	No. of Staff	No. of Years	Position	Country
1-Mar-18	NAP	Female	50	Grad	10	20	Partner	Thailand
12-Mar-18	WIL	Male	55	Grad	2	19	Partner	Hong Kong
29-Mar-18	SAM	Male	65	Pre-U	1	25	Founder	Malaysia
12-Jun-18	AKO	Male	62	Grad	5	30	MD	Singapore
4-Jul-18	BUR	Male	55	Grad	3	24	Founder	Indonesia
5-Jul-18	YOS	Male	58	Grad	3	25	Consultant	Japan
9-Jul-18	TRO	Male	52	Grad	40	10	Director	Malaysia
2-Aug-18	MAR	Male	49	Grad	4	12	MD	Australia
7-Aug-18	JAY	Male	36	Grad	15	10	MD	Australia
22-Dec-17	TJK	Male	45	Grad	20	20	MD	Singapore
23-Feb-18	UTO	Male	52	Grad	1	19	Consultant	Indonesia

3. The Leximancer Analysis

Figure 13.1 shows all the visible concepts within the respective themes that were important to this group. A single concept labelled in black type is linked to another concept by a grey line that shows the strength of the association between the two concepts. These concepts cluster to form a theme that appears in a larger type (Figure 13.1). The concept names are coloured, like the theme spheres, to show their importance. Concept proximity shows the strength of the association between two concepts. In the heat map (Figure 13.1), the largest sphere is 'franchise', but the 'hottest' theme is 'brand' (red amber), followed by 'franchise' (amber), 'country' (green), and 'market' (yellow green). The less important themes were 'franchisee' (green blue), 'food' (light blue), and 'local' (purple).

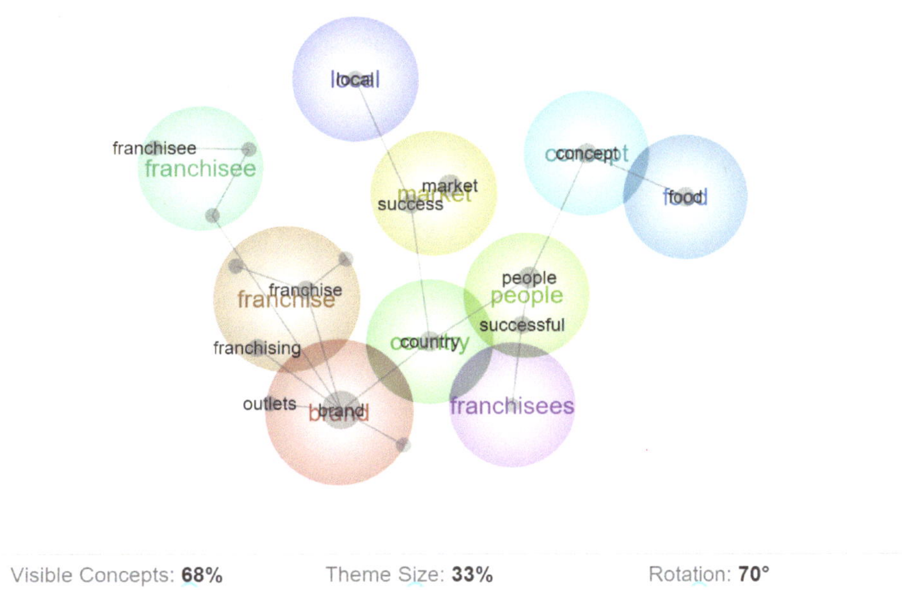

Figure 13.1: A concept map for the adviser group

There were several key nodes, namely, 'brand', 'country', 'franchise', and 'franchisee', reflecting the importance of the brand when venturing overseas, the choice of the country the brand owner sought to enter through franchising, and finding the right franchisee. Other prominent nodes were 'people', 'concept', and 'food', suggesting the importance of executing a concept and delivering food through the right people. 'Country', 'success', and 'local' highlight the importance of being 'local'. These contextual associations can be validated with the ranked concept relevance list shown in Table 13.2.

Table 13.2: The ranked concept list

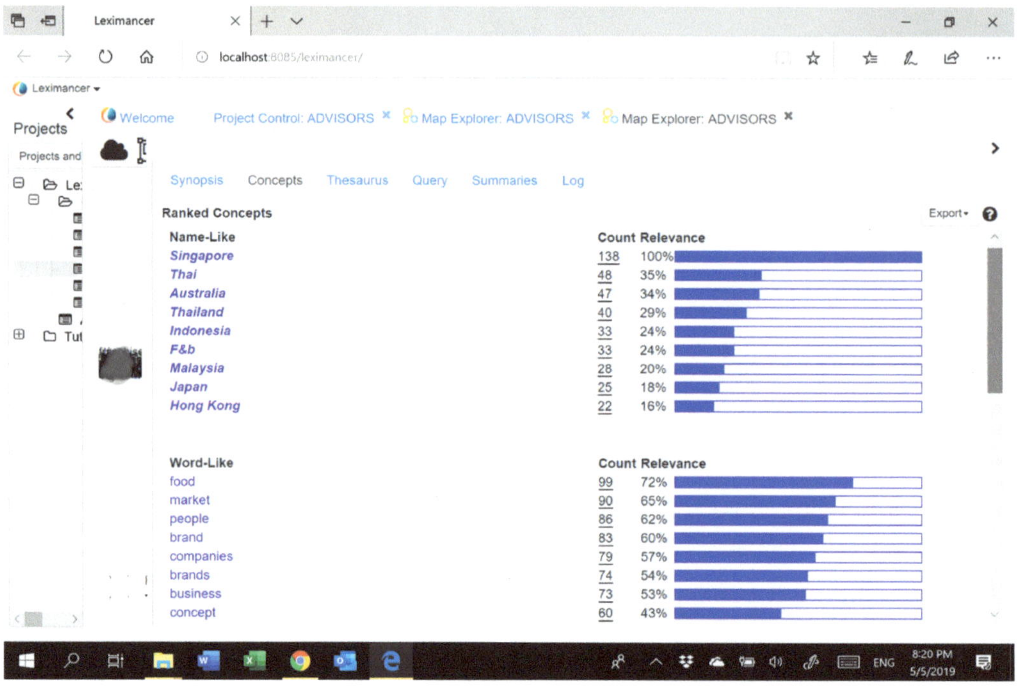

Name-Like	Count	Relevance
Singapore	138	100%
Thai	48	35%
Australia	47	34%
Thailand	40	29%
Indonesia	33	24%
F&b	33	24%
Malaysia	28	20%
Japan	25	18%
Hong Kong	22	16%

Word-Like	Count	Relevance
food	99	72%
market	90	65%
people	86	62%
brand	83	60%
companies	79	57%
brands	74	54%
business	73	53%
concept	60	43%

Ranked Concepts

Word-Like	Count	Relevance
brand	317	100%
food	99	31%
market	90	28%
concept	88	28%
people	86	27%
country	70	22%
success	53	17%
franchise	50	16%
successful	44	14%
franchising	43	14%
local	43	14%
franchisee	37	12%
outlets	29	09%
overseas	23	07%
partner	23	07%
government	23	07%
franchisees	22	07%
support	21	07%
marketing	20	06%

The Leximancer table (13.2) suggests that the most critical concepts for the advisers are 'brand', 'food', 'market', 'concept', 'people', 'country', and 'success'.

4. *The NVivo Analysis Findings*

The NVivo analysis found the top twenty words for this group of participants (Table 13.3), and the corresponding word cloud is shown in Figure 13.2.

Table 13.3: The top twenty relevant words for the advisers

Word	*Length*	*Count*	*Weighted Percentage*
brand	5	294	1.78
market	6	183	1.21
honest and respectful	4	281	1.16
companies	9	157	1.09
success	7	162	1.03
food	4	135	0.96
franchise	9	134	0.95
concept	7	134	0.88
people	6	118	0.79
local	5	146	0.79
business	8	120	0.74
country	7	127	0.73
help	4	136	0.71
disputes	9	82	0.58
franchisee	10	69	0.49
government	10	111	0.43
outlets	7	80	0.42
knowledge	4	101	0.42
price	5	68	0.41
support	4	58	0.35

Figure 13.2: A word cloud for the advisers

The findings from NVivo were like those obtained from the Leximancer analysis (excluding the name-like concept of Singapore, which was the focus of the study). This can be seen when the top ten themes from the Leximancer analysis and the top ten words from the NVivo analysis were compared (Table 13.4). The following section discusses the results based on the Leximancer and NVivo analyses for the adviser group.

Table 13.4: A comparison of the top ten Leximancer's themes and NVivo words

Ranking	Leximancer	NVivo	Ranking	Leximancer	NVivo
1	Brand	Brand	6	Country	Food
2	Food	Market	7	Success	Franchise
3	Market	Honest and respectful	8	Franchise	Concept
4	Concept	Company	9	Franchising	People
5	People	Success	10	Local	Local

5. *The Cross-Case Analysis*

This section provides an overview of the Leximancer concept map that is used to identify the emergent themes and the connectivity and relationships between these themes. It also highlights the importance of the various themes to the groups of participants as the Leximancer analysis enables groups to be examined when included in separate folders.

As can be seen in Figure 14.4, there are eight heat-mapped spheres, each representing a theme. All concepts and data categories are marked in grey nodes, with a label identifying the concept or the category. The size of the nodes shows the relative strength of the concept or the category, and the groups' positions show the differences in their views. The most prominent theme was 'brand' (red amber), followed by 'partners' (amber), 'support' (yellow green), 'food' (green), 'success' (blue green), 'customers' (blue), 'taste' (blue purple), and lastly 'staff' (purple).

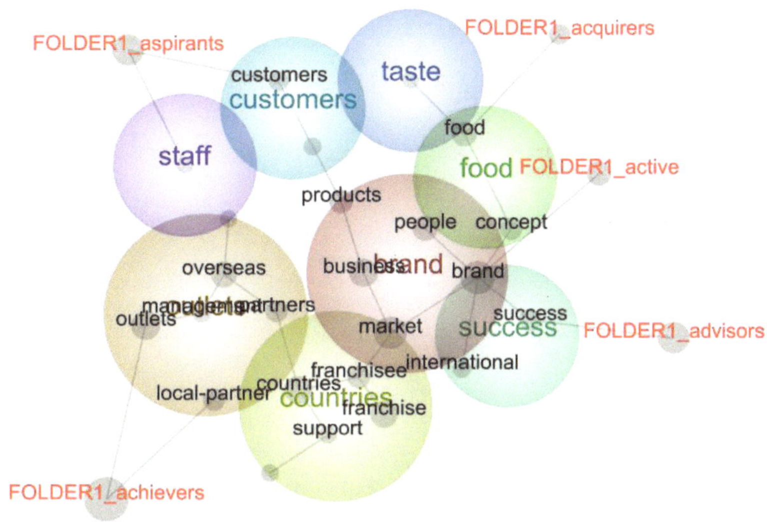

Figure 13.3: A concept map by category

Figure 13.3 shows that the concepts (in black) formed clusters that determined the themes, which appear in a larger type and are coloured the same way as the sphere. As an example, 'brand' is red (the same colour as the sphere) and is the central theme for that sphere. The related concepts in black type are 'people', 'market', 'brand' (as a concept), and 'business'. Grey lines linking two concepts suggest a relationship between the concepts while concept proximity shows the strength of the association. Data categories are shown in red (the outlying nodes of the map) (e.g. Folder1_achievers). Concepts and themes closest to a data category are more important to that category and less important to the other categories.

Figure 13.4 shows the dashboard quadrant map generated by the Leximancer analysis. The concepts towards the upper right-hand (magic) quadrant were the most important in the different cases. For the achievers, the most important themes and concepts were 'brand', 'markets', and 'countries', which were in the upper right quadrant. For the advisers, it was 'food'; and for the 'aspirants', it was going 'overseas'. The dashboard insight report suggested the cross-case data had 4,090 context blocks made up of 2 sentences in each block, 24 concepts, and 5 categories. In the next section, the discussion will focus on the participants' perceptions of the concepts' prominence..

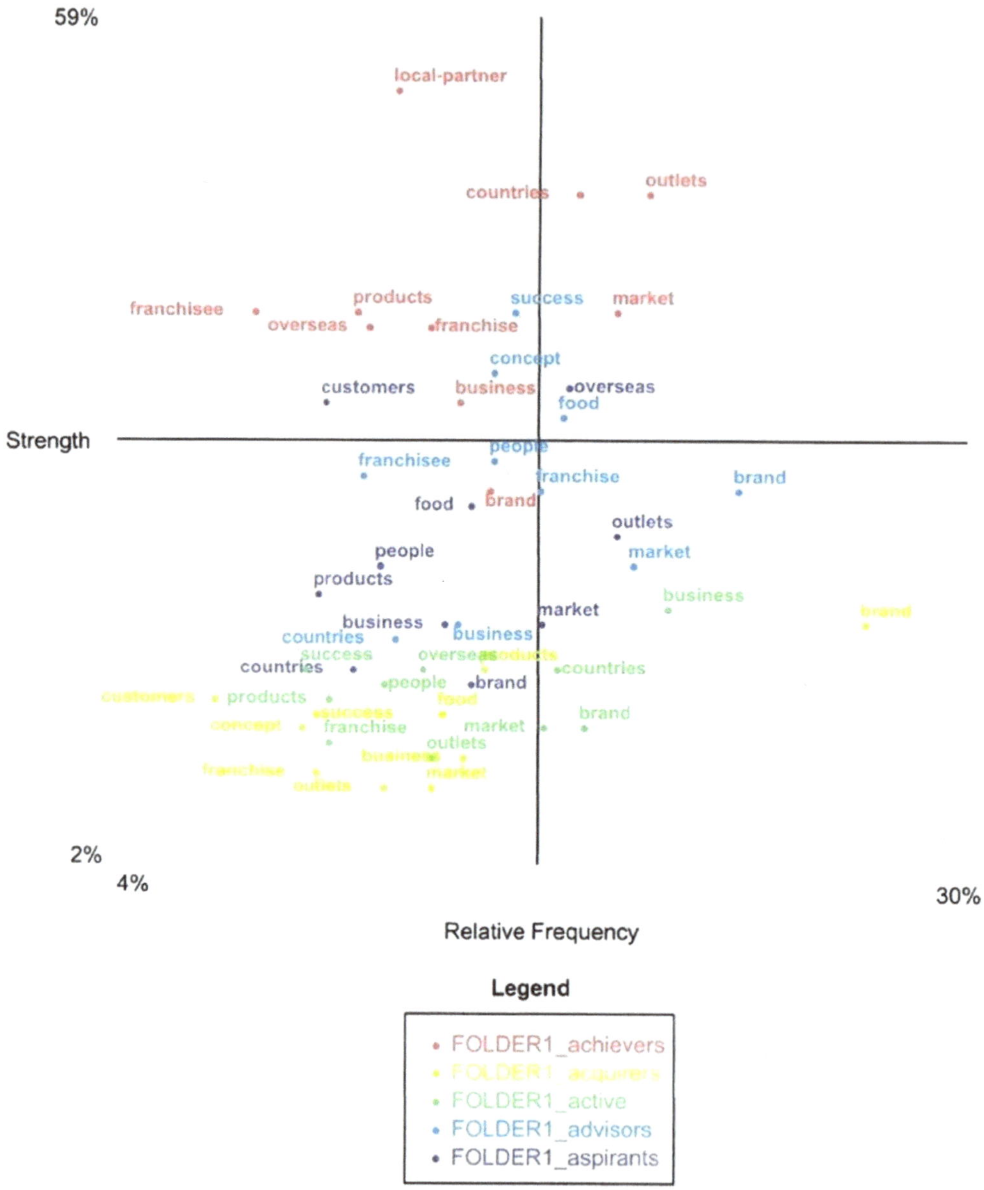

Figure 13.4: The dashboard quadrant map generated by the Leximancer analysis

5.1. Concept Prominence

In a Leximancer analysis, the prominence score combines the strength and frequency scores (Table 13.5), which 'are absolute measures of correlation between category and attribute and can be used to make comparisons over time' (Leximancer, 2018, p. 103). A score higher than 1.0 suggests that a co-occurrence happened more often than by chance. The table, which shows the top concepts for each category (i.e. a prominence score of at least 1.0), highlights the relative importance of each concept to the various groups.

Table 13.5: Prominence scores by category

Aspirants	Actives	Achievers	Acquirers	Advisers
Overseas (1.7)	Business (1.5)	The local partner (1.5)	Brand (1.8)	Success (2.0)
Customer (1.7)	Country (1.3)	Country (1.3)	Product (1.5)	Concept (1.7)
Food (1.3)	Success (1.2)	Outlets (1.3)	Customer (1.3)	Food (1.6)
Outlets (1.2)	Overseas (1.2)	Products (1.1)	Success (1.2)	People (1.4)
People (1.1)	People (1.1)	Franchisee (1.1)	Food (1.2)	Franchisee (1.4)
Products (1.0)	Products (1.0)	Market (1.1)	Concept (1.1)	Franchise (1.4)
		Overseas (1.1)		Brand (1.3)

The Leximancer analysis also computes a table of ranked compound concepts by category that reflects the same strength and frequency conditional probabilities. Prominence scores of 3.0 or higher (Table 13.6) suggest that such compound concepts are important to that category. These Leximancer outputs provide the basis for the discussion of the results that are provided in the next section.

5.2. Concept Prominence

Advisers are industry experts who have extensive experience in assisting local business people in importing or exporting brands and concepts. The inclusion of advisers is useful for data triangulation and strengthens the study's external validity (Yin, 2003). Their feedback and viewpoints should be helpful for Singaporean food service companies' internationalisation decisions.

Table 13.6: The top-ranking compound concept prominence scores by category

Aspirant Concept Prominence	Active Concept Prominence	Achiever Concept Prominence	Acquirer Concept Prominence	Adviser Concept Prominence
Overseas & Partner (7.2)	Franchise & Team (4.8)	Local Partner & International (3.5)	Customer & Quality (6.2)	Success & International (5.8)
Overseas & Team (6.2)	Overseas & Team (4.5)	Local Partner & Market (3.1)	Product & Taste (5.2)	People and International (5.7)
Food & Taste (5.3)	Overseas & Staff (4.3)	Local Partner & Overseas (3.0)	Brand & Product (4.8)	Franchise & International (5.4)
Customer & Food (5.1)	Overseas & Local Partner (4.2)		Food & Quality (4.6)	Food & Quality (4.7)
Food & Quality (4.2)	Success & International (4.0)		Customer & Staff (4.6)	Concept & Food (4.4)

In Figure 13.4, the themes that were important to the advisers included 'success', 'brand', 'market', 'people', and 'countries' amongst the critical nodes as well as 'food' and 'concept'. They focused on 'success' for the companies they advised. To achieve success, advisers looked at the 'brand', 'people', and 'markets' as they felt these factors influenced success. The advisers were understandably concerned about success because they were in the business of assisting companies to import or export brands.

The advisers felt Singaporean companies needed to pay heed to the 'brand' (1.3), 'concept' (1.7), and 'food' (1.6) as they were the crux of internationalisation. They argued that the brand must achieve success domestically and internationally, the overall concept must have the right appeal, and the food must be suitable and of consistently good quality. Other CSFs were the 'people' (1.4) and 'franchisees' (1.4). Most Singaporean companies expanded by franchising, and therefore, having good franchiser-franchisee relationships was critical to the success of both parties. Singaporean companies' ability to manage, support, and liaise with their franchisees was felt to be critical to success.

The list of important ranked compound concepts suggested that the advisers felt Singaporean companies needed a global mindset if they were to effectively manage diverse networks of overseas partners, especially as international franchising can be complex and challenging in the light of franchisees' opportunism and the chances of brands being hijacked.

4. Conclusion

This chapter highlights the theoretical findings and analyses from NVivo and Leximancer as well as the cross-case analysis. The findings provide the basis for the subsequent discussion and analysis of the keys to success and strategies that Singapore F&B companies could pursue in ensuring success in internationalisation in the next two chapters.

CHAPTER 14

THE KEYS TO SUCCESS

1. Introduction

The participants in the advisers group were highly experienced industry experts assisting and advising Singaporean franchisers venturing overseas and/or foreign franchisees acquiring Singaporeans brands into their local markets. They had seen successes as well as failures in internationalisation, and based on their responses in the study, the findings were discussed in the previous chapters. This chapter highlights the keys to success from the advisers' perspectives.

2. The Four Keys to Success

For the advisers group, the main critical success factors for internationalisation were the top five themes from the Leximancer analysis, namely, 'brand and concept', 'food', 'market', 'people', and 'partner'. All these themes were also the top five words generated by the NVivo software and would be elaborated on in the subsequent sections.

2.1. Brand and Concept

The advisers felt that a brand must have achieved success domestically before venturing internationally:

The general rule of thumb is that the brand must have some degree of domestic success in the home country. Some want to go abroad but only started the concept for a year or two. Proven in Singapore is a requirement, but being accepted in a foreign country is the other critical success factor. (TJK, managing director)

For JAY, a head of franchise sales and development in Australia, domestic success was critical to a brand concept's success overseas.

One of the reasons a brand might have difficulties making headway internationally is the lack of a USP that appeals to locals in a host country and a lack of commitment to internationalisation as noted by AKO, a managing director. The question of whether brands might perform well in a country depends on whether the concept is tailored to that market. JAY, a head of franchise and development, said this applies to all overseas brands entering Australia.

Another question is whether an established Singaporean heritage brand would have a better chance of success. AKO, a managing director, stated that heritage brands 'immigrated' to foreign territories because they appeal to people who resided in Singapore for a while. The brand did well, but after the euphoria, sometimes after two months, they then went quiet.

NAS, a partner in a market broking agency firm based in Thailand, argued that heritage brands and domestic success did not matter in Thailand as foreign concepts would succeed if Thai consumers accepted them:

Thais prefer the US and international brands. If they must spend money, they care about the brand; and for the price, they go for international brands as compared with Singapore's Ya Kun. It is 'cool' to be in Starbucks and drinking Starbucks versus Ya Kun. So it is the concept; it is the food, branding against a backdrop of a strong Thai F&B culture.

Despite being Singapore's closest neighbour, Malaysia is a challenging country as Singapore and Malaysia are culturally similar and have similar eating habits. Therefore, Singaporean companies need to have USPs to attract locals:

F&B is overcrowded, especially for Toast Box or Ya Kun. The critical question is, what is the differentiation or USP with PappaRich, Bangi, and OldTown? These are big players in Malaysia, and we have many Mamak [local Indian/Malay/Muslim shophouse] stores. (SAS, principal consultant)

Therefore, brand and concept are crucial in the host countries that Singapore F&B companies generally consider. However, how well companies succeed depends on several other factors as well, such as acceptance and uniqueness.

2.2. Food and Adaptation

The advisers suggested it was imperative that the food 'exported' was accepted and patronised by locals:

Hawker Chan is not popular in Hong Kong. It is staple food but may not compete with the HK versions, even if it is a Michelin Star. For roasted meat rice, Hong Kong residents swear by the local stores they patronise. (WIN, CEO)

Not only must there be patronage but there also must be 'repeaters' or loyal customers who come back to outlets as observed by YOS, a consultant. Ramen in Japan has enough repeaters compared with Singapore's chicken rice.

YOS also recommended that Singapore F&B brands must innovate their food and product offerings if they are to have sustainable success in Japan and compete for attention such as Maki-san, an example of maki sushi that travelled to California and later to Singapore and innovatively re-entered Japan.

For JAY, a head of franchise and development in Australia, understanding the food being served is a challenge for some Australians. If it is too localised, it might only appeal to Singaporeans who have migrated or are working or studying in Australia, which will mean it has limited appeal.

TJK, managing director of an established company in Singapore, pointed out that companies need to work hard to fit their food to local palates as it is not easy to change local eating habits. If not, Singaporean brands like Ya Kun are unlikely to succeed just like South Koreans felt that coconut jam (*kaya*) is exotic but not a daily food or a mismatch with the Taiwanese.

In summary, if Singaporean food is to be 'exported' successfully, it must be widely accepted by locals in host countries, have consistent food quality, and be adapted to suit locals' palates. Therefore, the choice of country for the venture is crucial as discussed in the next section.

2.3. Market Selection

According to TJK, a managing director, market selection is not difficult:

There is no hard science of market selection. Go into a market that would give you the least risk of failure. Conversely, go into a market that would give you a high chance of success.

Rather than be attracted to big countries like China and the glamour of the West, TJK advised Singaporean companies to consider regional countries first to reduce the risk of failure.

AKO, a CEO and managing director of another established Singapore consultancy firm for more than two decades, reiterated that, while it is just across the causeway, West Malaysia may not be an appropriate market extension for many Singaporean companies due to long-standing historical, nationalistic, and political factors. In addition, many locals in Malaysia perceive their Malaysian version of the food as 'equally good, if not better'.

One of the challenges in market selection is the barriers to entry that include franchise regulations, religious requirements such as halal, and even language:

In entering Japan, the company must have enough capital and proficiency in English. That is a hurdle, like English-speaking Japanese is a minority. Without the language, it is hard to proceed with negotiation, and it is a bottleneck. (YOS, consultant)

Franchise regulations can be a barrier for Singaporeans, and Australia is one of the most regulated countries. These restrictive regulations are not as complicated as the US, but there are difficulties in the franchise environment in Australia. (JAY, department head)

TRF acknowledged that venturing into Australia and the United States may not necessarily reap good returns for Singaporean companies and that their safer first bets might be in Asia and the Middle East:

I think it is a difficult place to make money, and I think that with the right strategy, Greater China, Taiwan, Japan, and Korea are attractive markets for Singapore brands: 'Asian food', meaning rice and noodle based, Asian desserts and sweets – this kind of product.

While it is not a hard science, there needs to be careful analysis when selecting international markets for expansion.

2.4. Partners and People

A prominent theme was 'partners and people', and this was crucial for Singaporean companies venturing overseas. Coordination, management, liaison, and good chemistry were all seen as affecting a brand's success:

I would say the prerequisite for international success is to have an excellent local partner you can work with and who understands the local market, your brand, and what it stands for. This partner must be capable of sourcing good locations, marketing, supporting operations, and even ensuring effective supply chain management. (TJK, managing director)

Selecting the right partner was a key to success. However, participants such as AKO, a CEO, suggested that selection processes and due diligence were often not rigorous and were overshadowed by financial considerations, which meant Singaporean companies often did not conduct much due diligence.

When selecting the right partner, Singaporean companies should look at critical attributes, such as the character of the partner, business ethics, financial resources, and other capabilities that would assist the expansion of the brand in the host country.

We must find a franchisee who is very understanding and transparent. Especially for F&B franchises, it is good to find someone who is in the business and has experience in running multiple outlets and not someone who is out of it and has much capital, even if they said that they have connections and even if they are members of the royal family. That is nice to have, but I do not think they are critical success factors. (TJK, managing director)

Having the right partner can create success for a Singaporean company, and that selection should be done carefully based on attributes set by each company and the team and management support given by the company:

Both Sushi Tei and Fish & Co. are successful because they have found the right partners, and they have an outstanding team. (UNO, principal consultant)

3. Strategies Recommended by Advisers

Bose's (2016) framework was again used to examine these factors. Table 14.1 shows the advisers' recommended strategies for successful internationalisation.

Table 14.1: The advisers' recommended strategies for internationalisation

Participant	Timing	Destination	Mode	Operations
NAP	The concept must be strong and suitable for the Thai market to be successful.	The product must be unique to make any headway in the competitive and insular Thai market.	Many successful international concepts open company-owned stores and expand thereafter on their own. Franchising is possible, but the expectation will be a few units.	• Marketing and branding are keys in attracting local Thais. • Project the USPs of the brand and the uniqueness of the taste to attract local customers. • Consider low-cost sourcing using local products and ingredients.
WIL	Ensure the taste is suitable for locals. Innovative and unique product offerings will be attractive to locals.	To enter Hong Kong, a product must be unique and high quality and have good customer service.	Consider setting up a company-owned outlet and ensure a proven concept before further expansion through franchising.	• Maintain quality. • Innovate continuously. • Focus on branding. • Ensure good management.

Participant	Timing	Destination	Mode	Operations
SAM	The uniqueness of the concept is vital when entering the Malaysian market.	It is difficult for the Singaporean concept to enter Malaysia as there is a lack of uniqueness in the concept.	It is difficult to find a franchise partner for a Singapore concept. Consider setting up company-owned outlets in Malaysia. After it is proven, then franchise throughout the country.	• Differentiate the product and the concept to suit the market. • Conduct due diligence on the market. • Ensure good supply chain management. • Adapt the concept and food to suit locals.
AKO	Timing is crucial. Suitability of the concept is key.	Being nearer to Singapore may not be good when considering Malaysia. It depends on the concept as both countries are culturally similar, which can be a strength and a weakness.	Franchising is preferred by many Singaporean companies but is subject to possible brand hijacking. Due diligence is required when selecting overseas franchise partners.	• Establish a proven and stable concept. • Invest in the brand. • Stress innovation and systematic improvement. • Use different strategies in different countries.

Participant	Timing	Destination	Mode	Operations
BUR	Suitable taste for Indonesians is key to success.	Singaporean companies tend to select Indonesia because of its market size. Indonesians are very open to Singaporean brands. In their views, what succeeds in Singapore is likely to work in Indonesia.	Franchising is preferred, especially master franchising. Do not overprice a master franchise. Spend resources to select the right franchise partner. It is good to have a joint operation venture for a start and, once established, hand it over to the local partner.	• Establish the concept and ensure there are good systems. • Adequate training must be provided to replicate the food and concept. • Be flexible in adapting to suit local tastes. • Make careful selections of key locations. • As most failures are due to poor management, ensure franchisees can manage well.
YOS	Japan is a tough and competitive market, so the food concept must be authentic and appeal to locals if it is to be sustainable. Education is needed before entering Japan.	Familiarity with the food product is key to success in Japan.	Franchising is preferred as joint ventures require capital and language barriers that need to be overcome. For significant food brands, such as US brands, the Japanese are open to joint ventures.	• Ensure quality and consistency. • Support and communicate well with local partners. • Be flexible when adapting the product to suit local tastes. • Ensure efficient supply chain management.

Participant	Timing	Destination	Mode	Operations
TRO	Venture overseas when you are ready (i.e. your franchise documents, support systems, and people are ready to support the expansion).	Find a market that suits the food concept and your products. Do not oversimplify –Singapore and Malaysia are not identical in tastes and preferences.	Franchising is preferred as joint ventures fail more often in Malaysia.	• Build the right foundation. • Find the right location as this is the key. • Innovate continuously. • Adapt to local tastes.
MAR	Consider whether the concept is suitable for Australia and whether the food is acceptable to Australians. Be prepared to incur time and cost when entering the market.	Consider the hurdles and costs of getting into the market. Have the necessary resources to do this.	Joint ventures and master franchising are both common in Australia. Subsequent sub-franchising is subject to a strict franchising code.	• Supply chain and logistic issues needed to be developed when importing into Australia. • Consider differences in terms of time, tastes, and logistical processes between the eastern and western states. • Labour and retail costs are higher in Australia.

Participant	Timing	Destination	Mode	Operations
JAY	Australia is increasingly open to Asian concepts, especially given its large Asian population.	Singaporean brands are welcome, but Malaysian concepts are more accepted.	It is difficult to sell a master franchise in Australia. Joint ventures make better sense in Australia, given its strict franchising code. Consider setting up a model outlet with local partners, and once the concept is proven, franchising can be used.	• Deal with the strict franchising code. • A deep understanding of the dining habits of Australians and delivery platform preferences is needed. • Adapt the food across the continent as east and west dining habits are different.

Participant	Timing	Destination	Mode	Operations
TJK	Before stepping out, the concept needs to be proven in Singapore. The readiness of the market to accept the food and the concept to be exported is crucial.	Go regional rather than trying to establish outlets in the UK, US, the Middle East, or even China as geographic proximity can ensure success. Indonesia is a good market for Singaporean brands to enter. Malaysia is not that easy as, often, there are similar and successful local options.	Franchising is preferred by Singaporean companies in venturing overseas. Franchising should not be the only strategy, but it should be an option in the 'internationalisation toolbox'. Joint ventures often bring higher returns with the right partner. In some markets, licensing can be a useful strategy as there are barriers to international entry such as Indonesia and Malaysia. In other countries like Australia, which is a developed country for franchising, entry via franchising can be onerous.	• Partner selection is key. • Support and good communication with local partners are important. • Efficient supply chain management is required. • The overseas partner who runs the business is crucial to a venture's success.

Participant	Timing	Destination	Mode	Operations
UTO	Have a presence in Singapore or Malaysia before entering Indonesia.	The Indonesian market is very open and welcomes Singaporean brands.	Licensing is preferred as franchising in Indonesia can be cumbersome. Indonesians generally have joint ventures with friends but are less likely to be open to joint ventures with foreigners. Opening a model store is a good way to start in Indonesia as there is no issue of 100 per cent foreign ownership.	• Marketing is key to success. • Finding the right partner is important but not easy. • The need to ensure the quality of the food and obtain local sourcing is critical. • Support and communicate with local partners.

3.1. Choice of Market Entry Mode

Table 14.1 highlighted the challenges and barriers to international market entry. The advisers felt that Singaporean companies in the food service sector preferred franchising as their choice for market entry as noted by many participants. TJK, a managing director, expanded on the idea that franchising should be a tool in the 'toolbox for internationalisation' depending on the host country's conditions:

In some markets, you can have franchising and joint ventures; you can end up taking a stake to show commitment, to get things going, to derive higher profits over there. Then you flash out the franchising and joint-venture tools. It may not be mutually exclusive.

For BUR, a founder, as well as JAY, a head of franchise and development, the choice of the market entry depends on the concept. If the concept is complicated, he argued that a joint venture will be more appropriate at least for the first outlet in the host country. However, UNO, a principal consultant, felt otherwise, arguing that a joint venture might not be the preferred mode as Indonesians only consider joint ventures with familiar people.

To penetrate specific markets, WIN, a CEO, suggested that Singaporean companies should take on more risks by setting up a wholly owned outlet from the outset and transferring it to the local partner once the business is established. While franchising is acceptable in mainland China, WIN recommended that Singapore F&B companies should have more control in Hong Kong:

Franchising is a good strategy for mainland China as the land mass is big, and you can afford to lose control. But for Hong Kong, you cannot afford to lose control because if one shop underperforms, it will affect the whole chain.

TRF, a chief operating officer, argued for a franchising-only model as he noted that joint ventures do not generally work unless they are between big corporates.

In the world of international franchising, there are few cases where joint ventures work. Joint ventures require a different set of skills, capabilities, and expectations than franchising.

Therefore, as noted by TJK, market entry options are akin to tools in a toolbox. Which tool Singaporean companies should prefer depends on factors such as the country, regulations, partners, capabilities, and company objectives. While the advisers felt that Singaporean companies prefer franchising, this is just one of the available tools in the toolbox.

3.2. Destinations

The importance of the right selection of markets and countries was discussed in an earlier section. The consequence of a wrong selection is likely to be severe. Indeed, many Singaporean companies have exited markets after failing to gain a foothold.

A heritage Singapore brand was in Vietnam in late 2008 or 2009 and ahead of time for foreign concepts. People were not ready or disposed to spend on expensive imported stuff. The owner was right to say the culture and the readiness of the market to accept imported stuff were factors for the failure. If that same heritage brand would go in today, it might be a different story. (TJK, managing director)

3.3. Operational Strategies

There are many operational capabilities Singaporean companies need to develop to be successful when internationalising, one of which is fine-tuning systems and support for overseas partners:

What the Americans eat day in and day out has been the same for decades. There is an economy of scale. They can fine-tune the food, and they have the operations and systems that work. They feel more secure taking a brand like this. (AKO, CEO)

To set up overseas ventures, Singaporean companies must 'clone' or 'replicate' their business model, food quality, and the DNA of the concept for foreign territories, which often requires the full transfer of know-how:

Most Singaporean companies failed because they are newly established and franchise their business right away before it is proven. They do not care about the target market. The transfer of knowledge is not complete, and they just open the business after four to five days of market study, which is not sufficient. (BUR, founder)

3.4. Timing

The internationalisation process for Singaporean companies should be a well-thought-out plan. Such careful planning should mitigate the chance of failures as noted by AKO, a CEO and managing director:

The key question is, How ready is the company to go international? Unfortunately, many may not care or plan for this; and when they failed, they quietly exit and come home.

TRF, a chief operating officer, suggested timing is critical and that Singaporean companies must consider all the issues carefully before venturing overseas.

In food franchising internationally, you are not opening a restaurant; you are launching your brand. The mindset of launching a brand is that you must think strategically, and you must plan the long term. (TRF, chief operating officer)

The advisers felt that Singaporean companies need to strategise and plan a road map, taking into consideration all possible obstacles and challenges that might thwart progress if they are to maximise the probability of success when internationalising.

4. Conclusion

This chapter examined a group of advisers' views. The eleven advisers were asked about the critical success factors for Singaporean companies in the food service sector when venturing overseas. They were also asked about the success strategies Singaporean brands should adopt when considering overseas ventures. The analysis suggested that they saw four keys to success: brand and concept, food and adaptation, market selection, and partners and people. The most CSFs for the advisers were concept, taste, and products when going international.

Although they felt most Singaporean companies preferred franchising, some advisers recommended that a concept store should be opened to provide a proof of concept, after which franchising could be implemented. A few advisers did support joint ventures or a 'franchise joint venture' for the first outlet in a host country. As TJK, managing director, noted, the various market entry modes are like 'tools in the toolbox', and the appropriate tool should be used to 'do the job'.

CHAPTER 15

THE NEW TSUNAMIS

1. Introduction

The research was completed in 2019, and in early 2020, the world faced an unprecedented external shock – a new 'tsunami' called Covid-19. Covid infections reportedly started in November 2019 and caused many countries to close their borders with lockdowns from 2020.

This external factor shocks the world, disrupts the economy, and affects the social and psychological fabric of society, creating widespread damage all over the world. The related impact also includes lockdowns and restricted movement for residents worldwide and disruptions to work and supply distributions of goods and services. Russia's war in Ukraine further complicates the situation and adds pressure on supplies. Consequently, inflation sets in, and retail businesses, especially dining in restaurants globally, are greatly affected by supply and increased prices. Singapore F&B companies operating overseas are not spared, and the impact cannot be understated.

For completeness, this chapter was added as an addendum to the research on how external factors can disrupt Singapore F&B companies' internationalisation process and journey. The author reconnected with some of the participants of the study to gather insights on the challenges of internationalisation in the Covid years and how that might affect some of the internationalisation strategies post-Covid. Sections 2 and 3 discuss the impact of external shocks, and section 4 summarises the various challenges faced by participants. Section 5 sums up the impact of Covid.

2. The New Tsunami – Covid-19 Pandemic

While finalising this research, Covid-19, a global pandemic, occurred in about December 2019 and created disruption worldwide. As of 27 March 2021, there were 126.7 million confirmed cases of the coronavirus and a death toll of about 2.8 million globally (Worldometers, 2021). Countries were in a partial or total lockdown, and the food sector has been greatly affected by border closures. Indeed, CNBC reported, 'Droves of unemployment at restaurants and bars made March one of the worst months for US employment in the modern era, with the unemployment figure for the United States exceeding a total of 36.5 million' (Franck, 2020).

A Monetary Authority of Singapore report on 28 April 2020 suggested, 'Covid-19 will hit wages more than jobs; retail, F&B, recreation sector workers most at risk of lay-offs.' The impact of just this exogenous factor can put internationalisation on the back burner for years.

Many notable F&B brands in Singapore such as Swee Kee, Starker, Grub Burger, Yan Kee Noodle House, Rice Table, Slate, and Ben's Cookies closed during the pandemic (https://vulcanpost.com/765389/restaurants-closed-down-in-2021-covid-19/). The impact of Covid on the local F&B players varied as noted by Mr Kung Teong Wah, a member of the Executive Committee of Singapore's Food and Beverage Management Association. He noted that while bigger players such as hotel and restaurant chains were able to weather out, smaller business owners may not survive long if the pandemic drags on (https://www.straitstimes.com/singapore/consumer/fb-associations-warn-of-impending-closures-with-operators-hard-hit-by-go-no-go).

On the international front, Singapore F&B companies faced challenges, but there is little current data at this juncture on the impact overseas, and this research will provide some insights into how Singapore F&B companies were affected during the pandemic years.

The new normal of social distancing, restrictions on dining capacity, and working from home (WFH), as well as the interrelated impact on catering and food delivery platforms, will affect critical success factors for Singaporean companies operating locally, as well as those venturing overseas (Choo, 2020).

3. *Other Tsunamis*

The Covid-19 pandemic, with its lockdowns, WFH, and border closures worldwide, caused significant disruption to the global supply chain. The impact was rising costs and short supply of key ingredients. Other disruptions, such as climate change, resulted in massive floods as seen in Pakistan in October 2022, severe storms in the Philippines, and raging wildfires in Australia in 2021, which will impact Singapore F&B companies overseas.

Other disruptions such as wars, earthquakes, and civil unrest in the host countries could affect the profitability and success of food service operations in and out of Singapore. Singapore F&B companies operating overseas suffered delays in the supply of the key ingredients, rising costs, and any movement restriction measures in the host countries that would impact the viability of its operations.

4. *External Factors Moderating the Success of Internationalisation*

This section discusses how the changes in the external factors or environment can affect Singapore F&B companies' internationalisation considerations, strategies, and mitigating plans.

4.1. Aspirants

For the aspirants, the new change in the external environment affected the internationalisation plans for many Singapore companies. Statistics from a report from Enterprise Singapore on 28 March 2022 revealed that, in 2020, 1,000 out of the previous year's 2,600 Singapore companies shelved their plans to internationalise due to the onset of the pandemic. The figure of 1,600 remained constant in 2021 (https://www.channelnewsasia.com/singapore/big-read-covid-19-local-firms-overseas-expansion-business-2588266).

There were many enquiries for franchising of our brand pre-Covid, and with the onset of COVID in early 2020, the discussions went dead, and everything was put on hold. (ATS, CEO)

Many companies remained resolved in seeking international expansion and laying the groundwork as post-pandemic strategies.

With the pause in internationalisation during the Covid years, we dedicated our time to focus on our local business with digitalisation and remodelling of our domestic business. We also had to relook at our 'venturing overseas' strategies knowing that the business overseas would be badly hit during Covid. (ASL, CEO)

Another established F&B company, an achiever in this study, shared that they were suspending all internationalisation ventures during the pandemic.

We had an enquiry from Japan during the pandemic period and had to turn it down and informed the overseas party that our focus is on the domestic market and will revisit this when borders reopened. (EIL, business development manager)

4.2. Actives and Achievers

For Singapore F&B companies with international presence (both actives and achievers in this study), they faced the domestic challenge of staying afloat, with sales plummeting with only a pale fraction of less than 50 per cent as compared with pre-Covid. The immediate task was to sustain sales domestically and remain viable to tide through the rough road ahead.

Domestic sales have dropped significantly with zero sales during the pandemic lockdowns. With movement restrictions eased to allow limited dining, sales were less than half of what we would clock in pre-Covid.

For our international outlets, the situation was dire with limited support from the landlords overseas. Some of the outlets were closed, and many struggled to stay open with little dine-in customers. (LIA, managing director)

The other challenge was to assist their international franchisees and partners. So this was a double task that Singapore F&B companies needed to address simultaneously during that period.

A. Termination of Contracts

One of the outcomes of this long pandemic that Singapore F&B companies faced was the closures of outlets overseas. One of Singapore's heritage brands which had an overseas presence in three countries had that experience.

We lost our Indonesian operations as the local partner could not hold on to the last outlet that they had with Covid, and that was unfortunate. The years of demanding work in establishing the brand and outlet overseas were lost.

We also lost two outlets in China as the franchisee had to scale back and refocus during the pandemic. The latest in Chengdu just closed in January 2023.

In Vietnam, we started with two outlets, but one of these outlets had to close due to Covid which was opened a month before the onset of Covid and could not sustain due to the country's lockdown. (NIC, managing director)

Another established Singapore F&B company which had a franchisee in Malaysia and had signed a master franchise agreement for Indonesia in December 2019 suffered similar setbacks.

During Covid, our Malaysian franchisee decided to terminate the agreement and cease the operations. We had to take over the outlets ourselves.

For Indonesia, we signed a promising master franchise agreement with an established F&B company in December 2019. A few months later in March, with lockdowns in Indonesia, the Indonesia master franchisee asked to delay the store opening and shared about the impact of Covid on their current business. We empathised with their predicament and unilaterally agreed to terminate the contract and refund their franchise fees without any preconditions. (SSN, managing director)

One of the acquirers of Singapore brands in Indonesia also shared that his company had to rationalise their portfolio of imported brands. The consequence of that exercise was to terminate all the outlets of an acquired Thai brand.

We had a portfolio of local, Singapore, and other international brands. During the pandemic, we had to rationalise our operations. We do not know how long this pandemic will last. The property owners in Indonesia are not given many waivers on rentals; we had no choice but to offer fourteen outlets of an international brand for takeover. If there are no takers, we have to close the entire operation. It is *sayang* [a waste], but we had to decide on this based on the business model, profitability of the concept, and the dealings with the brand owner. (MOG, head)

B. Waiver of Royalties and Digitalisation

With businesses being affected, overseas partners would inevitably seek help during the pandemic. Singapore F&B companies can transfer or share their experience with digitalisation in the domestic market with their overseas franchisees and partners. The other aspect would be financial relief such as a waiver of royalty payment during the pandemic years and suspension of unpaid royalties.

One of Singapore's established advisers, AKO, echoed during a Zoom meeting that the Covid response to internationalisation involves helping overseas partners and franchisees with digitalisation and even financial relief.

Franchisees and overseas partners require help from brand owners and franchisors during these challenging times. They would require help to remodel the Singapore concept to adapt to these challenging times where dining in is not an option. Home delivery and digitalisation would be the new normal.

The other aspect of assistance would be a huge discount on royalties, or even a waiver would be helpful. These are unprecedented times that require unprecedented measures.

LIA, the owner of another Singapore heritage brand, shared that waiver of royalty payment was helpful during this difficult period.

I suspended the royalty payments during the pandemic. Everyone is suffering, and just like what the Singapore government has done for the F&B industry, I would like to help my overseas franchisees by waiving any royalty payments until the sky is clear.

C. Food Adaptation

The Covid-19 pandemic created the new normal in internationalisation. The business concept and food were most assimilated with the local culture and accepted by the locals in the host country.

We continued the business for the Singapore brand as it was readily accepted by our customers, and despite lockdown with no dining in, we could still do home delivery, and that could sustain our business. For the other international concept, while we could do delivery, the products offered were drinks and desserts, and these items are not stable for the locals. While there were sales, it could not sustain the entire business, and that was the reason we gave up the business. (MOG, head)

NIC, a managing director of one of Singapore's heritage brands, shared that food adaptation which include items that are traditionally not on r menu was necessary.

For our Vietnamese partners, we allowed them to include other Vietnamese food in their menu for home delivery during the pandemic. This enabled the food offered to be broader based and suited for home dining. With that, our partner was able to sustain its operations and at least keephat outlet going. The other outlet near the business district was unfortunately closed as WFH was the new normal in Vietnam. With these changes, at least our Singapore brand can tide through those difficult years for that one remaining outlet.

D. Mitigating Future Tsunamis

One of the considerations that acquirers would have for future Singapore brand acquisition would be how the Singapore brand could weather or mitigate the impact of future tsunamis such as another pandemic and/or supply side shocks. FRE, a managing director who acquired several Singapore brands, felt that Singapore F&B brands need to address these issues when they prospect for any acquirers.

When we next acquire any foreign or Singapore F&B brand, we would need to know how the concept and brand mitigate the crushing impact of a pandemic like Covid, how the brand owner intends to help us to tide through the tough times, and how the food could be adapted to cushion the impact of these external shocks.

NAP, an established consultant, also concurred with these observations.

As advisers, we would like to know the strategies that brand owners have in addressing the challenges of a pandemic and how the brand could move from a 'dine in' concept to a hybrid concept of 'dining in and delivery'. The brand owners' openness in addressing issues of royalty payments and support during these unprecedented times would be needed for acquirers seeking to take a brand into their home territory.

Foreign acquirers will want to know how digitalisation, food delivery platforms, and adaptation of the concept will make it possible to deal with such external shocks. Acquirers will also want to know how flexible Singaporean franchisers will be in terms of contractual obligations in such circumstances and what help they can offer overseas partners. These are new areas that will have to be addressed considering the current Covid-19 pandemic, and research needs to be carried out to better understand such situations and how they should be handled.

E. Remote Management

The Covid-19 pandemic resulted in the closure of international borders. There were restrictions for international travel, and face-to-face meetings were not possible. That affected the supervisory work for many Singapore F&B companies' international network.

As highlighted by Mr Tan, Enterprise Singapore's chief executive officer, the pandemic created the need for digital solutions that changed the social lifestyle of many people (https://www.channelnewsasia.com/singapore/big-read-covid-19-local-firms-overseas-expansion-business-2588266). Working from home was the new normal then. Singapore F&B companies had to move into web conferencing and virtual events to promote their brands internationally and maintain the advisory support of their overseas franchisees and partners:

Before the pandemic, we always need to visit our foreign franchisees and partners to discuss issues and address challenges. When travel was not possible during the pandemic, we had to resort to Zoom meetings to maintain contact and resolve issues.

Moving forward, we see that we can have more contact with our foreign franchisees and partners via both remote and face-to-face meetings. That is a significant development out of this pandemic. (CHI, general manager)

Consequently, Singaporean companies will need to have continuity plans to support overseas franchisees and partners in such situations. Singaporean companies must gear up to face these challenges.

5. Conclusion

With the opening of borders in mid-2022, the outlook became positive and encouraging for Singapore F&B companies. Covid-19 infections had not subsided globally, with China still experiencing lockdowns in many key cities and with infections in Korea and Japan in the tens of thousands. On 25 November 2022, Singapore's Ministry of Health reported a weekly moving average of at least 1,400 infections (www.moh.gov.sg/Covid-19).

The annual franchise expo organised by the Franchising and Licensing Association of Singapore returned in November 2022. While the recovery was ongoing and China opened its borders without the need for quarantine on 8 January 2023, the outlook for Singapore F&B companies remained cautiously optimistic in the next two years.

The new tsunamis have disrupted the internationalisation scene massively and call for innovative solutions to address the underlying foundations for Singapore F&B brands in venturing overseas. In addition to the critical success factors discussed thus far in the earlier chapter, Singapore F&B companies need to factor in sudden external shocks such as these new tsunamis with new measures to face the onslaught of any pandemic, war, or acts of God that might occur from time to time.

CHAPTER 16

NO SINGLE RECIPE FOR SUCCESS

1. Introduction

Bee Cheng Hiang, Sushi Tei, Crystal Jade, and the TungLok Group were the first four Singaporean food service sector companies to venture overseas in the 1990s. Since then, many other such companies have followed. However, the path to internationalisation is not always easy, as was evident in the case studies examined here. The project's key findings were as follows:

1. Singapore F&B companies have made some headway in internationalisation over the past several decades.
2. Several critical success factors vary depending on the stage of internationalisation.
3. These success factors affect the capabilities and strategies companies need during their journeys.

The present study suggests an integrative framework for the complexities facing Singaporean food sector companies as they internationalise. The internal and external factors determine a firm's readiness to expand overseas. However, the success of its internationalisation drive is affected by moderating factors and the strategies that are adopted.

Section 2 summarises the critical success factors as well as the key capabilities and competencies for the internationalisation of the various groups. Section 3 discusses the key strategic propositions for internationalisation for Singapore F&B companies while section 4 considers whether an Asian model of internationalisation exists, and section 5 looks at future trends that may affect internationalisation for Singapore F&B companies.

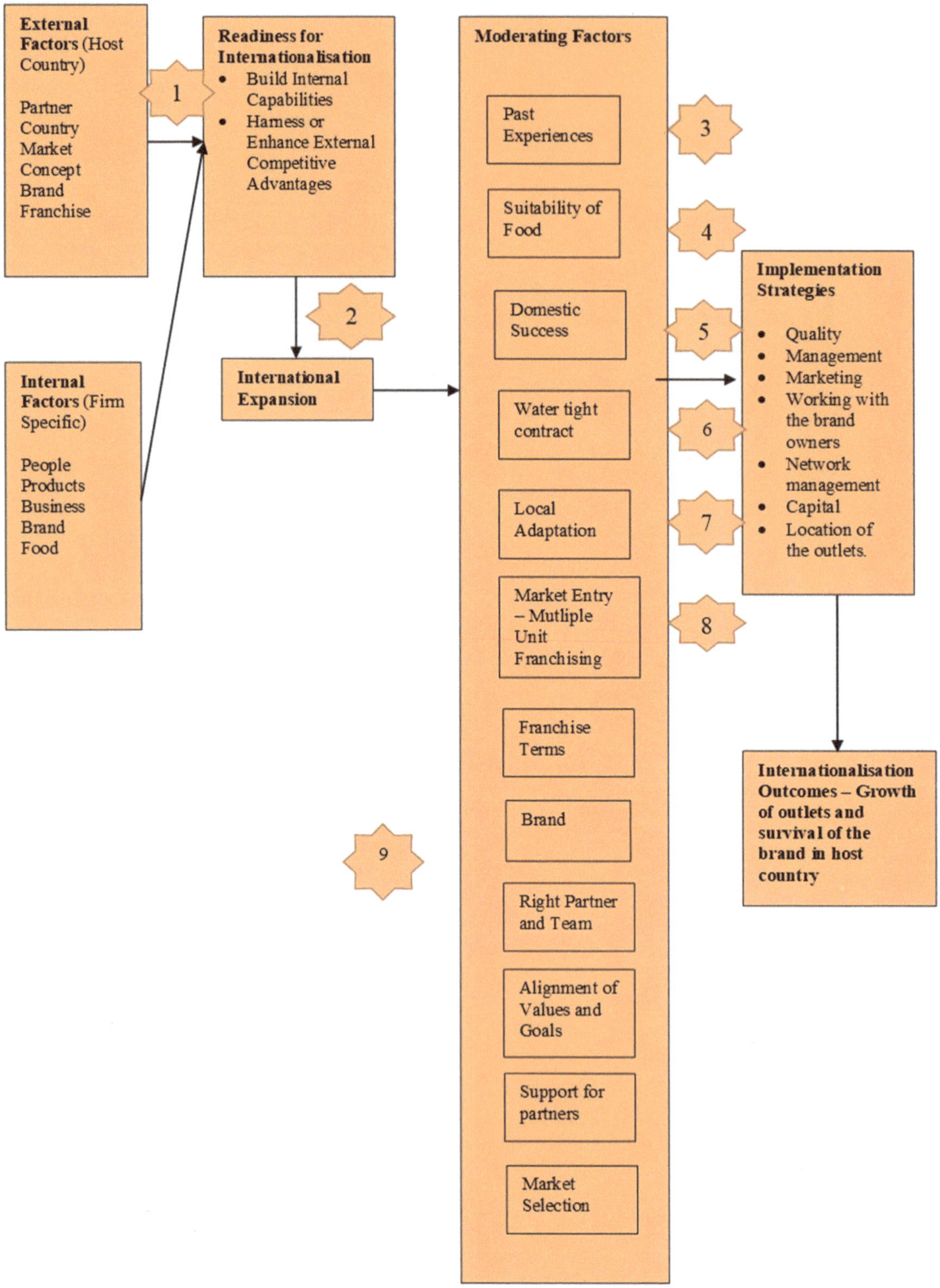

Figure 16.1: An integrative framework suggested by the case studies

2. *Critical Success Factors*

Unlike Cavusgil and Nevin's (1981) research, which suggested that firm-specific characteristics were determinants of success, this study highlighted the importance of both firm characteristics (internal) and environmental (external) factors as propellants for internationalisation success. Indeed, the study found many internal and external factors that were critical to the various groups examined (Table 16.1). The author also developed an integrative framework based on the findings of the study in Figure 16.1, which would be central to the discussion in this chapter.

Table 16.1: Critical success factors for the various groups

Aspirant (companies that have intentions to go overseas shortly) concept prominence	**Active (companies which have an overseas presence in one or two countries) concept prominence**	**Achiever (companies that have an overseas presence in three or more countries) concept prominence**	**Acquirer (overseas buyers of Singapore concepts) concept prominence**	**Adviser (companies that advise and assist Singapore F&B companies in overseas expansion) concept prominence**
Right Fit	Right Appeal and Offering	Global Aspirations	Suitable Brand	Brand and Concept
Right Food	Right Alignment	Global Branding	Suitable Owner	Food and Adaptation
Right Location	Right Team	Global Adaptation	Suitable Business	Market Selection
Right Partner	Right Foundation	Global Support	Suitable Adaptation	Partners and People
			Suitable Terms	
			Suitable Location	

Notably, there was a difference in the internal and external critical success factors across the various categories. For the external factors, the most prominent issues across the categories were

1. brand appeal,
2. suitability of the food,
3. the concept,
4. location,
5. market selection,
6. overseas partners,
7. terms.

These external critical success factors could impede or enable future internationalisation prospects as they determined patronage and the viability of Singaporean brands in overseas markets. Firm-specific characteristics or internal factors also differed across the groups. However, seven such factors were identified:

1. Brand development
2. Management
3. Staff and people
4. Training and support
5. Governance
6. R & D capabilities
7. Local sourcing expertise

Table 16.2: Key capabilities and competencies for the various groups

Aspirant (companies that have intentions to go overseas shortly) concept prominence	**Active (companies which have an overseas presence in one or two countries) concept prominence**	**Achiever (companies that have an overseas presence in three or more countries) concept prominence**
Know yourself	Build the brand	Restructure networks
Know your capacity	Brand the framework with overseas partners	Realign support structures
Know your 'enemies'	Build the foundation	Rebrand
Know your allies	Build the team	Readapt food, services, and products
Know your advocates		Rekindle working relationships with overseas partners

3. *Strategic Issues and Propositions*

This exploratory study provides strong empirical evidence of the critical success factors for Singaporean food sector companies that have ventured overseas and the capabilities and strategies they need to be successful. The CSFs for the different groups (i.e. aspirants, actives, and achievers) are different, suggesting changes are needed as such companies extend their international operations. There is, therefore, no single recipe for success. The study highlights the need for Singaporean food sector companies to examine their internal strengths and consider external factors before deciding on their internationalisation journey.

The qualitative case study approach used in this study has proved useful in extending our understanding of the complexities of internationalisation and enabled 'sensitive information' about failures and the challenges encountered in the internationalisation journey to be obtained, which will not have been possible even with a large-scale quantitative survey. Arising from this study, the following will be the discussions on the key statements as well as strategic propositions that Singapore companies should focus on as they seek to venture overseas.

3.1. Success in Internationalisation Can Never Be Certain

The study made clear that international success is an elusive idea and that there is no broad measure of success for all companies. As Sir Winston Churchill once said, 'Success is not final, and failure is not fatal; what matters is the courage to continue that count.'

Internationalisation pathways are 'different strokes for different folks'. Each company must evaluate its unique selling propositions and critical success factors, both internally and externally, and consider these for any host country it is thinking of entering. Each such country is likely to require a unique set of franchiser and franchisee capabilities, and these will suggest different market entry strategies and ongoing operational approaches if long-term success is to be achieved.

3.2. Success Is about Managing All Factors – Internal and External Factors – Well

International outcomes and performance form a constant loop of feedback, adjustment, and reframing of original strategies. The ability of Singapore F&B companies to manage such factors consistently and effectively is key to achieving continuing success. However, constant adjustments and adaptations affect internationalisation frameworks, which explains why there is no set recipe or fixed formula. Companies must manage uncertainty and react to external changes as each expansion into a new host country requires a unique set of resources, capabilities, and strategies. Singapore F&B companies will need to continually develop an appropriate repertoire of experience, knowledge, and insight as they move to confront their next frontier.

The internal (firm-specific) and external (environment-driven or host-country-specific) critical success factors can obstruct (be a barrier) or enable (be a benefit) Singapore F&B companies' future internationalisation prospects, suggesting:

Proposition 1: Managing internal and external CSFs well will enhance Singapore F&B companies' internal capabilities and external preparedness for internationalisation.

3.3. Success in Internationalisation Requires Key Capabilities and Competencies

To succeed overseas, Singapore F&B companies must possess the right capabilities and competencies as suggested by the groups in Table 16.2. To be successful, Singapore F&B companies need to have the right team to spearhead overseas expansion, standardise their operating procedures, and assist their overseas partners to find local sources.

3.4. Readiness for Internationalisation Is a Key to Success

The study also suggested that Singapore F&B companies' readiness for internationalisation was fundamental to achieving success. It is unclear how many of the 180 aspirants found by the researcher will venture overseas in the next few years as their readiness is not clear in many cases. The aspirant case studies provided a list of internal and external factors that can be used as a diagnostic tool for any aspirant to ascertain their readiness for internationalisation. Indeed, the aspirant case studies suggested:

Proposition 2: Improving internal capabilities and external preparedness will enhance a company's internationalisation readiness and affect future internationalisation outcomes.

3.5. The Past Internationalisation Experience Affects the Present and Future Success

Earlier internationalisation experiences have an impact on prospects. Several companies had experienced failures and have not gotten out of them. Consequently, they shunned internationalisation for fear of another failure. Reasons for the failures varied from fraud, non-compliance, wrong choice of markets, inadequate market study, and choosing the wrong overseas partners. Another good example was the Jumbo Group of restaurants' experiences, which was shared by its CEO, Mr Ang Kiam Meng:

Flush with domestic success and recognising the competitiveness and limited size of Singapore's Food & Beverage market, the company ventured overseas [into] Indonesia in 1995. 'We failed,' said Mr Ang, with a chuckle. 'It was all due to our inexperience in opening branches [overseas]. These were earlier years of training. The school fees we had to pay.'

It took Jumbo almost twenty years before it tried to go overseas again. It was only in 2013 that the company opened its second international outlet (in Shanghai). The company's second overseas expansion was different as Jumbo was thriving in China. So what changed? According to Mr Ang:

'Everything [in China] we took a quite different approach,' he said. 'You know, once bitten, twice shy, so we were cautious. When it comes to F&B, you must be patient. If you rush into it, if you do not do your homework well, it will all go down the drain in less than six months.' (Enterprise Singapore, 2020)

Where initial success could lead to further success, initial failures often deterred further internationalisation efforts. Therefore, it is important that Singapore F&B companies set off on the right foot and achieve initial success as this will instil confidence and greater enthusiasm for subsequent success. This suggests:

Proposition 3: The initial failure in internationalisation and the fear of subsequent failure are obstacles to further internationalisation efforts and achieving success in internationalisation.

3.6. The Suitability of Food Concepts, Tastes, and Products Determines Success

While there is limited information about the impact that food concept, taste, and products have on internationalisation, this study found that these were critical by acquirers, actives, and advisers (Table 16.1). Acceptance of the brand in foreign markets is crucial. However, the study found food suitability preceded the brand, unlike the Western internationalisation model, in which brand prominence ensured expansion into Asia first before locals acquired a taste for Western food. Taste suitability was assumed to be a given, but often, it was a problem if overseas customers did not accept the original taste. When this happened, brand expansion internationally was difficult. As an example, *bak kut teh* (peppery pork ribs soup, Singapore Teochew-style version) had limited success in Thailand:

This is a very niche kind of food and only found in certain segments of Bangkok. For Thais, the taste is not suitable, and they do not go to a single type of food. They would order this in a Chinese restaurant together with other Chinese dishes and not as a single type of food even with its condiments. (NAP, director)

Thus, the study supports Doherty and Quinn's work (1999) as does Levitt's (1993) suggestion that the success of a foreign food service brand concept is dependent on taste acceptance and cultural adaptation. Taste suitability is what CSF potential partners or franchisees consider when acquiring an overseas food service franchise, suggesting:

Proposition 4: The suitability of taste, food concept, and products in foreign countries are critical determinants of success.

3.7. Domestic Success Is a Key to Brand Acquisition in Overseas Markets

The study supports the suggestion that domestic success opens the door to international success. While it does not automatically guarantee success (Huszagh et al., 1992), it is the basis for attracting suitors and the eventual adoption of a brand in a host country. It was also the yardstick that advisers used when evaluating a company's readiness for internationalisation. The study found that acquirers, particularly Indonesians, only buy a Singaporean franchise if its brand enjoyed domestic success, suggesting:

Proposition 5: Success in a domestic market is critical to foreign partners' brand acquisition decisions.

Only two Singaporean brands had born global aspirations from the outset, which is consistent with previous research. As ADW, a managing director, noted:

It is in the plan that we go overseas from the start.

Another managing director, VIT, pointed out:

We plan to go overseas, but we have lots of worries such as the untried logistics and whether the food is suitable in the host country.

While born global food service companies may become more common in the future, many organisations are still likely to prefer to evaluate their brand locally and expand internationally only after they have achieved success domestically.

3.8. A Win-Win Contractual Agreement Ensures Continuing Success

This study adds further weight to the importance of administrative efficiency (Choo, 2005), which suggests the need for contractual arrangements that align franchisers' and franchisees' interests (Brickley and Dark, 1987; Alon et al., 2020). Contractual terms must be attractive for acquirers. Brand hijacking often happens in Asia (e.g. the LiHO, Yole, and Tealive cases in recent years) as has been reported by the media and in this thesis. Consequently, Singapore F&B companies need monitoring capabilities and to enforce contracts if they are to prevent future occurrences. Most Singapore F&B companies wanted a watertight contract that prevented franchise opportunism from taking place, and there were instances where franchisees were removed for under-declaration of sales and royalties and non-conformance to quality standards. This suggests:

Proposition 6: A well-crafted franchise contract reduces franchisee opportunism and helps ensure the survival of the brand in host countries.

3.9. The Importance of Local Adaptation

JAG, an achiever, aptly noted, 'Once you are out of Singapore, do not expect just to copy and paste your concept, food, and operations.' The study showed adaptation was critical to overseas success. Even across the causeway in Malaysia, Singaporean food needed to be adapted to local conditions given the large Muslim Malay population and the need to have halal certification when catering for this large segment.

Taste suitability is always the key concern when internationalising. No food is always suitable for new countries, and even the US giants – like McDonald's, KFC, Pizza Hut, and Subway – invest heavily to educate locals about their food. They also constantly innovate and adapt their food to local palates. The introduction of a nasi lemak burger in Singapore and Malaysia is a case in point. The burger was so popular that it was brought back for Ramadan, the fasting month for Muslims (Channel News Asia, 2019).

The abilities to innovate and adapt the food to local palates are dependent on the efforts of the company and its overseas partners. This capability needs to be intensified as overseas networks grow from one or two countries for the actives to more than two countries for the achievers.

Cultural adaptability (Yaprak, 1985; Huszagh et al., 1992; Choo, 2003) was found to be critical by all participants. However, the key questions were as follows:

1. What do we adapt?
2. How do we adapt?
3. When do we adapt?

Indeed, the balance between standardisation and adaptation was highlighted throughout the case studies.

The issue of authenticity of the food relates to customers familiar with it. One participant (HRE), who invited a famous Michelin one-star restaurant to cook a dish in a foreign country using local ingredients, found the taste was not suitable. The prospective master franchisee had to impress the owner that food acceptability is critical. However, if the concept is only to serve travelling Singaporeans, then being genuinely Singaporean will be most important as many Singaporeans feel food can never be better than in original Singaporean outlets. Taste is personal and varies over time. The key to success is to appeal to enough customers to sustain the concept. Therefore, every company must determine the extent of adaptation that is acceptable without losing its soul and DNA.

The study suggested that aspirants and actives did not conduct a host country risk assessment before entering. Rather, they opted for franchising and relied on overseas partners to manage compliance risks. While many achievers did not conduct feasibility studies and risk assessments before entering new countries, some established achievers, such as those listed on the Singapore stock exchange, did undertake such studies before entering the new countries, suggesting:

Proposition 7: The right local market adaptation to align with a host country will improve patronage and increase network growth in host countries.

3.10. Market Entry Mode

The study suggested Singapore F&B companies preferred franchising over other foreign market entry modes, such as joint ventures or self-owned subsidiaries, in their initial phase of international expansion. Multiple units and joint-venture franchising were preferred options, with single-unit franchising being less preferred due to the costs involved in supporting one unit outside Singapore.

Unlike the dominant master franchising mode used by brands from developed nations, this study found that Asian brand owners had to adapt not only the food but also their franchise systems. The choice of market entry mode was a key to success in many Asian countries.

Choosing the right mode of entry depends on the resources available, local knowledge, and the complexities of the legal framework in a host country. For example, in Indonesia, owned and operated foreign entities are not allowed in some areas. Further, Singapore's immediate neighbours (Malaysia and Indonesia) have franchise regulations that impose constraints on international expansion. For example, Indonesia requires 80 per cent of ingredients to be locally sourced. Other countries also have franchise regulations that affect market entry mode choices, which have led some companies to opt for other market entry options.

Local knowledge of franchisees or overseas partners was also seen as crucial to governance as was the need for Singapore F&B companies to have control over their franchise networks, explaining the attractiveness of the master franchise. Participants also realised the need to collaborate closely with overseas partners to ensure that the business ran well.

3.11. Franchise-Related Terms

Many scholars have found that franchise-related terms have to be suitable for franchisees if they are to be successful (Gikroyo et al., 2015; Combs and Castrogiovanni, 1999). This study lends support to this idea. Further, it is clear that overseas franchisees in developing countries cannot afford to pay exorbitant franchise fees or royalties. While the cost of operations can be lower, the revenues are correspondingly lower, which affects profitability and return on investment.

Multiple units and joint-venture franchising are preferred over master franchising as outlays are lower and thus more attractive to overseas partners. However, this gives rise to some form of franchisee opportunism (e.g. under-reporting of sales or brand hijacking). Such practices will reduce Singapore F&B companies' chances of success as reduced profits will affect the continuing growth of their international networks, suggesting:

Proposition 8: Suitable franchise-related terms ensure a better take-up rate of the brand and reduce franchisee opportunism.

3.12. Brand Power Determines Success

Brand power is an important success factor (Gikonyo et al., 2015). Indeed, Shane and Spell (1988) suggested that a company must build its brand to ensure long-time success and noted that brands could provide a competitive advantage because they were not replicable, unlike outlet operations. All groups in this study confirmed this point, noting that building the brand and ensuring its appeal to local consumers were crucial.

Although participants recognised each brand's importance, they also recognised that its continuing contribution to success was dependent on its ability to evolve. Sakae Sushi, once a leading player in the conveyor-belt sushi and Japanese food segment, was one of Singapore's successful food service companies. However, this was not enough as was pointed out by Mr Nick Foley, president for Southeast Asia, the Pacific, and Japan at brand consultancy Landor, who commented:

Brands need to stand for something while never standing still. In a disruptive market, more now than ever, brands must adapt. Sakae failed to read the market and did not adapt to changing tasting and preferences of younger consumers. Just because you had a winning formula in the past does not guarantee you a robust future.

Interestingly, Lau Kong Cheen, deputy CEO at A. S. Louken, also noted some additional problems, commenting:

Sakae built its brand in the era where decent Japanese food was in demand and operations costs in terms of labour and rentals were low. Today, despite having a good brand, Sakae Sushi's sheer number of outlets are not able to support the organisation due to high operations cost. (Marketing Interactive, 2017)

3.13. The Importance of the Right Overseas Partner

Singapore F&B companies saw franchising as the preferred international market entry mode. Overseas franchisees who were able to develop and competently manage multiple stores were preferred. This is consistent with previous research that suggested franchising occurs because of franchisers' need to have partnered with financial capital (Park and Jang, 2018), human capital (Rhou et al., 2019), managerial talent (Gillis et al., 2019), and local knowledge (Combs and Castrogiovanni, 1993). Against this backdrop, the selection of the right partner and an effective working relationship with that partner is crucial to international success.

The study supports the critical success factors described in Fladmoe-Lindquist's (1996) model. The right partner or franchisee will be dependent on the attributes required to run operations in a host country. Prerequisites are critical, such as having relevant business or industry-related experience, maturity, and entrepreneurship related to the acquired brand. Consequently, franchisers need to have a set of clear expectations and guidelines that guide the selection process.

While prior research tends to focus on 'hard skills', in this study, 'softer issues' (e.g. integrity, business ethics, and character) surfaced and were emphasised by participants. Many talked about an alignment of values, goals, and expectations being needed in any long-term working relationship.

The study support Choo's (2005) work that suggested that an overseas partner's management capability was critical to success. One participant, JAT, suggested that poor local management would not help even famous brands get established in a host country, but a mediocre brand with good management would have a better chance of success. While the brand was critical, overseas partners' ability to establish the brand and their ongoing brand building were more critical, suggesting:

Proposition 9: Continuing support for the overseas partner will help the alignment of goals, prevent franchisee opportunism, and enhance performance.

Once overseas partners are selected, continuing support is needed. The study supported the importance of franchisers providing training, maintaining communication, and providing product updates to maintain good relations with their partners. As Choo (2005) noted, the franchiser-franchisee relationship is also critical to the long-term survival of the franchise. While conflicts are inevitable in any partnership, the key is to manage conflicts well so that they do not disrupt operations (Saraogi, 2009). This study found that franchisers and their overseas franchisees felt they had good relationships. There were some conflicts, but these were managed well, and potential crises were averted.

The study highlighted the need to have a systematic screening process and to invest in finding the right partners. As Mahizhnan (1994) noted, Singapore F&B companies, particularly SMEs, found it challenging to assess trust, compatibility, and competence when selecting international partners. There was a lack of due diligence when evaluating partners as many participants relied on gut feel. However, some had good processes, with one participant noting that to accurately assess overseas partners, it was essential to visit their homes and offices and know the books they liked to read. Credit bureau reports, checks with industry suppliers, and online reports were also seen as helping find the right partner.

3.14. Market Selection

Uppsala's theory suggests that companies expand outwards based on their consideration of psychological comfort and cultural distance (Johanson and Vahlne, 2009). However, this study did not find compelling evidence to support this position. On one hand, Malaysia is just 1 km from the northern tip of Singapore via a causeway, yet few Singaporean food sector companies operate there. Malaysians and Singaporeans have the same racial mix, although with differing proportions. Malays make up 69.3 per cent of Malaysia (Department of Statistics, Malaysia, 2019), while in Singapore the Chinese population is about 76 per cent (Department of Statistics, Singapore, 2019). Malays in Singapore constitute about 15 per cent of the population, which is like the Chinese in Malaysia (22.8 per cent). Indians, the other significant ethnic group, only make up about 7.5 per cent of the population in Singapore and Malaysia. Thus, it is attractive for Singapore F&B companies to venture first into Malaysia given its physical proximity and small cultural and administrative distance (Ghemawatt, 2001, 2007).

However, this study found that participants did not wish to enter the Malaysian market. As noted by AKO, cultural similarities have proved to be an obstacle due to a commonly held belief that 'what they have in

Singapore, they have too'. Further, JKT noted there was a strong rivalry between the two countries over versions of chicken rice, *bak kut teh*, nasi lemak, or prawn *mee*. Established brands, such as Jumbo and Wee Nam Kee, have had an overseas presence in many countries but hesitated to venture into Malaysia, and many who have ventured into Malaysia have subsequently shut their operations.

Many Singaporean food sector companies have chosen to venture into China, Taiwan, and Hong Kong, although few do so in the first phase of their development. Like Singapore, Hong Kong is a cosmopolitan city; and as noted by a participant (WNA), to enter Hong Kong, the brand, concept, food, and service must be close to perfect. Expectations are high, and the food must be suitable for residents. Taiwan, on the other hand, prides itself on food and what it can create. So it will be very niche for Singaporean concepts to make a foothold in the country.

While many Singapore F&B companies want to venture into China, they are wary of the difficulties of entering and sustaining their operations there. China is not homogeneous, and food tastes differ from region to region. The study found that many participants would only enter China in the later phases of their internationalisation.

Everyone has made the same mistake, including me. As Singaporeans, we think Singaporeans are good, so we send them to China. However, a manager manages fewer people here than in China. Going to China will not be a bed of roses. (George Quek, BreadTalk Group chairman, Enterprise Singapore, 2019)

The study also highlighted the need to focus on international expansion and that it is better to do well in a few countries than to spread too thinly with a wide coverage:

If I open ten shops, I would rather open them in one city than in ten. I want to focus on doing one thing first [to] maximise human resources and do an outstanding job. (Ang Kiam Meng, CEO, Jumbo Group)

For the more established achievers and big players, such as BreadTalk and Bee Cheng Hiang, the next step is globalisation by expanding to the United States and Europe:

We have been successful with the Asian market, and we are always keeping an eye on the European and American markets. About 20 years ago, the company used to get only a handful of inquiries from Europe and the United States. It now gets hundreds of inquiries but has yet to find a suitable partner. (Daniel Wong, general manager, https://e.beechenghiangvn.com/the-family-bak-kwa-business-that-grew-and-grew-6-lessons-of-bee-cheng-hiangs-success/)

3.15. Implementation Strategies

While the broader literature has not focused on implementation strategies, this study highlighted the importance of successful implementation by overseas partners. Phin's (2020) study suggested that knowledge transfer practices were critical to the success of franchise networks. Achieving mimetic institutional isomorphism, even by coercion, is crucial to brand conformity, which is important to international franchising success. Singaporean brands are new to host countries and are likely to fail if plans are not well implemented (Phin, 2020). Thus, Singapore F&B companies need to be actively involved in implementation strategies. While this has often been left to overseas partners as they are responsible for managing the outlets, participants have stressed the importance of transferring know-how (in food preparation and management) to overseas partners.

Choosing the first outlet location is also critical as its success will affect growth in that host country. This study has noted the importance of Singapore F&B companies being actively involved in the selection of all outlet locations. Although the local partner is likely to be better versed in location selection, Singapore F&B companies can add value through a combination of accumulated knowledge, insight, and experience.

4. An Asian Internationalisation Model

This study adds weight to the suggestion that the Asian internationalisation model is different from the Western model. The differences are in how companies deal with their overseas partners and the approach taken. There are distinct differences even in market entry mode as there is a preference for multiple-unit franchises and for joint-venture franchises in which the Singaporean company owns a percentage of the joint-venture company that operates the first outlet and then franchises other locations. The attractiveness of this approach for overseas partners is the clear commitment of the Singaporean company, as well as lower start-up costs as a franchise fee is not needed. The advantage for the Singaporean company is the ease of entry into the host country and the financial benefit overall if the JV outlets perform well.

Another key aspect of this 'Asian' model is the management of overseas partners. Against the background of brand hijacking of high-profile companies such as Gong Cha, IlaoIlao in Singapore, and Cha Time in Malaysia and other forms of franchisee opportunism (Choo, 2005), the Singapore F&B companies included in this study were increasingly mindful of such risks and sought to safeguard themselves against overseas franchisee opportunism. TJK, a group chairman, highlighted the 'Asian approach' in dealing with overseas partners:

Especially for Asian franchising, both franchisor and franchisee need to have clear communication. In the West, it is entirely by the book. In Asia, the relationship does count.

The study suggested, being 'Singaporean and Asian', many companies preferred to refrain from issuing warning letters and seeking litigation or terminating franchise contracts. Instead, they sought regular updates, consensus, and talking regularly with their overseas partners to resolve conflicts. Many waited until a contract was complete and then did a reset by selecting new partners.

5. Future Trends That Will Likely Affect Internationalisation

The world is changing rapidly, and Singapore F&B companies will have to deal with trends that affect their success and sustainability. They will affect aspirants, actives, and achievers differently, and these companies need to strategise to deal with an evolving and disrupted landscape in which the basis of success will change rapidly and unpredictably. *Forbes* (2019) suggested the top ten macro-trends:

1. Factory automation affecting quick-service restaurants (for that matter any food concept)
2. Plant-based food
3. New Age: sea to cell

4. Sweetness preference shifting
5. The new fizz buzz (beverages)
6. Cannabis compound – subject to regulator's approval
7. Clean label commoditisation driving brand importance
8. Food innovation
9. Eco-friendly packaging (reduce or remove single-use plastics)
10. The devaluing and de-socialising of dining out (food delivery and eating at home)

The reality is that such trends will change rapidly from year to year and that disruption will be continuous (Stuckey, 2019). Consequently, Singapore F&B companies venturing overseas will need to brace themselves for changes that are going to happen in their networks. As the surrounding region is developing rapidly, Singapore F&B companies will need to innovate to ensure their concepts suit buyers' changing needs and aspirations.

This study suggested that participating companies were mindful of such trends. SSN, the chief financial officer of a heritage brand, noted that healthier choices were needed to cater to millennials while FRE, managing director of a Singaporean brand based in the Philippines, commented:

Health in F&B is a big trend; healthy food, a tasty and hip concept, will be attractive. It is health and wellness. Basic concepts are doing well, and our brand is in that category, and thus, it is doing well with growth of at least 15 per cent year on year without any big marketing expenses on our side.

Another issue that is likely to affect Singapore F&B companies is that Singaporean concepts can lose their popularity as many entrepreneurs in the region are likely to create concepts that best suit their countries as was highlighted by FRE, a managing director in the Philippines.

Mr Ip Yiu Tung – consultant, founder, and ex-chairman of Crystal Jade Culinary Concepts Holdings (Crystal Jade) – argued that Singapore F&B companies must revitalise and refresh their menus if they are to stay relevant (Cai, 2014).

Some changes we have made include revitalising and refreshing menu items; retaining the essence of traditional Chinese cuisine while incorporating some inventive approaches in light of food trends and drawing influence from modern gastronomy.

Further, millennials are becoming franchisees. These are better-educated managers, and this has implications for parent companies, said TJK, a managing director:

Millennials are becoming franchisees and buying concepts. Their way of thinking and philosophy of life are different, and it does not mean it is all bad. They have different drives and visions and [are] willing to take different risks.

There is also a growth in the number of food halls and large-scale food courts. The question for Singapore F&B companies is whether their food concept is suitable for such food courts and whether to evaluate their impact on the franchise and the brand:

Food halls are a trend right now, and every shopping mall needs to have them. We have one food hall opening in every CBD. Manila has three busy business areas, namely, Ortigas, Makati, and FBC, amazingly fast and everyone within six months. (FRE, a managing director)

IAC, a managing director, suggested that there will be lots of disruption in the retail scene and that the retail mix in shopping malls is changing. There are more food options, and competition is keener, which means customers' loyalty will wane due to the greater choice they have:

With retail, people are not coming more often to the shopping malls, and with new concepts coming on stream, people are very fickle. Today they tried something delicious, but they have not tried many others, and it would be a long time before they tried the same store again. That is the challenge with retail.

While finalising this thesis, Covid-19, a global pandemic, occurred in about December 2019 and created disruption worldwide. As of 27 March 2021, there were 126.7 million confirmed cases of the coronavirus and a death toll of about 2.8 million globally (Worldometers, 2021). Countries are currently in a partial or total lockdown, and the food sector has been affected. Indeed, CNBC reported, 'Droves of unemployment at restaurants and bars made March one of the worst months for US employment in the modern era, with the unemployment figure for the United States exceeding a total of 36.5 million' (Franck, 2020).

Other disruptions, such as climate change, wars, floods, or other acts of God, could affect the profitability and success of food service operations in and out of Singapore. Consequently, Singapore F&B companies will need to have continuity plans to support overseas franchisees and partners in such situations. Singapore F&B companies must gear up to face these challenges. Foreign acquirers will want to know how digitalisation, food delivery platforms, and adaptation of the concept will make it possible to deal with such external shocks. Acquirers will also want to know how flexible Singaporean franchisers will be in terms of contractual obligations in such circumstances and what help they can offer overseas partners. These are new areas (external factors) that will have to be addressed considering the current Covid-19 pandemic, and research needs to be conducted to better understand such situations and how they should be managed.

6. Conclusion

This study suggested many recommendations for Singapore F&B companies in the food service sector that wish to venture overseas. As Choo (2005) noted, there are plenty of how-to success tips on the internet. However, these recommendations are 'contextual, largely opinionated, disorganized and unsubstantiated'.

This book is the first in-depth study of the internationalisation of Singaporean food sector companies, and the suggested model shows relevant processes, critical success factors, needed capabilities, and appropriate strategies for successful internationalisation.

Several critical internationalisation lessons were suggested in the earlier chapters for Singapore companies in various stages of the internationalisation journey. However, as the groups examined differed, the recommendations also differed for these different groups of companies. Some of these recommendations were discussed in relevant chapters, but the more salient recommendations (which are not exhaustive) are repeated here.

The present study provided sufficient results to support and challenge some findings in prior research. The study suggested participants are, and will be, dealing with many disruptions to their external environments and will need to brace themselves for the changes that will happen in the future. Although many participants were not prepared for such disruptions and will never be, it is the preparedness to deal with endogenous and exogenous changes that will be key to sustainable success on the internationalisation road.

Success for Singapore F&B companies must come down to food and service, and these are determined by local customers in the host countries. What is a success then? It is a complex process of winning the hearts, minds, and souls of new customers so they accept, embrace, and adopt a foreign brand, food, quality, service, and all the other critical attributes as their own.

Finally, following Sunzi's *Art of War*, when all the critical success factors (the right partner, the right food, the right country, the right location, and the right brand and all the internal and external factors) are in place (or addressed) and mitigated against any unprecedented external factors such as wars, pandemics, and disruptions of supplies, that elusive success can be inevitable. The difference between success and failure is knowing the critical success factors that matter at the various stages of internationalisation and how these CSFs can be managed in new host countries with key competencies and capabilities.

The road ahead for Singapore F&B companies is peppered with key successes and failures, and each company must have its game plan in mapping the road it intends to walk in with a good chance of success. As our founding prime minister, Lee Kuan Yew, once said, let us look at that horizon, follow the rainbow, and go ride it with success or failures; we shall learn and pursue the pot of gold at the end of the rainbow.

'May your voyage beyond Singapore be blessed with abundance.'

Successes and Struggles:

SINGAPORE F&B COMPANIES' VOYAGES

The author would like to thank the following companies for approving to feature the companies' voyages, successes, and struggles. Many other companies were approached but due to printing deadlines, we were unable to get the necessary approvals on time.

1. Wee Nam Kee Hainanese Chicken Rice
2. Founder Bak Kut Teh
3. Barcook Bakery
4. Old School Delights
5. Ponggol Nasi Lemak
6. White Restaurant
7. Rong Hua Bak Kut The
8. greendot
9. ROOST
10. SAYBONS
11. SALADSTOP!

Thank you!
Dr James Mok

Wee Nam Kee Hainanese Chicken Rice

Wee Nam Kee's outlet in Jakarta, Indonesia
Photo by Wee Nam Kee

Wee Nam Kee Hainanese Chicken Rice was founded in 1987, and it serves one of Singapore's favourite and iconic dishes – Hainanese chicken rice. The founder, the late Mr Wee Toon Ouut, was known to be a gracious host. He often credited his father, who worked as a head chef aboard ships, for helping him develop a discerning palate.

According to him, Wee Nam Kee's success is based on a very simple principle, 'the chicken rice that Mum cooks'. So the chefs were told to cook with the passion that mothers had, with love and concern for their families.

It is this uncompromising commitment to quality and culinary heritage that has garnered Wee Nam Kee a loyal following, various accolades from the press, and prestigious commissioning by the Singapore government to serve its famous chicken rice at various overseas events.

Voyages

1987 – first outlet in Singapore
2010 – Manila, Philippines
2016 – Tokyo, Japan, with outlets at Tamachi, Ginza, and Shinjuku
2016 – Seoul with three outlets
2017 – Jakarta BSD and currently eight outlets
2017 – Surabaya
2018 – Taipei City
2020 – Semarang, Indonesia

Mr Wee Liang Lian – the second-generation owner
Photo by Wee Nam Kee

Success Factors

1. Market and brand acceptance
2. Commitment and passion of the overseas partner
3. Understanding of the host country's culture and customs

Struggles

We exited South Korea after twelve months. It was a wrong selection of overseas partners, and the business concept in concessionaires employed by them was not suitable for the Korean market; we would rather prefer an outlet model.

Founder Bak Kut Teh

Founder Bak Kut Teh's HCMC outlet
Photo by Founder Bak Kut Teh

Founder Bak Kut Teh (發起人骨茶) have been serving aromatic *rou gu cha* (肉骨茶, also known as *bak kut teh* in the Hokkien/Teochew dialect) since 1978. It has established a reputation as one of the best *bak kut tehs* in Singapore.

The customers come first and foremost for the *bak kut teh* and hail from all over Singapore as well as other regional countries (Malaysia, Indonesia, China, Thailand, Hong Kong, Japan, etc.). The multitude of celebrity photographs that fill the walls of the eatery and the crowds that throng the restaurant during its opening hours are proof of Founder Bak Kut Teh's appeal and the authenticity of the food served.

Voyages

1978 – First outlet in Singapore
2014 – Jakarta with two outlets
2018 – HCMC, Vietnam, with two outlets
2018 – Taipei with one outlet
2019 – Hangzhou with two outlets
2020 – Chengdu
2021 – Hainan Island

Mr Chua and his son, Nigel Chua
Photo by Founder Bak Kut Teh

Success Factors

1. Right overseas partner
2. Location
3. Support for overseas partners

Struggles

For Japan, the deal did not go through due to trademark issues. We cannot register our trademark as someone in Japan has registered our trademark, and so we cannot award the franchise despite firm interest from a potential franchisee. After a few years, we managed to register our trademark in Japan with legal help and incurred costs.

Barcook Bakery

吧台料理
BARCOOK

Barcook Bakery Bangsar South outlet in Malaysia
Photo by Barcook Bakery

Barcook Bakery was started in 2008 as a small takeaway kiosk at Hong Lim Complex when two ex-colleagues came together with the same dream of making healthy, handcrafted buns and cakes available to all and with the same philosophy of uncompromising excellence through the finest, freshest ingredients.

All confectionery items are carefully handcrafted by a dedicated team of passionate and experienced chefs who are based on site. All the bread is made from fresh dough using their recipes and served warm all day – literally from the oven to the customers. The cakes are also baked from scratch in-house.

Voyages

2008 – first outlet in Singapore
2014 – Kuala Lumpur, Malaysia, with two outlets

Mr Sim, managing director of Barcook Bakery
Photo by Barcook Bakery

Success Factors

1. Brand acceptance

2. Right partner

3. Adaptation to suit the locals in foreign territories

Struggles

On venturing overseas, we started venturing overseas much earlier than 2014 with Vietnam in 2009. At that time, we failed as we were not very experienced, and our brand has not been properly developed. We also had consistent quality, and our management system was not developed, and thus, we failed.

Old School Delights

Old School Delights at the Esplanade Singapore
Photo by Old School Delights

At Old School Delights, customers will feel that they have stepped back in time to the days when they were still in school when things were much simpler. Step into the family-run cafe's tuck-shop-style interior for a taste of homely, authentic, home-cooked food such as nasi lemak that is prepared traditionally. Owners Olivia and her brother Aaron Teo started Old School Delights at Upper Thomson in 2010. Soon after, Olivia's husband, Koh Choon Chye, joined the business when Aaron decided to relocate to Western Australia.

It is a step-by-step progress, and only in 2017, when the Esplanade approached them, that OSD, as it is more commonly known, decided to venture into their second restaurant. It turned out to be a hit, and then they took another outlet at the Esplanade, and it was well received by the family crowd. Although it is a mall, it is a destination place, and the human traffic is not great. It is a step forward for the brand to go beyond the first outlet to open at Esplanade. It makes the company more aware of the need to standardise and make the processes more efficient.

Voyages

2010 – First outlet in Singapore
2017 – Opened the second outlet at Esplanade

Chye and Olivia, owners of Old School Delights
Photo by Old School Delights

Success Factors

1. Brand
2. Consistent quality
3. Joint-venture overseas partners

Struggles

Venturing overseas is risky, and we admire the success of others. If we have the right partner, it will be good; but with the wrong partner, it can be disastrous when we invest our capital.

The other alternative would be franchising. However, we cannot guarantee that the conviction of the overseas partners would be the same, and the food may vary drastically. To mitigate this, while we hope for conviction on the part of our overseas partners, we must place emphasis on processes and standard operating procedures (SOP) to ensure that quality.

Ponggol Nasi Lemak

PONGGOL
NASI LEMAK

Ponggol Nasi Lemak's outlet in Jakarta
Photo by Ponggol Nasi Lemak

Established in 1979, Ponggol Nasi Lemak is a heritage brand serving one of the most iconic foods in Singapore. Under the guidance of founders Mr Ang Chye Choon and Madam Koh Ah Tan, their family started delivering traditional pre-packed nasi lemak in banana leaves to the distributor and hawker stores in Singapore.

Today the brand consists of three speciality stores, namely, the Kovan outlet, the Tanjong Katong outlet, and the latest Jalan Besar flagship outlet. At its third and latest outlet at Jalan Besar, Ponggol has successfully combined its years of cooking experience with automated kitchen technology through tireless product research and innovation. The company is now able to scale their operations effortlessly and efficiently to realise its goal of franchising and overseas expansion very shortly. Ponggol Nasi Lemak seeks to create the best with their insatiable hunger for perfection.

Voyages

1979 – first outlet in Singapore
2020 – Jakarta, Indonesia

Mr Edmund Ang, third-generation owner of Ponggol Nasi Lemak and staff in Jakarta
Photo by Ponggol Nasi Lemak

Success Factors

1. Right overseas managing partner
2. Acceptance of food and business model
3. Readiness to go international

Struggles

Franchise regulations are challenges for us. We understand that, sometimes, the laws in other countries are not strong regarding intellectual property rights, and there is a certain amount of fear in running businesses in these countries.

That is the reason why we thought the best way is to have strong branding, and when you have that, it is a deterrent to switching brands. Would anyone want to switch brands, for example, from McDonald's to another brand? It is stupid to do that. The strategy for us is to build strong branding for Ponggol Nasi Lemak.

White Restaurant

WHITE
三巴旺白米粉

White Restaurant at Urban Hawker, New York, USA
Photo by White Restaurant

Originally prepared as a homely dish by founder Mr Tay King Huak, White Restaurant's signature Original Sembawang White Beehoon has since become a uniquely Singaporean dish well loved by both local and overseas gastronomes. The home-grown brand had humble beginnings in 1999, operating from a small hawker stall in Chong Pang Market before moving to Jalan Tampang in 2000 when the market closed. The immense popularity of their signature dish made customers refer to them fondly as the 'Sembawang White Beehoon Restaurant' instead of the official name of You Huak Restaurant.

As their brand's reputation grew, so did the number of outlets. In 2013, they officially rebranded as the White Restaurant we know today, having earned the revered reputation of the namesake dish.

Voyages

1999 – First outlet in Singapore
2022 – Eight outlets in Singapore
2022 – First overseas store in New York's Urban Hawker

Second-generation owner, Victor Tay
Photo by White Restaurant

Success Factors

1. Food and brand acceptance
2. Right partner
3. Marketing

Struggles

We have plans to expand overseas and have our struggles as venturing overseas is untried and untested; we have many questions and factors to consider, such as logistics and mode of market entry. As we are not planning to operate the overseas outlet[s] by ourselves, we are also considering the type of franchise model -– single, multi, or area franchise. Other questions will be how we send our food overseas, whether it is suitable for the locals and the host countries, and whether they have the disposable income to afford the desired pricing. Those hard questions need to be addressed before we rush into overseas expansion.

Rong Hua Bak Kut Teh

榮華 肉骨茶

Rong Hua Bak Kut Teh

Rong Hua Bak Kut Teh's Manila outlet
Photo by Rong Hua Bak Kut Teh

The originating roots of Rong Hua Bak Kut Teh can be traced back to the early years when their founding grandfather, Mr Chua Ah Hua, migrated to Singapore or Nanyang in search of a better life and fortune for his family. When Mr Chua arrived in Singapore, *bak kut teh* was already being served by the Teochews around Char Jung Tao (Clarke Quay).

In the early days, Ah Hua started work as a manual labourer, and he discovered that by consuming his favourite *bak kut teh* regularly in the morning, he found the energy boost he needed for his back-breaking work of unloading sacks of rice off the sampans. His interest in this dish soon led him to find pupillage as a kitchen apprentice at a well-known Teo Chew Bak Kut Teh stall owned by his village elder Uncle Rong.

As the years went by, the young Ah Hua grew in culinary skills and experience under the discipleship of Uncle Rong. What truly impressed Uncle Rong was the hard work and dedication displayed by Ah Hua in his personal goal to perfect the culinary art of *bak kut teh*. In Uncle Rong's own words, the highest level of culinary success is when *bak kut teh* becomes a dish prepared 'using your own heart and soul'. Before the late uncle Rong passed away, he named Ah Hua his successor; and together with the younger Ah Hua, they went on to develop their very own unique blend of popular pork ribs soup recipe, which eventually went on to be known as Rong Hua Bak Kut Teh.

Voyages

2014 – First outlet in Singapore
2019 – Manila, Philippines

Opening night at Rong Hua outlet in Manila
Photo by Rong Hua Bak Kut Teh

Success Factors

1. Committed overseas partner
2. Brand and products appealing to the host country
3. Adaptation to suit the locals while maintaining the core

Struggles

We must establish a good system and update our concept before we venture overseas. The system plays an important role, the system (logistics, processes, stocks, and ingredients); and without the system, everything will break down. The system must be in place before venturing overseas. Our concept must appeal to the locals, and adaptation is a must to interest them. These are challenges.

greendot

Photo by greendot

Greendot was founded with a single intention of making plant-based meals convenient, accessible and affordable. We pride ourselves in using wholesome and fresh ingredients to create healthy and memorable plant-based food.

At Greendot, we hold a common belief that everyone can make a positive difference to the world by consciously choosing what you eat. Beyond food that nourishes the mind and body, it also reflects the intrinsic qualities of the brand - Inspiring people to create a positive ripple impact that brings lasting good to themselves and to others.

Backed by over a decade of experience in serving delicious plant- based meals with a local spin, Greendot is a lifestyle F&B concept brand that truly embraces the "Green Transformation".

Green is all about green earth, green food, green lifestyle.

True to our brand ethos, Greendot creates positive and meaningful experiences beyond plant-based food. We empower people to renew their mind and embrace new habits, and help them to become kind to themselves and to others, creating a positive ripple effect.

Our Vision - Inspiring people to embrace a Green Lifestyle that brings lasting good to themselves, their loved ones and their community.

Our Mission – We want to seed and spread care, love and hope daily through our people food and services

Voyages

2011 – First outlet in Singapore
2022 – Thirteen outlets in Singapore including One Full Vegan Patisserie

Justin Chou, CEO of Glife Technologies, and Fu Yong Hong, CEO of Greendot
Photo by greendot

Success Factors

1. Brand acceptance and durability
2. Supply chain
3. Strong local partner

Struggles

Internally, the struggle is the availability of people that is key in venturing overseas. Do we have a team of four or five that we can send to the overseas outlets?

Even for franchising, we are trying to transfer not only our expertise and operations but also our culture, value, and vision of the brand. For overseas franchising, we are trying to do these transfers within two weeks of training, which is quite a challenge. For our local outlets, this is possible as the people are with me for half a year. So the alternative is to infuse our overseas outlets with our people and transfer the hard as well as the soft aspects of our business. So if I do not have the overseas-ready team, I do not want to expand overseas.

Roost

Roost's Singapore outlet at Resorts World Sentosa

Entrepreneur Alson Teo and the late chef Toh Tian Ser set to work on an innovative way to distil their passion for and expertise in making chicken rice in 2003. Paying equal attention to craftsmanship and industrialisation, the duo designed an automated process that ensures every carefully sourced ingredient is cooked to exacting perfection. In doing so, their chicken rice traditions can not only be preserved but also flourish in the future.

Their revolutionary efforts have culminated in Roost, which opened in 2016 with the first proof of concept, a convivial space where everyone can enjoy a taste of exceptional chicken rice. Alson went on to open its quick-service Roost restaurant in Resorts World Sentosa in 2019.

Thanks to the precision of iKook, their proprietary automated cooking system, and the use of thoughtfully sourced ingredients, Roost's chicken rice is unfailingly succulent, flavourful, and unmistakably authentic.

Voyages

2016 – First proof of concept outlet in Singapore
2019 – First quick-service Roost restaurant

Alson Teo, CEO Roost
Photo by Roost

Success Factors

1. Right partner
2. Profitable and meaningful growth of outlets
3. Quality and consistency to scale the business with proprietary iKook equipment, sauces, paste, and the robust SOP in place

Struggles

One of the key challenges of internationalisation is quality and consistency. We would be able to send paste overseas in a few forms, chilled or frozen; technically, that could be done, but the shipping costs will be very high. We need to be able to develop our paste and ship at ambient temperature so that the shipping costs will come down by three times at the same time and also ensure the product shelf life is longer. Once we can do that, we bought a passport to export to the world.

Saybons

Saybons Singapore
Photo by Saybons

Saybons is inspired by the French phrase *c'est bon*, which means 'it's good'. A common phrase used in the everyday French language, it can be used as a response to anything from the weather to the food. To make it easier for all to pronounce, they anglicised the phrase and added an *s* at the end so that they can trademark this name that they coined.

Saybons started back in 2007, when their founder, Daphane Loke, decided to pursue her dreams of being in the food industry. She started Saybons to make French food affordable and accessible to everyone. No more exorbitant 'ambience charges' nor three-hour course-after-course dinners. Using the freshest of food ingredients, classical French culinary techniques, and a collection of fresh insights, she packaged the goodness of French food into convenient takeaways, one that allows you to enjoy on the go, in your office, or the comfort of their cafes. They hope everyone in this time-pressed world can enjoy French goodness without fuss.

Voyages

2007 – First outlet in Singapore
2018 – Saybons' range of soups and ready-to-eat meals launched

Saybons sales and marketing director Ian Choo
Photo by Saybons

Success Factors

1. Food and brand acceptance
2. Right partner
3. Marketing

Struggles

Many countries, when it comes to food, are very protectionist, so the concern is to bring the ingredients and secret recipe overseas. It will be an advantage to have a trusted OEM factory in the host countries so that the quality of our food can be maintained.

Alternatively, it would be to have a big factory in Singapore or Malaysia and export our food at ambient temperature to overseas locations. My preference is the latter. We need to be targeted as we do not have many resources with where we are going.

SALADSTOP!

SALADSTOP! outlet at the Exchange Square, China Hong Kong
Photo by SALADSTOP!

SALADSTOP! came together with a shared dream – a more conscious way of eating that is truly GOOD.

SALADSTOP! was founded in 2009 to bring a new dimension to salads and a new approach to fast food.

We currently operate in Singapore, the Philippines, Hong Kong, Indonesia, Japan, Spain, Korea, and Vietnam. As we expand our footprint in the region, we remain committed to ending 'pre-made culture' and ensuring a more conscious way of eating. For us, every bowl that you enjoy is the result and catalyst of a positive cycle of change.

Voyage

2009 – First outlet in Singapore
2015 – Philippines
2015 – japan
2017 – Seoul, South Korea
2017 – Barcelona, Spain
2018 – China, Hong Kong
2018 – Jakarta, Indonesia
2018 – Ho Chi Minh City, Vietnam
2022 – Bangkok, Thailand
2023 – 14 outlets in Singapore

Adrien Desbaillets, CEO and Co-founder of SALADSTOP!

Success Factors

1. Right mix of overseas partners
2. Supply Chain
3. Suitable local adaptation

Struggle

The main challenge is to find the right partner whose key consideration may vary from country to country, the other challenge will be the supply chain. SALADSTOP! requires the freshest supply of ingredients. If the food chain is not developed and people do not trust food safety and we need to make sure that we could get at least the supply chain sorted out before we enter the country. Sometimes, if we cannot source directly from the supplier, we go to the farms directly and help them to sort out the supply chain. This is imperative before we start the business. We need to get the fundamentals right.

REFERENCES

Aaker, D. A. 1984. 'How to Select a Business Strategy'. *California Management Review*, 26(3), 167–175.

Aggarwal, R., Erel, I., Ferreira, M., and Matos, P. 2011. 'Does Governance Travel around the World? Evidence from Institutional Investors'. *Journal of Financial Economics*, 100(1), 154–181.

Aliouche, E. H., and Schlentrich, U. A. 2011. 'Towards a Strategic Model of Global Franchise Expansion'. *Journal of Retailing*, 87(3), 345–365.

Alon, I. 2000. 'The Organizational Determinants of Master International Franchising'. *Journal of Business and Entrepreneurship*, 12(2), 1–18.

—— 2006. 'Key Success Factors of Franchising Systems in the Retailing Sector'. *International Journal of Emerging Markets*, 1(1), 9–20.

—— and Mckee, D. L. 1999. 'The Internationalization of Professional Business Service Franchises'. *Journal of Consumer Marketing*, 16(1), 74–85.

—— Apriliyanti, I. D., and Parodi, M. C. H. 2020. 'A Systematic Review of International Franchising'. *Multinational Business Review*, 29(1), 43–69.

Alonso, D. A., and Kok, S. K. 2020. 'Understanding Critical Success Factors and Perceived Future among Micro and Small Firms through Entrepreneurial Action Theory'. *European Business Review*, 33 (2), 383–406.

Altinay, L., and Altinay, M. 2003. 'How Will Growth Be Financed by the International Hotel Companies?' *Journal of Contemporary Hospitality Management.* 15(5), 274–282.

Altheide, D. L., and Johnson, J. M. 1994. 'Criteria for Assessing Interpretive Validity in Qualitative Research,' in N. K. Denzin and Y. S. Lincoln (eds.), *Handbook of Qualitative Research.* Sage Publications: Thousand Oak, CA, 485–499.

Antonowicz, A. 2011. 'The Dissemination of Franchising All over the World: An Attempt to Assess the Scale of the Phenomenon'. *Problems of Management in the Twenty-First Century*, 2, 8.

Anderson, R. D. 1983. 'A Consolidation and Appraisal of Science Meta-Analyses'. *Journal of Research in Science Teaching*, 20, 497–509.

Andersson, S., Evers, N., and Gliga, G. 2018. 'Entrepreneurial Marketing and Born Global Internationalisation in China'. *Qualitative Market Research*, 21(2), 202–231.

Antoncic, B., and Hisrich, R. D. 2000. 'Intrapreneurship Modelling in Transition Economies: A Comparison of Slovenia and the United States'. *Journal of Developmental Entrepreneurship,* 5(1), 21–40.

Barney, J. 1991. 'Firm Resources and Sustained Competitive Advantage'. *Journal of Management*, 17(1), 99–120.

Beamish, P. W., and Banks, J. C. 1987. 'Equity Joint Ventures and the Theory of the Multinational Enterprise'. *Journal of International Business Studies*, 18(2), 1–16.

Bhasin, N., and Paul, J. 2016. 'Exports and Outward FDI: Are They Complements or Substitutes? Evidence from Asia'. *Multinational Business Review*, 24(1), 62–78.

Bose, T. K. 2016. 'Critical Success Factors of SME Internationalization'. *Journal of Small Business Strategy*, 26(2), 87–109.

Bowen, R. 2017. The Internationalisation of Food and Drink SMEs: Towards a Recipe for Success'. Unpublished Doctoral Thesis, Aberystwyth University.

—— 2019. 'Motives to SME Internationalisation'. *Cross-Cultural and Strategic Management*, 27(1), 51–74.

Bradford, H., Guzmán, A., and Trujillo, M. A. 2017. 'Determinants of Successful Internationalisation Processes in Business Schools'. *Journal of Higher Education Policy and Management*, 39(4), 435–452.

Brickley, J. A., and Dark, F. H. 1987. 'The Choice of Organizational Form: The Case of Franchising'. *Journal of Financial Economics*, 18(2), 401–420.

Brochado, A., Lobo, C. A., Pacheco, L. M., and Maldonado, I. 2020. 'Drivers of and Barriers to the SME Internationalisation Process in a Small Open Economy'. *Economics Bulletin*, 40(4), 2932–2942.

Brodzicki, T. 2017. 'Internationalisation and Innovation Intensities of Polish Manufacturing Firms: A Close Nexus?' *Entrepreneurial Business and Economics Review*, 5(1), 91–109.

Brotherton, B., and Shaw, J. 1996. 'Towards an Identification and Classification of Critical Success Factors in UK Hotels'. *International Journal of Hospitality Management*, 15(2), 113–115.

Brown, E. 2018. 'The Definition of an Advisor: Comprehending the Mission to Advise Foreign Security Forces'. *Small Wars Journal.*

Burton, F., and Cross, A. R. 1997. 'International Franchising: Market versus Hierarchy. Internationalisation Strategies'. *Academy of International Business (UKI) Series*, 135–152.

——— and Rhodes, M. 2000. Foreign Market Servicing Strategies of UK Franchisors: An Empirical Enquiry from a Transactions Cost Perspective. *Management International Review*, 40(4), 373–400.

Buzavaite, M., and Korsakiene, R. 2019. 'Human Capital and the Internationalisation of SMEs: A Systemic Literature Review'. *Entrepreneurial Business and Economics Review*, 7(3), 125–142.

Cahen, F. R., Jr, M. D. M. O., and Borini, F. M. 2017. 'The Internationalisation of New Technology-Based Firms from Emerging Markets'. *International Journal of Technology Management*, 74(1–4), 23–44.

Campbell, D., Datar, S. M., and Sandino, T. 2009. 'Organizational Design and Control across Multiple Markets: The Case of Franchising in the Convenience Store Industry'. *The Accounting Review*, 84(6), 1749–1779.

Casson, M. 2018. *The Multinational Enterprise: Theory and History.* Edward Elgar Publishing: Camberley, UK.

Cavusgil, S. T. 1994. 'A Quiet Revolution in Australian Exporters'. *Marketing News,* 28(11), 18–21.

Chaplin, L. 2017. 'Is Continuous Improvement Taking Place in Franchise Operations? An Exploratory Study'. Working Paper, School of Marketing and Management, Coventry University.

Chiang, J., and Chathoth, P. K. 2013. 'International Expansion Strategy of Foodservice Firms: An Exploratory Study'. *Journal of Hospitality Marketing and Management*, 22(2), 204–228.

Choo, S. 2001. 'Critical Success Factors of International Franchising: Case Studies of Foreign Franchisors in Asia'. Unpublished Master of Commerce Thesis, School of Management, Curtin University of Technology.

—— 2003. 'Determining the Critical Success Factors of International Franchising: Cases of Foreign Franchisors in East Asia'. Working Paper, School of Management, Curtin University of Technology.

—— 2005. 'Determinants of Monitoring Capabilities in International Franchising: Foodservice Firms within East Asia'. *Asia Pacific Journal of Management*, 22(2), 159–177.

—— Mazzarol, T., and Soutar, G. 2007. 'The Selection of International Retail Franchisees in East Asia'. *Asia Pacific Journal of Marketing and Logistics*, 19(4), 380–397.

Christmann, H. 2019. 'Exploring the Role of the Entrepreneur in Retail SME Internationalisation: An Analysis of Retail Cases in North-Western Europe'. Doctoral Thesis, University of Surrey.

Cicic, M., Patterson, P. G., and Shoham, A. 1999. A Conceptual Model of the Internationalization of Services Firms. *Journal of Global Marketing*, 12(3), 81–106.

Coelen, R. J. 2009. 'Ranking and the Measurement of Success in Internationalisation: Are They Related? Measuring Success in the Internationalisation of Higher Education'. *EAIE Occasional Paper*, 22, 39–48.

Combs, J.G., and Castrogiovanni, G. J. 1993. 'Franchising Strategy: A proposed Model and Empirical Test of Franchise versus Company Ownership'. *Academy of Management Proceedings*, 1, 7–11.

—— —— 2004. 'Franchising: A Review and Avenues to Greater Theoretical Diversity'. *Journal of Management*, 30(6), 907–931.

—— and Strauss, A. 1990. 'Grounded Theory Research: Procedures, Canons, and Evaluative Criteria. *Qualitative Sociology*, 13(1), 3–21.

Cortellazzo, L., Bonesso, S., and Gerli, F. 2020. 'Entrepreneurs' Behavioural Competencies for Internationalisation'. *International Journal of Entrepreneurial Behavior and Research* 26(4), 723–747.

Creswell, J. W., Hanson, W. E., Clark Plano, V. L., and Morales, A. 2007. 'Qualitative Research Designs: Selection and Implementation'. *The Counseling Psychologist*, 35(2), 236–264.

Crick, J. M., Crick, D., and Chaudhry, S. 2020. 'Entrepreneurial Marketing Decision-Making in Rapidly Internationalising and De-Internationalising Start-Up Firms'. *Journal of Business Research*, 113, 158–167.

Cristiano, E. 2018. 'Internationalisation and Corporate Governance in Family Businesses: A Case Study'. *International Journal of Business Performance Management*, 19(1), 75–86.

Dant, R. P. 2008. 'A Futuristic Research Agenda for the Field of Franchising'. *Journal of Small Business Management*, 46(1), 91–98.

—— Weaven, S. K., Baker, B. L., and Jeon, H. J. J. 2013. 'An Introspective Examination of Single-Unit versus Multi-Unit Franchisees'. *Journal of the Academy of Marketing Science*, 41(4), 473–496.

Dar, I. A. 2019. 'Internationalisation of SMEs: How Does Global Mindset and Network Relationships Impact in India'. *International Journal of Business and Globalisation*, 23(4), 568–581.

Demir, R., Campopiano, G., Kruckenhauser, C., and Bauer, F. 2021. 'Strategic Agility, International Speed and International Success: The Role of Coordination Mechanisms and Growth Modes'. *Journal of International Management*, 27(1), 100838.

Demirbag, M., Tatoglu, E., and Glaister, K.W. 2009. Equity-Based Entry Modes of emerging Country Multinationals: Lessons from Turkey'. *Journal of World Business*, 44(4), 445–462.

Doherty, A. M., and Quinn, B. 1999. International Retail Franchising: Evidence from Theory and Practice'. *International Journal of Retail and Distribution*, 27(6), 354–372.

Dubé, F. N., Haijuan, Y., and Lijun, H. 2016. 'Halal Certification System as a Key Determinant of Firm Internationalisation in the Philippines and Malaysia'. *Asian Academy of Management Journal*, 21(1), 73.

Edwards, J. S. 2013. 'The Foodservice Industry: Eating Out Is More than Just a Meal'. *Food Quality and Preference*, 27(2), 223–229.

Eisenhardt, K. M. 1989. Building Theories from Case Study Research. *Academy of Management Review*, 14(4), 532–550.

Fayaz, A., Kamal, Y., Amin, S., and Khan, S. 2017. 'Critical Success Factors in Information Technology Projects'. *Management Science Letters*, 7(2), 73–80.

Felzensztein, C., Crick, D., Gonzalez-Perez, M. A., Jurado, T., and Etchebarne Lopez, M. S. 2020. 'Capabilities and the Internationalisation of Smaller-Sized, Service-Oriented Firms in the Southern Hemisphere'. *Journal of Strategic Marketing*, https://doi.org/10.1080/0965254X.2020.1815235.

Fladmoe-Lindquist, K. 1996. 'International Franchising: Capabilities and Development'. *Journal of Business Venturing*, 11(5), 419–438.

Fletcher, M., and Harris, S. 2012. 'Knowledge Acquisition for the Internationalization of the Smaller Firm: Content and Sources'. *International Business Review*, 21(4), 631–647.

Frazer, L., and Merrilees, B. 2005.' Brand Piracy by Franchisees'. Working Paper, Griffith University.

——— 2012. 'Pioneering Asian Franchise Brands: Pho24 in Vietnam'. *Journal of Marketing Channels*, 19(4), 295–309.

—— —— and Bodey, K. 2007. 'Franchisors Do Their Homework before Entering International Markets: Experiences from the Australian Franchising Sector'. *International Entrepreneurship and Management Journal*, 3(4), 437–452.

—— and Weaven, S. 2003. 'Franchising', in J. McColl-Kennedy, (eds.), *Service Marketing*. Wiley, Brisbane, Australia, 418–441.

Gahan, C., Hannibal, C. G. M., and Hannibal, M. M. 1998. *Doing Qualitative Research Using QSR NUD* IST*, Sage Publishing: London, UK.

Galloway, N., Numajiri, T., and Rees, N. 2020. 'The "Internationalisation", or "Englishisation", of Higher Education in East Asia'. *Higher Education*, 80(3), 395–414.

Gao, Y. 2018. 'A Set of Indicators for Measuring and comparing University Internationalisation Performance across National Boundaries'. *Higher Education*, 76(2), 317–336.

Gerschewski, S., Evers, N., Nguyen, A. T., and Froese, F. J. 2020. 'Trade Shows and SME Internationalisation: Networking for Performance'. *Management International Review*, 60, 573–595.

Ghantous, N., and Das, S. S. 2018. 'International Franchising and Performance: A Resource-Based Perspective. *International Journal of Retail and Distribution Management*, 46(8), 744–763.

Ghemawat, P. 2001. 'Distance Still Matters'. *Harvard Business Review*, 79(5), 137–147.

—— 2007. 'Distance Still Matters'. *Harvard Business Review*, 85(3), 58–68.

Gillis, W. E., Combs, J. G., and Yin, X. 2020. 'Franchise Management Capabilities and Franchisor Performance under Alternative Franchise Ownership Strategies'. *Journal of Business Venturing*, 35(1), 1–20.

Gikonyo, L., Berndt, A., and Wadawi, J. 2015. 'Critical Success Factors for Franchised Restaurants Entering the Kenyan Market: Franchisors' Perspective'. *SAGE Open*, 5(4), 1–8.

Giles, L. 2013. *Sun Tzu on the Art of War*. Globusz Publishing: New York, NY.

Glaser, B. G., and Strauss, A. L. 2017. *Discovery of Grounded Theory: Strategies for Qualitative Research*. Routledge: New York, NY.

Goxe, F., and Belhoste, N. 2019. 'Be Global or Be Gone: Global Mindset as a Source of Division in an International Business Community'. *European Management Review*, 16(6), 617–632.

Graves, C., and Thomas, J. 2006. 'Internationalization of Australian Family Businesses: A Managerial Capabilities Perspective'. *Family Business Review*, 19(3), 207–224.

Grünhagen, M., and Mittelstaedt, R. A. 2005. 'Entrepreneurs or Investors: Do Multi-Unit Franchisees Have Different Philosophical Orientations? *Journal of Small Business Management*, 43(3), 207–225.

Gruenhagen, J. H., Sawang, S., Gordon, S. R., and Davidsson, P. 2018. 'International Experience, Growth Aspirations, and the Internationalisation of New Ventures'. *Journal of International Entrepreneurship*, 16(3), 421–440.

Harris, S. G., and Sutton, R. I. 1986. 'Functions of Parting Ceremonies in Dying Organizations'. *Academy of Management Journal*, 29(1), 5–30.

Haverland, M., and Blatter, J. 2012. 'Two or Three Approaches to Explanatory Case Study Research'. American Political Science Association, Annual Meeting Paper.

Hennart, J.-F. 2007. 'The Theoretical Rationale for a Multinationality-Performance Relationship'. *Management International Review*, 47(3), 423–452.

Hinson, R. E., Osabutey, E., Kosiba, J. P., and Asiedu, F. O. 2020. 'Internationalisation and Branding Strategy. Qualitative Market Research: An International Journal'. *Qualitative Market Research*, 23(4), 747–766.

Hollender, L., Zapku, F. B., and Schwens, C. 2017. 'SME Foreign Market Entry Mode Choice and Foreign Venture Performance: The Moderating Effect of International Experience and Product Adaptation'. *International Business Review*, 26(2), 250–263.

Huberman, A. M., and Miles, M. B. 1994. *Data Management and Analysis Methods*. Sage Publications: London, UK.

Hussain, D., Grünhagen, M., Panda, S., and Hossain, M. I. 2020. 'Franchising in South Asia: Past, Present, and Future Developments'. *Journal of Marketing Channels*, 26(4), 1–23.

Huszagh, S. M., Huszagh, F. W., and Mcintyre, F. S. 1992. 'International Franchising in the Context of Competitive Strategy and the Theory of the Firm'. *International Marketing Review*, 9(5), 5.

Hutchison, A. J., Johnston, L. H., and Breckon, J. D. 2010. 'Using QSR-NVivo to Facilitate the Development of a Grounded Theory Project: An Account of a Worked Example'. *International Journal of Social Research Methodology*, 13(4), 283–302.

Ibeh, K. I. 2003. 'Toward a Contingency Framework of Export Entrepreneurship: Conceptualisations and Empirical Evidence'. *Small Business Economics*, 20(1), 49–68.

Idris, B., and Saridakis, G. 2018. Local Formal Interpersonal Networks and SME Internationalisation: Empirical Evidence from the UK'. *International Business Review*, 27(3), 610–624.

Igwe, P. A., and Kanyembo, F. 2019. 'The Cage around Internationalisation of SMEs and the Role of Government', in M. Y. Haddoud, P. Jones, and A.-K.E. Onjewu (eds.), *International Entrepreneurship in Emerging Markets: Nature, Drivers, Barriers and Determinants* (*Contemporary Issues in Entrepreneurship Research*, vol. 10), Emerald Publishing Limited: Bingley, UK, 161–176.

Jang, S. S., and Park, K. 2019. 'A Sustainable Franchisor-Franchisee Relationship Model: Toward the Franchise Win-Win Theory'. *International Journal of Hospitality Management*, 76 (part B), 13–24.

Javalgi, R. G., Griffith, D. A., White, S., and Barbara, S. 2003. 'An Empirical Examination of Factors Influencing the Internationalisation of Service Firms'. *Journal of Service Marketing*, 17(2), 185–201.

Javidan, M., and Walker, J. L. 2019. 'A Whole New Global Mindset for Leadership'. *People and Strategy*, 35(2), 37–41.

Jin, X. 2017. 'Challenges Facing Leadership of Australian Universities for Partnership-Driven Internationalisation with Chinese Universities: Rhetoric, Realities and Implications'. Unpublished PhD Thesis, School of Education, Western Sydney University.

Johanson, J., and Vahlne, J.-E. 2003. 'The Internationalisation Process of the Firm – A Model of Knowledge Development and Increasing Foreign Market Commitments'. *International Business*.

———— 2009. 'The Uppsala Internationalization Process Model Revisited: From Liability of Foreignness to Liability of Outsidership'. *Journal of International Business Studies*, 40(9), 1411–1431.

Jones, M., and Diment, K. 2010. 'The CAQDA Paradox: A Divergence between Research Method and Analytical Tool'. Working Paper, Faculty of Commerce, University of Wollongong.

Justis, R. T. and Judd, R. J. 2003, *Franchising* (3rd ed.). Thomson Custom Publishing: Stamford, CT.

King, C., Grace, D., and Weaven, S. 2013. 'Developing Brand Champions: A Franchisee Perspective'. *Journal of Marketing Management*, 29(11–12), 1308–1336.

Kirschling, K. M. 2019. *How Franchise Terms Impeded Private Subway Construction in New York City: Comparison with Concession Agreements for Early Subterranean Transit in Great Britain.* Kyle Mark Kirschling, 1–13.

Klein, B. 1995. 'The Economics of Franchise Contracts'. *Journal of Corporate Finance*, 2(1–2), 9–37.

Knight, G. A., and Cavusgil, S. T. 1996. 'The Born Global Firm: A Challenge to Traditional Internationalization Theory'. *Advances in International Marketing*, 8, 11–26.

—— and Liesch, P. W. 2016. 'Internationalization: From Incremental to Born Global'. *Journal of World Business*, 51(1), 93–102.

Kong, L. 2018. 'Emerging Market Small and Medium Enterprises Internationalisation: A Meta-Analysis'. Unpublished Doctoral Dissertation, Auckland University of Technology.

Korsakienė, R., Bekešienė, S., and Hošková-Mayerová, Š. 2019. 'The Effects of Entrepreneurs' Characteristics on Internationalisation of Gazelle Firms: A Case of Lithuania'. *Economic Research-Ekonomska istraživanja*, 32(1), 2864–2881.

Kotler, P., and Gertner, D. 2002. 'Country as Brand, Product, and Beyond: A Place Marketing and Brand Management Perspective'. *Journal of Brand Management*, 9(4), 249–261.

Kruesi, M., Kim, P. B., and Hemmington, N. 2017. 'Evaluating Foreign Market Entry Mode Theories from a Hotel Industry Perspective'. *International Journal of Hospitality Management*, 62, 88–100.

Kyvik, O. 2011. 'The Internationalisation of Small Firms: The Importance of a Global Mindset'. *International Journal of Technology Transfer and Commercialisation*, 10 (3–4), 1–18.

Lafontaine, F., and Shaw, K. L. 1999. 'The Dynamics of Franchise Contracting: Evidence from Panel Data'. *Journal of Political Economy*, 107(5), 1041–1080.

Lee, C., Hallak, R., and Sardeshmukh, S. R. 2016. 'Drivers of Success in Independent Restaurants: A Study of the Australian Restaurant Sector'. *Journal of Hospitality and Tourism Management*, 29, 99–111.

Lee, J. E., and Lee, S. S. 2021. Effects of Fairness on Relationship Quality and Re-Contract Intentions in Food Service Franchise System: Comparison between Global and Domestic Franchise. *Management Research Review*, 44(3), 509–532.

Lewins, A., and Silver, C. 2007. *Using Software in Qualitative Analysis: A Step-by-Step Guide*. Sage Publications, Thousand Oaks, CA.

Lin, F.-J., and Ho, C.-W. 2019. 'The Knowledge of Entry Mode Decision for Small and Medium Enterprises'. *Journal of Innovation and Knowledge*, 4(1), 32–37.

Liu, Y. 2017. 'Born Global Firms' Growth and Collaborative Entry Mode: The Role of Transnational Entrepreneurs'. *International Marketing Review*, 34(1), 46–67.

Lo, T. Y. J., and Pan, S. 2020. 'The Internationalisation of China's Higher Education: Soft Power with "Chinese Characteristics"'. *Comparative Education*, 57(2), 227–246.

Luoma-Aho, V., Virolainen, M., Lievonen, M., and Halff, G. 2018. *Brand Hijack: Why Campaigns and Hashtags Are Taken over by Audiences*. Communication Case Studies, Lexington Books, 57–68.

Maček, A., Kros, J., and Bobek, V. 2019. 'International Franchising in the Fashion Industry from the Franchisor's Perspective'. *Journal for International Business and Entrepreneurship Development*, 12(1), 49–66.

Madanoglu, M., Alon, I., and Shoham, A. 2017. 'Push and Pull Factors in International Franchising'. *International Marketing Review*, 34 (1), 29–45.

Madsen, T. K., and Servais, P. 1997. 'The Internationalization of Born Globals: An Evolutionary Process?'. *International Business Review*, 6(6), 561–583.

—— 2013. Early and Rapidly Internationalizing Ventures: Similarities and Differences between Classifications Based on the Original International New Venture and Born Global Literature'. *Journal of International Entrepreneurship* 11(1), 65–79.

Mahizhnan, A. 1994. Developing Singapore's External Economy. *Southeast Asian Affairs*, 21(1), 285–301.

Marshall, C., and Rossman, G. B. 2014. *Designing Qualitative Research*, Sage Publications: Thousand Oaks, CA.

Mazzarol, T., and Choo, S. 2003. 'A Study of the Factors Influencing the Operating Location Decisions of Small Firms'. *Property Management*, 21(2), 190–208.

—— Soutar, G. N., and Thein, V. 2001. 'Critical Success Factors in the Marketing of an Educational Institution: A Comparison of Institutional and Student Perspectives'. *Journal of Marketing for Higher Education*, 10(2), 39–57.

McKinsey & Co. 1993. *Emerging Exporters. Australia's High Value-Added Manufacturing Exporters*, Melbourne: McKinsey & Company and the Australian Manufacturing Council.

Merrilees, B. 2014. 'International Franchising: Evolution of Theory and Practice'. *Journal of Marketing Channels*, 21(3), 133–142.

—— and Frazer, L. 2006. 'International Franchising Success Factors: Front End Risk Management'. Working Paper, Griffith Business School and Services Industries Research Centre.

Michael, S. C., and Combs, J. G. 2008. 'Entrepreneurial Failure: The Case of Franchisees'. *Journal of Small Business Management*, 46(1), 73–90.

Miles, M. B., and Huberman, A. M. 1994. *Qualitative Data Analysis: An Expanded Sourcebook.* Sage Publishing: London, UK.

Moen, O. 2002. 'The Born Globals: A New Generation of Small European Exporters'. *International Marketing Review* 19(2), 156–175

Moeuf, A., Lamouri, S., Pellerin, R., Tamayo-Giraldo, S., Tobon-Valencia, E., and Eburdy, R. 2020. 'Identification of Critical Success Factors, Risks and Opportunities of Industry 4.0 in SMEs'. *International Journal of Production Research*, 58(5), 1384–1400.

Morais, F., and Ferreira, J. J. 2020. 'SME Internationalisation Process: Key Issues and Contributions, Existing Gaps and the Future Research Agenda'. *European Management Journal*, 38(1), 62–77.

Nhan, T. T., and Le, K. A. T. 2019. 'Internationalisation of Higher Education in Vietnam', in C. Nguyen and M. Shah (eds.), *Quality Assurance in Vietnamese Higher Education.* Palgrave Macmillan: Cham, Switzerland, 1–23.

Oliveira, S. M. 2017. 'Partner Selection in International Joint Ventures: A Framework for the Analysis of Factors Relevant to the Selection of Partners'. *The Marketing Review*, 17(2), 199–215.

Ooi, S. M., and Richardson, C. 2019. 'The Internationalisation of Service-Sector SMEs in an Emerging Market'. *Review of International Business and Strategy*, 21(1), 44–60.

Oviatt, B. M., and McDougall, P. P. 2005. 'Toward a Theory of International New Ventures'. *Journal of International Business Studies*, 36, 29–41.

Oxenfeldt, A. R., and Kelly, A. O. 1969. 'Will Successful Franchise Systems Ultimately Become Wholly Owned Chains'. *Journal of Retailing*, 44(4), 69–83.

Parkhe, A. 1993. '"Messy" Research, Methodological Predispositions, and Theory Development in International Joint Ventures'. *Academy of Management Review*, 18(2), 227–268.

Park, K., and Jang, S. 2018. 'Is Franchising an Additional Financing Source for Franchisors?'. *Tourism Economics*, 24 (5), 541–559.

Paswan, A. K., and Wittmann, C. M. 2009. 'Knowledge Management and Franchise Systems'. *Industrial Marketing Management*, 38(2), 173–180.

Patton, M. Q. 2002. 'Two Decades of Developments in Qualitative Inquiry: A Personal, Experiential Perspective'. *Qualitative Social Work*, 1(3), 261–283.

Paul, J., and Dikova, D. 2016. 'The Internationalization of Asian Firms: An Overview and Research Agenda'. *Journal of East-West Business*, 22(4), 237–241.

Pfoser, S., Treiblmaier, H., and Schauer, O. 2016. 'Critical Success Factors of Synchromodality: Results from a Case Study and Literature Review'. *Transportation Research Procedia*, 14, 1463–1471.

Pham, V. Q., Nguyen, B. K. Q., and Le, T. Q. 2020. 'Success Factors Affecting Internationalization Process of Large Vietnamese Companies: A Conceptual Framework'. *Journal of Asian Finance, Economics, and Business*, 7(11), 905–913.

Phin, P. 2020. 'Achieving Institutional Isomorphism in International Franchising through Knowledge Transfer: Evidence from the Food and Beverage Industry in Cambodia. Doctoral Dissertation, ResearchSpace@Auckland.

Pinfield, L. T. 1986. 'A Field Evaluation of Perspectives on Organizational Decision Making'. *Administrative Science Quarterly*, 31(3), 365–388.

Preble, J. 1995. Franchising Systems around the Globe: A Status Report'. *Journal of Small Business Management*, 33(2), 80–88.

Ranker, G., Huang, D., and McLeod, M. 2014. 'Navigating the U.S. and Chinese business Cultures Using Global Mindset Leadership'. *Leader to Leader*, 75, 23–30.

Rask, M. 2014. 'Internationalization through Business Model Innovation: In Search of Relevant Design Dimensions and Elements'. *Journal of International Entrepreneurship*, 12(2), 146–161.

Rasmussen, E. S., and Madsen, T. K. 2002. 'The Born Global Concept'. Conference paper, 28th EIBA Conference, Athens, Greece.

Rhou, Y., Li, Y., and Singal, M. 2019. 'Does Managerial Ownership Affect Franchising in the Restaurant Companies?'. *International Journal of Hospitality Management*, 78, 122–130.

Ridha, R., and Hidayat, N. K. 2020. 'Impact of Innovation and Certification to SME Performance in the F&B Sector'. EasyChair Preprint.

Rienda, L., Claver, E., and Andreu, R. 2020. 'Family Involvement, Internationalisation and Performance: An Empirical Study of the Spanish Hotel Industry'. *Journal of Hospitality and Tourism Management*, 42, 173–180.

Robson, M. J., Kadile, V., Watson, K., and Clegg, L. J. 2018. 'International Franchising Relationships', in L. Leonidou, C. Katsikeas, S. Samiee, and B. Aykol (eds.), *Advances in Global Marketing*, Springer: Cham, Switzerland, 427–446.

Rockart, J. F. 1979. 'Chief Executives Define Their Own Data Needs'. *Harvard Business Review*, 57(2), 81–93.

Rosado-Serrano, A., and Paul, J. 2018. 'A New Conceptual Model for International Franchising'. *International Journal of Hospitality Management*, 75, 179–188.

Rugman, A. M., and Verbeke, A. 'A Perspective of Regional and Global Strategies of Multinational Enterprises'. *Journal of International Business Studies*. 35(1), 3–18.

Ruzzier, M., Antončič, B., and Konečnik, M. 2006. 'The Resource-Based Approach to the Internationalisation of SMEs: Differences in Resource Bundles between Internationalised and Non-Internationalised Companies'. *Zagreb International Review of Economics and Business*, 9(2), 95–116.

Sanghavi, N. 1998. 'Franchising as a Tool for Small Medium-Sized Enterprises (SME) Development in Transitional Economies-The Case of Central European Countries'. *Management Research News*, 21(11), 35–44.

Saraogi, A. 2009. 'Exploring Franchisor Franchisee Relationship: Building a Predictive Model of Franchisee Performance'. *Vision,* 13(1), 31–58.

Sasha, F., Charabsarn, A., Ahmad, N. H., and Mohaidin, Z. 'Driving Food and Beverage SMEs Innovation'. *Advances in Economics, Business and Management Research*, 141, 17–19.

Seige, L. C., and Weers, L. K. 2020. 'One-Click Internationalisation through E-Commerce Marketplaces? A Qualitative Study of the Key Capabilities for SMEs'. Unpublished Master's Thesis, Lund University.

Sen, K. C. 1998. 'The Use of Franchising as a Growth Strategy by US Restaurant Franchisors'. *Journal of Consumer Marketing*, 15(4), 397–407.

Shane, S. A. 1996. 'Why Franchise Companies Expand Overseas'. *Journal of Business Venturing*, 11(2), 73–88.

—— and Spell, C. 1998. 'Agency Costs, Search Costs, Transaction Costs, Managerial Limits to Firm Growth and New Franchisor Survival 1984–1994'. Conference paper, Society of Franchising Conference.

Shih, T.-Y. 2017. 'An Empirical Study of Food and Beverage Chains' Internationalisation: Advancing Intangible Resource Theory and Research'. *European Journal of International Management*, 11(6), 660–687.

Shockley, J., and Turner, T. 2016. 'A Relational Performance Model for Developing Innovation and Long-Term Orientation in Retail Franchise Organizations'. *Journal of Retailing and Consumer Services*, 32, 175–188.

Silverman, D. 2016. *Qualitative Research.* Sage Publications: Thousand Oaks, CA.

Smith, A.E., and Humphrey, M. S. 2006. 'Evaluation of Unsupervised Semantic Mapping of Natural Language with Leximancer Concept Mapping'. *Behavior Research Methods*, 38(2), 262–279.

Sotiriadou, P., Brouwers, J., and Le, T.-A. 2014. 'Choosing a Qualitative Data Analysis Tool: A Comparison of NVivo and Leximancer'. *Annals of Leisure Research*, 17(2), 218–234.

Steinberg, P., and Lescatre, G. 2004. 'Beguiling Heresy: Regulating the Franchise Relationship'. *Dickson Law Review*, 109(1), 101–353.

Sun, K.-A., Park, S., and He, Z. 2019. 'Effect of Franchising on Restaurant Firms' Risk Evaluations in the Bond Market'. *International Journal of Hospitality Management*, 83, 19–27.

Teramae, F., Makino, T., Lim, Y., Sengoku, S., and Kodama, K. 2019. 'International Strategy for Sustainable Growth in Multinational Pharmaceutical Companies. *Sustainability*, 12(3), 867.

Torkkeli, L., Nummela, N., and Saarenketo, S. 2018. 'A Global Mindset; Still a Prerequisite for Successful SME Internationalisation?', in N. Dominguez and U. Mayrhofer (eds.), *Key Success Factors of SME Internationalisation: A Cross-Country Perspective*. Emerald Publishing Limited: Bingley, UK.

Tran, L. T., and Marginson, S. 2018. 'Internationalisation of Vietnamese Higher Education: An Overview', in L. T. Tran and S. Marginson (eds.), *Internationalisation in Vietnamese Higher Education*. Springer: New York, NY.

Uzhegova, D., and Baik, C. 2020. 'Internationalisation of Higher Education in an Uneven World: An Integrated Approach to Internationalisation of Universities in the Academic Periphery'. *Studies in Higher Education*, https://doi.org/10.1080/03075079.2020.1811220.

Virglerova, Z., Kliestik, T., Rowland, Z., and Rozsa, Z. 2020. 'Barriers to Internationalisation of SMEs in Visegrad Group Countries'. *Transformations in Business and Economics*, 19(3), 58–73.

Wach, K. 2017. 'Exploring the Role of Ownership in International Entrepreneurship: How Does Ownership Affect Internationalisation of Polish Firms?' *Entrepreneurial Business and Economics Review*, 5(4), 205–224.

Wang, Y., Sung, M.-C., and Vong, K.-I. P. 2019. 'The Foreign Moon Is Fuller: Chinese Academics' Perception of Internationalisation'. *Compare: A Journal of Comparative and International Education*, 50(6), 1–17.

Wang, Z. J., Zhu, M., and Terry, A. 2008. 'The Development of Franchising in China'. *Journal of Marketing Channels*, 15(2–3), 167–184.

Welch, L. S., and Luostarinen, R. 1988. 'Internationalization: Evolution of a Concept'. *Journal of General Management*, 14(2), 34–55.

Weaven, S., and Frazer, L. 2007. 'Mature Franchise Systems Use Multiple Unit Franchising to Leverage Learning Economies and Sustain Systemwide Growth'. *Asia Pacific Journal of Marketing and Logistics*, 25 (2), 173–205.

Whyte, W. F. 1955. *The Street Corner Society*. University of Chicago Press: Chicago, IL.

Wilk, V., Soutar, G. N., and Harrigan, P. 2019. 'Tackling Social Media Data Analysis: Comparing and Contrasting QSR NVivo and Leximancer'. *Qualitative Market Research*, 22(2), 94–113.

Wong, H. Y., and Merrilees, B. 2008. 'The Performance Benefits of Being Brand-Orientated'. *Journal of Product and Brand Management*, 17(6), 372–383.

Yaprak, A. 1985. 'An Empirical Study of the Differences between Small Exporting and Non-Exporting US Firms. *International Marketing Review* 2(2), 72–83.

Yin, R., 1994. 'Evaluation: A Singular Craft'. *New Directions for Program Evaluation*, 61, 71–84.

—— 2003. *Case Study Research: Design and Methods*. Sage Publications: Thousand Oaks, CA.

Zhang, Z. 2017. 'English-Medium Instruction Policies in China: Internationalisation of Higher Education'. *Journal of Multilingual and Multicultural Development*, 39(6), 542–555.

APPENDIX 1

Online News Articles References

Vasko, L. (2018), 'A Taste of Singapore Abroad', *Straits Times* [online]. Available at https://www.straitstimes.com/lifestyle/travel/a-taste-of-home-abroad, accessed 21 July 2019.

Lim, S. (2019), '70% of Singapore Consumers Order from Food Delivery Apps at Least Once a Month – and Most Are Spending More Money in Recent Years', *Business Insider* [online]. Available at https://www.businessinsider.sg/70-of-singapore-consumers-order-from-food-delivery-apps-at-least-once-a-month-and-most-are-spending-more-money-in-recent-years/, accessed 22 July 2019.

Siow, L. (2017), 'Singapore SMEs Going Places', *Business Times* [online]. Available at https://www.asiaone.com/business/singapore-smes-going-places, accessed 23 July 2019.

Shiao, Vivien (2018), 'Only 14% of SMEs Intend to Internationalise: A Survey', *Business Times* [online]. Available at https://www.businesstimes.com.sg/sme/only-14-of-smes-intend-to-internationalise-survey [Accessed 24 July 2019].

Heng, J. (2018), 'Singapore Firms Urged to See Innovation and Internationalisation as a Single Process', *Business Times* [online]. Available at https://www.businesstimes.com.sg/asean-business/singapore-firms-urged-to-see-innovation-and-internationalisation-as-a-single-process, accessed 25 July 2019.

Daley, J. (2013), 'What Is the Real Survival Rate of Franchised Businesses?', *Entrepreneur Asia Pacific* [online]. Available at https://www.entrepreneur.com/article/227394, accessed 26 July 2019.

Teo, N. (2015), 'Wendy's Singapore Closes Last Outlets, Pulls Out of Singapore Again', *Yahoo! News* [online]. Available at https://sg.news.yahoo.com/wendy-singapore-closes-last-outlets-010059989.html, accessed 28 July 2019.

Ho, J. (2019), 'Rooting for You: A&W Returns to Singapore after 16 Years with Jewel Changi Airport Outlet', *Channel News Asia* [online]. Available at https://cnalifestyle.channelnewsasia.com/trending/a-w-jewel-changi-airport-singapore-root-beer-float-coney-dog-11432850, accessed 30 July 2019.

Loh, D. (2019), 'American Diner Chain Chili's Closes All Branches in Singapore', *Straits Times* [online]. Available at https://www.straitstimes.com/lifestyle/food/american-diner-chain-chilis-closes-all-branches-in-singapore, accessed 30 July 2019.

Cheok, J. (2017), 'Bubble Tea – Goodbye Gong Cha, Hello LiHO', *Business Times* [online]. Available at https://www.businesstimes.com.sg/sme/bubble-tea-goodbye-gong-cha-hello-liho, accessed 9 August 2019.

Tang, S. K. (2017), 'Frozen Yoghurt Chain Llaollao to Be Replaced With New Brand Yole', *Channel News Asia* [online]. Available at https://www.channelnewsasia.com/news/singapore/frozen-yogurt-chain-llaollao-to-be-replaced-with-new-brand-yole-9474914, accessed 16 August 2019.

Adilah, A. (2010), 'Tealive, Chatime Owners Settle Bubble Tea Dispute', *Malay Mail* [online]. Available at https://www.malaymail.com/news/malaysia/2018/08/30/tealive-chatime-owners-settle-bubble-tea-dispute/1667586, accessed 22 August 2019.

Tegos, M. (2017), 'Study: Singapore Should Invest in More Risks and Stop Supporting 'Zombie' Startups', *Tech in Asia* [online]. Available at https://www.techinasia.com/nus-enterprise-startup-study-singapore-2017, accessed 29 August 2019.

Bloomberg (2018), 'Singaporean Companies on a Global Acquisition Spree with the Value of Overseas Deals More than Doubling This Year', *Straits Times* [online]. Available at https://www.straitstimes.com/business/economy/singapore-companies-on-global-acquisition-spree-value-of-overseas-deals-more-than, accessed 7 September 2019.

Bloomberg (2018), 'Singaporean Companies Doubling up on Overseas Acquisitions This Year: Bloomberg Report' Connect to India'. Available at https://www.connectedtoindia.com/singapore-companies-doubling-up-on-overseas-acquisitions-this-year-bloomberg-report-4636.html, accessed 10 September 2019.

Lee, U. W. (2018), 'Beyond Asia, BreadTalk Has Sights Set on Europe and US', ***Business Times*** [online]. Available at https://www.businesstimes.com.sg/companies-markets/beyond-asia-breadtalk-has-sights-set-on-europe-and-us, accessed 16 September 2019.

Yusof, H. (2018), 'Is There Anyone in Singapore More Avuncular than Old Chang Kee's Founder Han Keen Juan?', *Business Times* [online]. Available at https://www.businesstimes.com.sg/lifestyle/weekend-interview/han-keen-juan, accessed 20 September 2019.

Cai, H. (2014),'LVMH Adds Crystal Jade to Singapore Jewel Box', *Business Times* [online]. Available at https://blogs.wsj.com/moneybeat/2014/05/02/lvmh-buys-controlling-stake-in-singaporean-restaurant-chain/, accessed 24 September 2019.

Retail New Asia (2018), 'First BreadTalk India Has Opened'. Available at https://www.retailnews.asia/first-breadtalk-india-has-opened/, accessed 28 September 2019.

Chiew, S. (2018), 'BreadTalk Signs Franchise Agreement to Expand into India', *Edge Singapore* [online]. Available at https://www.theedgesingapore.com/breadtalk-signs-franchise-agreement-expand-india, accessed 30 September 2019.

Gittleson, K. (2014), 'Meet Singapore's Coffee King Adrin Loi', *BBC News* [online]. Available at https://www.bbc.com/news/business-26677290, accessed 7 October 2019.

Tang, S. (2019), 'Becoming Less Reliant on Foreign Manpower: Why Is It So Hard for Singapore's F&B Industry?' *Channel News Asia* [online]. Available at https://www.channelnewsasia.com/news/singapore/less-reliant-on-foreign-manpower-singapore-f-b-challenges-11446190, accessed 16 October 2019.

Soon, W. (2016), 'Singapore Needs to Accept Risk and Failure to Create an Innovative Economy: Iswaran,' *Business Times* [online]. Available at https://www.businesstimes.com.sg/government-economy/singapore-needs-to-accept-risk-and-failure-to-create-innovative-economy-iswaran, accessed 18 October 2019.

SBS Consulting (2019), '6 Reasons Behind the Failure of Singapore Start-ups', *SBS Consulting* [online]. Available at https://www.sbsgroup.com.sg/blog/6-reasons-behind-the-failure-of-singapore-start-ups/, accessed 19 October 2019.

Channel News Asia Lifestyle (2019), 'McDonald's to Bring back Nasi Lemak Burger ahead of Ramadan'. Available at https://cnalifestyle.channelnewsasia.com/trending/mcdonalds-nasi-lemak-burger-desserts-ramadan-11474030, accessed 20 October 2019.

Tay, V. (2017), 'Sakae Sushi Shutters More Outlets in Singapore', *Marketing* [online]. Available at https://www.marketing-interactive.com/sakae-sushi-shutters-more-outlets-in-singapore/, accessed 21 October 2019.

Chan, F. (2016) 'Foreigners Can Own up to 67% of Indonesian Firms', *Straits Times* [online]. Available at https://www.straitstimes.com/asia/se-asia/foreigners-can-own-up-to-67-of-indonesian-firms, accessed 21 October 2019.

William, N. (2019), 'Is the Nasi Lemak from Malaysia or Singapore?', *South China Morning Post* [online]. Available at https://www.scmp.com/magazines/style/travel-food/article/3018591/nasi-lemak-malaysia-or-singapore-and-how-did-it-get-its, accessed 22 October 2019.

Lee, L. (2017), 'Why Are Malaysia and Singapore Fighting over a Burger?' *Asian Correspondent* [online]. Available at https://asiancorrespondent.com/2017/08/nasi-lemak-burger/, accessed 23 October 2019.

Chor, K. (2018), 'The Family Bak Kwa Business That Grew and Grew: 6 Lessons of Bee Cheng Hiang's Success', *Channel News Asia* [online]. Available at https://www.channelnewsasia.com/news/cnainsider/bee-cheng-hiang-family-business-bak-kwa-barbecued-meat-9965004, accessed 25 October 2019.

Stuckey, B. (2019), '10 Macro Trends Impacting Food and Beverage Innovation in 2019', *Forbes* [online]. Available at https://www.forbes.com/sites/barbstuckey/2019/01/08/10-macro-trends-impacting-food-beverage-innovation-in-2019/#682d2f2842f7, accessed 27 October 2019].

Lee, M. (2015), 'Going Regional: Pushing Singapore Firms to Expand Overseas', *Straits Times* [online]. Available at https://www.straitstimes.com/singapore/going-regional-pushing-singapore-firms-to-expand-overseas, accessed 28 October 2019.

Tan, S. (2018), 'BreadTalk's George Quek on Conquering the World, One Loaf at a Time', *Straits Times* [online]. Available at https://www.sgsme.sg/news/towkays/breadtalks-george-quek-conquering-world-one-loaf-time, accessed 29 October 2019.

Enterprise Singapore, 'Inspiring Stories'. Available at https://www.enterprisesg.gov.sg/overseas-markets/asia-pacific/asean/inspiring-stories, accessed 30 October 2019.

Singapore. Department of Statistics, Yearbook of Statistics (2014) [online]. Available at https://www.singstat.gov.sg/find-data, accessed on 31 October 2019.

APPENDIX 2

A Diagnostic Tool for Aspirants

Target Market: __________ **Target Year: _____________**

Please assign a score of 1 to 10, with 10 being most important for perceived importance and perceived readiness.

Critical Success Factors and Key issues	Perceived Importance	Perceived Readiness
A. Motivation for Internationalisation • Profits • Brand value • Non-economic value (please specify: ___________) • Others _____________		
B. Right Team • Leadership • Commitment to internationalisation • Team to support internationalisation • The capability of the team – able to deal with an overseas partner • Able to support overseas operations – logistics, marketing, and R & D • Training (please specify: ___________) for the team		
C. Right Foundation • Terms and contract (right offering) • Standard operating procedures • Training schedules, manuals, and content • Governing structure		
D. Right Appeal • Brand awareness in the target market • Brand acceptance • USPs for the market		

Critical Success Factors and Key issues	Perceived Importance	Perceived Readiness
E. Marketing • Marketing support for overseas partners • Marketing collateral • Website support • Merchandising • E-commerce (if applicable)		
F. Innovation • Able to innovate and adapt to foreign markets • R & D expertise • Food quality and consistency • Delivery platforms • Digitalisation for FOH and BOH		
G. Market Study (Right Fit) • Commitment to undertake the market study. • Suitability of food for the market • vailability of key ingredients • Competitive analysis • Pricing • Profitability analysis		
H. Overseas Partner (Right Partner) • Selection criteria (right alignment) • Due diligence checks • Goals and aspirational assessment • Personality tests • Resolution of conflicts and disagreements		
I. Right Location • Criteria for selecting locations • Development plan for outlets		
J. Regulations • Any franchise regulations in the target country • Import restrictions • Foreign exchange controls • Repatriation of fees, royalties, and dividends (if applicable) • Competitive practices restrictions • Restricted trade provisions		

Critical Success Factors and Key issues	**Perceived Importance**	**Perceived Readiness**
K. Market Entry • Choice of market entry • The rationale of the mode of market entry • Terms of contract		
L. Exit Strategy • Any exit strategy • Disruptions (wars, supply, costs, pandemics, or any other acts of God) • Dissolution of agreement • Business continuity plan		

caw+ Academy
Towards Greater Hospitality

CAW Academy offers specialised F&B continuing professional education programmes for the industry. Online lessons and in-classroom two- to four-day courses cover specialised topics such as F&B entrepreneurship, intellectual property rights, and franchising systems, which are taught by experienced industry practitioners.

www.cawacademy.com

CPSIA information can be obtained
at www.ICGtesting.com
Printed in the USA
LVHW071109130423
744263LV00002B/10

9781543773194